BID

BID

How Australia won the 2000 Games

**Rod McGeoch with
Glenda Korporaal**

William Heinemann Australia

Published 1994 by William Heinemann Australia
a part of Reed Books Australia
22 Salmon Street, Port Melbourne, Victoria 3207
a division of Reed International Books Australia Pty Limited

Typeset in Janson Text by DOCUPRO, Sydney
Printed and bound in Australia by Griffin Paperbacks

National Library of Australia
 cataloguing-in-publication data:

McGeogh, Rod, 1946– .
  The bid: how Australia won the 2000 Olympics.
  ISBN 0 85561 626 1.
  1. Sydney Olympics 2000 Bid. 2. Olympic Games (27th: 2000;
  Sydney, N.S.W.) – Planning I. Korporaal, Glenda II. Sydney
  Olympics 2000 Bid. III. Title.

786.48

To
Deeta,
Lucie
and
Anna,
who shouldered the burden,
bore the absences,
shared the pain and pleasures

Contents

Olympism is a philosophy of life, exalting and combining in a balanced whole the qualities of the body, will and mind. Blending sport with culture and education, Olympism seeks to create a way of life based on the joy found in effort, the educational value of good example and respect for universal fundamental ethical principles.

The goal of Olympism is to place everywhere sport at the service of the harmonious development of man, with a view to encouraging the establishment of a peaceful society concerned with the preservation of human dignity.

The goal of the Olympic Movement is to contribute to building a peaceful and better world by educating youth through sport practiced without discrimination of any kind and in the Olympic spirit, which requires mutual understanding with a spirit of friendship, solidarity and fair-play.

The activity of the Olympic Movement is permanent and universal. It reaches its peak with the bringing together of the athletes of the world at the great sport festival, the Olympic Games.

From The Olympic Charter

List of Abbreviations

AENOC	Association of European National Olympic Committees
ANOC	Association of National Olympic Committees
ANOCA	Association of National Olympic Committees of Africa
AOC	Australian Olympic Committee
ASOIF	Association of Summer Olympic International Federations
FIFA	International Federation of Football Associations
GAISF	General Assembly of International Sports Federations or IFs (*pron.* 'gafe')
IAAF	International Amateur Athletics Federation
IF	International (sports) Federation
IOC	International Olympic Committee
NOC	National Olympic Committee, eg Australian Olympic Committee
OCOG	Organising Committee of the Olympic Games
ONOC	Oceania National Olympic Committee
PASO	Pan-American Sports Organisation
TOP	The Olympic Program, the IOC's international sponsorship scheme

1
Success

The important thing in the Olympic Games is not to win but to take part, the important thing in life is not the triumph but the struggle.

Baron de Coubertin

And the winner is . . . Sydney!'
There was pandemonium in the Stade Louis 11 in Monte Carlo after International Olympic Committee President Samaranch read out the verdict at 8.28 pm on Thursday, 23 September 1993. We had no idea how the vote had gone — only that we had won. Sydney would host the 27th summer Olympics in 2000.

John Fahey, a St Christopher medal in one hand, had gripped my hand with the other, waiting for the decision. When the announcement came, he jumped up into the air, dragging me to my feet, a scene repeated over and over on television. Graham Lovett, who was sitting behind me, let out a tremendous cry, like a scream. Bruce Baird walked up the room to me. He couldn't get down the aisles, so he walked over the chairs. Phil Coles clipped me on the side of the ear — his way of saying wasn't it great.

Everyone in our team was rushing for their wives and hugging them. I could see Deeta, my wife, a few rows behind, fighting to get to me, but finding everyone else was around me. Everyone was coming up and hugging me, but the one person that I wanted to hug couldn't get to me because of the throng.

I was the eye of the storm, quiet, but all around me incredible activity. People hugging and kissing. I didn't feel elation, just relief. Quite detached. The job had been done. The goal I had worked towards for almost three years — consuming almost every moment of my waking life — had been achieved. It was all over. Or almost.

Six of us from the Sydney team were supposed to go up on the stage. That was the arrangement agreed beforehand, when we were one of five candidate cities bidding. We had to nominate a spokesman. John Fahey, the Premier, was to give a speech.

But when we got there it was chaos. The Australians in the room had gone berserk. They walked down aisles and over chairs to get to the front. The media was everywhere, trying to interview us all. And we were meant to be signing the contract.

François Carrard, the director-general of the IOC said to me, 'Do you want the Games? You won't get them unless you sign the contract.' I couldn't sign of course. I had no such status. Frank Sartor, the Lord Mayor of Sydney, and John Coates, president of the Australian Olympic Committee sat down and signed. I stood back and watched.

Then Margaret, my wonderful, loyal assistant of 12 years, completely broke down on the stage. She just couldn't control herself. I put my arm around her and said, 'Come on. You're all right.'

There were microphones and cameras everywhere and politicians running around.

I had a cold, and now a terrible headache. I thought, I don't need to be in all this. I wanted to pull away from it all. So I went to the back of the stage which was only two or three metres wide — and just stood there for a minute with my head in my hand. A newspaper photographer snapped a photo of me which was published later under the heading:

McGEOCH OVER-COME

I wasn't overcome, I had a headache.

With all this pandemonium, they couldn't go ahead with the rest of the official proceedings.

It seemed as if all 250 Australian supporters who had come to Monte Carlo for the week were on the stage, dressed in their orange Sydney 2000 tee-shirts.

John Fahey never spoke. I don't know what Prince Rainier thought. He was on the stage and there was meant to be more of the program. But eventually we all just looked at each other and I said to President Samaranch: 'What do we do now?' And he just gestured that we should all go off and have a drink. It seemed like a good idea. It was impossible to go on. So that's where things ended.

After the announcement I had to go back to give an international press conference with the rest of the Sydney team. But by the time we got to the exit, everyone else had taken the official cars. Deeta and I didn't have any transport so we had to find our own way back to the press centre, which was about 20 minutes away. We caught a bus. We didn't say much, just tried to collect our thoughts. But Deeta was a lot more excited than I was. She seemed to have a much better perspective on what had happened. I was still coming to terms with it.

By the time I got to the press conference everyone was on the stage. The Prime Minister, the Premier, the Lord Mayor and everyone else. There had been a scramble for seats and I could barely fit at the table. But it didn't matter. I wasn't going to push in. It was the politicians' time. I pulled my chair back about half a metre and sat for a while. I had my cold and everyone else had their speeches.

Eventually somebody asked: 'Could we hear from Rod? What does he feel?'

'I've only got one thing to say at the moment. We've had tremendous support from Australia, particularly from some of the companies.' I pointed out Pat Stone from CUB and Brian Kirkham from Qantas in the audience. 'These sort of people put a huge investment into us and I hope they feel we've paid them back.'

The press centre was attached to the Loews Hotel where many Sydney supporters and a lot of our staff were staying — and where our victory party was to be held. We walked past the room where the Manchester team were having their function. They may have lost but they sure seemed to be having a riot of a time.

We had planned to have our party — win or lose — on the Pistou Terrace on roof of the Loews Hotel which had a wonderful view over the Mediterranean. But it was pouring rain and we switched to a function room in the hotel. The Sydney 2000 bid team had done a power of organising for the week at Monte Carlo — for the whole three years of the bid for that matter — but when it came to organising what turned out to be a victory party, we were caught short.

Paul Clark, our 'office' manager for the week at Monte Carlo, had arranged a party for 250, but we ended up with 1200. The hotel management wouldn't deliver room service for that many. So the food finished in about 20 minutes and there was nothing to eat. People were drinking champagne and eating apples because there was nothing else. By the time Deeta and I got there we couldn't get any food. I was starving. I hadn't had any breakfast, I couldn't remember having any lunch, and it was well past dinner time.

The room was terribly crowded. I kept losing Deeta and walking around the room, trying to find her. At one point Barbara Wild and I and some other people actually sat down on the floor to get away from the crowd. There was singing and a lot of backslapping, and alcohol was starting to take over.

Margaret came up to me and said she and Alan Hoskins and Sue Bushby were going to open up our IOC hospitality suite in the Hotel de Paris. They had run the suite, which was open for members to drop in and chat about the Sydney bid, until midnight every night that week. I couldn't believe it. We had won and Margaret and Alan and Sue were *still* working. They said it was something they wanted to do. They said if any IOC members wanted to come by and talk about it all, they wanted to be there.

Then Deeta said to me, 'Don't you think it would be nice if you walked in and said hello to Bob Scott?'

Bob was the chief executive of the Manchester bid. It was Manchester's second unsuccessful bid for the Games and he had been on the road for years, campaigning to have the Games in the city. We had a few cross words over the bid, but only the sparring of serious but friendly rivals. Nothing damaging. He was a great guy and had worked hard for Manchester. I thought it would be a good thing to do, so I walked into the Manchester room. Somebody was just finishing a speech, standing on a chair. I starting wallking down the room where I could see Bob when one of the Manchester guys said, 'Rod's here. Please say a few words.' So I got up on the chair.

'I'm very glad we've won but I feel sorry for you people. You've been wonderful and supported us as we travelled together on the road. I just want you to know that I've seen your team the entire time we've been bidding and they've represented you proudly. They were worth every penny you put into them. They gave their best for you. That's the message you should take home to Manchester.'

It wasn't one of my best speeches, but it was appreciated.

The Sydney supporters partied on. We had to keep putting pressure on David Smithers, the chairman of our finance commission, to extend the hospitality to everyone for another half an hour; then another half an hour; then another one. Gradually, everyone just wore out. About 3 am Deeta and I walked up the hill to our room at the Hotel Metropole. We were exhausted but there were still a few things to be done.

We rang our two daughters in Sydney, who were at horse camp. They were trying not to sound too excited but they were. We just wanted to be home with them as soon as possible.

I had already spoken to my mother on a mobile phone from the stage. She had seen it all on television and was very excited. The whole McGeoch family had been phoning each other to talk about it. My younger brother, Andrew, had been very emotional.

Then I rang one of my oldest friends, Peter Kidney, a stockbroker who was working in his office at Hambros in Sydney. Peter and I used to drive to work together every morning and lunch about twice a week. But after I became chief executive of the Sydney 2000 Olympic bid, I hardly ever saw him. In June, Peter had come to see me in my office and broke down. His doctors had confirmed he had motor neurone disease. He was dying. I realised then how much your friends rely on you — and how much my work on the bid had taken me away from my friends, and my family.

When I got onto the switchboard at Hambros, the girl couldn't believe I was on the phone. She quickly ran and got Peter. He was very happy.

Then I rang the Sydney Olympics 2000 office. All the staff were all in my office, which has lots of glass with great views of Darling Harbor, and they put me on the speaker phone. Gavin Blatchford, a young guy in our office, was sitting in my chair, imitating me as he was wont to do. He got a bit of a shock when he found out it was really me on the phone. I could hear everyone laughing. In all the press interviews I had done in Monte Carlo I always mentioned how hard my staff had worked and how great they were. They had heard them and it was much appreciated.

By 4 am Deeta and I realised we'd hardly eaten anything all day, so we rang for room service. There was a mix up and somehow we ended up getting double our order. We got two huge club sandwiches and two chicken salads each. We ate the lot.

2
'Oh, No, I'm too Busy'

If you want something done, ask a busy person
                                            Business adage

It seems strange looking back on it now, but in the first months of 1991 I had no idea Sydney was bidding for the Olympic Games, much less that the New South Wales Government was looking for someone to run the whole campaign.

I've always had a passionate interest in sport, Olympic sport in particular, but I was so absorbed with the work of helping to pull together a major national law firm, I wasn't paying attention to much else that was going on that summer.

All that was to change with one phone call.

I was working as usual in my office at the law firm Corrs Chambers Westgarth in March 1991 when a guy in the NSW Attorney General's Department phoned. We weren't close friends but we had known each other through the Law Society.

He pointed out an advertisement in the *Australian Financial Review* for the position of chief executive of the company that would run the Sydney Olympic bid and asked if I was interested. I didn't even know what he was talking about. My first reaction was, 'Oh, no, I'm too busy.'

There were good reasons for my lack of knowledge about the job — but it was also those reasons that may have left me open to a career change at that point. I had had a pretty tough 12 months. I had just been elected chairman of the Sydney office of Corrs, one of the biggest law firms in Australia, and was deeply involved in a number of mergers involving the firm.

I started my law career in Sydney at the age of 23 after graduating from Sydney University. I joined the long-established firm of Law and Milne as a partner. In 1990 Law and Milne merged with the Sydney office of Corrs Australian Solicitors and I became managing partner of the whole Sydney office. Corrs was a Melbourne-based firm of solicitors that had opened a branch in Sydney and was in the process of building itself up to become a national law firm. Not long before I joined it merged with Chambers, McNab in Brisbane and other firms in Perth and Adelaide. Corr's chief executive, James Strong, who was based in Melbourne, then proposed the merger with Westgarth Middleton which had offices in Sydney and Melbourne. In the end Middleton, the Melbourne arm of that firm, didn't join in the merger. But in Sydney we had to amalgamate the offices of three firms — Corrs, Westgarth and Law and Milne.

We were all in different premises around Sydney. We had to put people together, combine various specialty departments and merge the cultures of each firm so that they become part of the one big Corrs' Sydney office. It was a major exercise. I became chairman of the Sydney office and Ron Finlay, who had been the managing partner of Westgarth, became the Sydney managing partner. I got caught up in negotiations about the mergers and a lot of the organisational details. It was very intensive work which often took me interstate. It was also a very difficult financial time for law firms. I was under a lot of pressure and it affected my home life. I was definitely not my usual relaxed self at home. I had no idea at all about the Sydney bid but I guess I was open to suggestions of an attractive alternative.

A little later on, someone else also urged me to look at the advertisement, a lawyer in my firm, a Fijian-Indian called Prafel Patel. He was very well connected in Fiji and always looking at new ideas. He walked into my office one day with the ad and said, 'I reckon this is you.' By that time I was already thinking about it, but I couldn't say anything. So I said, 'No. I couldn't do that. I'm chairman here.'

As I began to think about it, I felt in my bones that Sydney must have a good chance of winning. I didn't know Melbourne had bid for the 1996 Games. I had no idea what bidding for the right to host an Olympic Games was all about. But being very involved in sport and knowing a lot about Olympic statistics, I thought Sydney would be hard to beat.

I may not have known about the Sydney bid, but I knew a lot about Olympic sport. It was said I had an encyclopaedic knowledge for all sport — but particularly about Olympic Games.

My passion for Olympic statistics was fuelled by the 1956 Olympics in Melbourne. I was a boy of 10 at the time, living in Brisbane. I was the second of three brothers and have a younger sister. I remembered listening to the Games on the radio, but what really got me in was a book about the Melbourne Games. Every Olympic city has to publish a book about the Games afterwards and we had the Melbourne book in our house. Called simply, *The Olympic Games, Melbourne 1956* it gave a day-by-day account of the Games. It had black and white photos of the heroes of the Games — Ron Clarke holding the Olympic torch, Betty Cuthbert and Marlene Mathews holding their medals — and listed every medal won. I can still remember the front cover: green with a picture of a hand holding the flaming Olympic torch. It was very important to me. I would read it whenever I had an idle moment. It wasn't just about Betty Cuthbert and her three gold medals on the track. It was everything — the weight lifting and the wrestling. The book was the most distinctive thing about the 1956 Olympics.

I have a good memory for facts and figures. I'm not sure what a photographic memory is, but I can still see the photographs in that book in my mind today. When I went into law school exams I could actually see the page of the text book which had the case on it to do with the question they were asking. I can do it 90 per cent of the time and I do it with sports. I used to read everything on sport — all the baseball results, all the golf results, all the horse-racing results — and I don't even go to the races. I could name all the first, second and third placegetters in the Melbourne Cup and the jockey and trainer from 1896 to 1980. I read all the sports results every weekend in the Sunday papers and it sticks in my head.

I used to watch a Saturday morning sports program on television with Ron Casey and Ray Stehr. Halfway through the program they had a phone-in quiz. I always knew the answer, but I could never get through. Then somebody told me you should dial all the numbers except the last one, wait for the question and then dial the last number. It worked. I got on and got the answer right. The prize was an Onkaparinga rug. But then somebody said, 'How old are you?'

'Twelve.'

And then they said, 'We're terribly sorry but you're too young to win.'

Well, that wasn't fair. So I got my mother to write in and complain and they sent me a pen as a consolation prize. And of course I always loved watching and playing sport. When I was 11 or 12 in Brisbane, I used to go to the Brisbane Boys' College and sit on the hill overlooking the oval, watching the athletics and the football. I knew all the people on the teams and I wasn't even at the school. I can still see Alan Martin playing on the wing and John Prowse winning the 100 yard dash.

Watching these players, who remained local heroes, I first saw a very talented young Aboriginal sprinter. I had gone along to a combined athletics meeting to see John Prowse run. I thought nobody could beat him — but someone did. It was a young guy from the Church of England Grammar school who ran the 100 in 10 seconds flat. His name was Lloyd McDermott and he later became the first Aboriginal to play rugby union for Australia. A magnificent sprinter, he played on the wing with the Wallabies.

Then I got interested in boxing. My mother had some surgery which put her out of action for a while. So Dad got a guy who was an old army cook to come and look after us. This man, John Pybus, (we used to call him 'Pie') was mad on boxing and wrestling and he took me to the fights on Monday nights and the wrestling on Friday nights at Brisbane Stadium — every week for about five years. They were very famous days in boxing. There was George Barnes and Clive Stewart and the Sands brothers. I saw them all. I've been interested in boxing ever since. I followed the careers of Lionel Rose and Johnny Famechon as well as the fortunes of those on the American professional circuit.

To me, there is no greater athlete than Mohammed Ali. Carl Lewis is the second greatest athlete in the world, but Mohammed Ali is the best. To go 15 three-minute rounds of boxing is an extraordinary feat — but to do it when you are 16 or 17 stone and box as gracefully as Ali did is unbelievable. There's no ballet dancer that is 18 stone. To have the grace and movement that he had shouldn't have been possible with a body that size.

And of course I've always loved to compete. As a school boy,

I played First XV Rugby and Second XI Cricket and represented my school in swimming and athletics. But rugby union was always been my big passion. I played more than 300 games of sub-district rugby. I was well into my thirties before Deeta finally confiscated my boots and mouthguard.

So it didn't take much for me to become interested in the idea of running the Sydney bid to stage the Olympic Games. But I already had a successful career and a wife and two children to support. I knew the job would involve a pay cut. At 44, I had to think carefully about such a big change. Could I do the job and then resume my career at Corrs?

Deeta and I went for a number of walks around Cremorne Point, near where we live, and talked about it. Deeta and I both lead very busy lives. When we met in 1976, Deeta Colvin was the assistant manager of the Wine and Brandy Corporation of Australia. After we married, in 1978, she started her own public relations consultancy, Colvin Communications International. She speaks French and her client list includes top French companies such as Perrier, Remy Martin, Krug and Louis Vuitton. The job was demanding and often took her overseas. When we had something important to discuss we would often take a walk around Cremorne Point, a lovely spot with a great view of Sydney Harbor. We talked about the possible demands of the job. The advertisement said there would be a lot of travel and I knew that would mean time away from my family. We agreed that I would telephone the executive search firm, Rochford Williams International, and find out more about it.

I telephoned anonymously and asked two questions:

- Was it possible to apply for the job on the basis that you could take leave of absence from your existing job for three years? They said the government would consider it.
- Was it possible for someone to apply if they had to give three to six months' notice to leave their present job? I felt I couldn't leave Corrs immediately. Again, the answer was: the government would consider it.

So I thought I had nothing to lose. I did my first ever *curriculum vitae* and submitted it. As I prepared it, I realised there was an unusually good parallel between what the advertisement wanted and what I had done. They wanted someone with international experience, a good knowledge of sport and experience in managing money and dealing with the press.

I had been chairman of the Young Lawyers Committee of the NSW Law Society for seven years until 1980, head of the NSW Young Lawyers' Association and created the National Young Lawyers section of the Law Council of Australia. I had been president of the Law Society in 1984, the society's centenary year. I had travelled many, many times overseas and had built up a personal network of lawyers all around the world which I had maintained. I had been chairman of the planning committees for the American Bar Association Meeting in Sydney in 1979 and the International Bar Association Meeting in Sydney in 1980. I had represented Australia at many overseas conferences, including the American Bar Association meetings in Atlanta, New York, Chicago and Hawaii.

The ad said candidates needed sporting knowledge. Well, I could certainly show that I had that.

It said that one needed media experience. I had had a very extensive dealings with the media as president of the Law Society of NSW and had been one of the Law Society's media spokesmen for many years. I had also done a lot of talkback radio. I was into the fifth year of a weekly program about the law every Friday morning on Radio 2BL, the ABC's Sydney metropolitan station, with Margaret Throsby. The program had developed a good following and in 1989 Margaret and I won the Golden Gavel Award in 1989 for excellence in legal reporting.

I always used to get there early for the program so Margaret would know I was there. On one occasion I came into the studio and Peter McCormack, the producer, had a book about the Olympics. And I bragged, 'Pete. You can ask me anything on that and I'd know it.'

Unbeknown to me, Peter took the book into Margaret during a break with a piece of paper on it saying: 'McGeoch says he can answer anything on this. You try him.'

Over the years on the show, Margaret often had a dig at me about rugby on the program. She knew I was mad about sport. And all of a sudden, while the program was on, she put the book down and opened it up and said:

'Who won the long jump at the Melbourne Olympic Games?'

'Gregory Bell.'

'Who won the decathalon?'

'Milton Campbell.'

'You actually do know all this, don't you?'

Peter Wall, a senior executive with ABC Radio, was listening. At that stage they were planning to revamp the weekend radio sports program, *Grandstand*. He called me in and asked me if I would be interested in hosting the program for them. He said they wanted to put a whole new 'face' on radio sport. We had some discussions and I became excited about it: to actually be paid to talk sport all weekend seemed to me to be a pretty good deal.

After a while I realised that to work from noon to 7 pm each day for 48 weekends of the year was a big job. But I was still interested and a contract was given to me to do this job for more than $50,000. Then I asked my partners at Corrs if anybody had any problems with me doing this. They didn't object — but they said the money I was to make had to go to the firm.

That set me back a bit. I had thought it was an extra bit of money I would be able to put in my pocket. A number of partners said, 'We work all day Saturday and Sunday for clients and the money goes to the firm. So surely yours must go as well.' I knew I couldn't win that argument, so I backed away from the job.

But when I had to put in my application for the job, and answer the question about sport and media, I simply annexed the ABC contract and said, 'There you are. I'm apparently good enough to run a radio program and obviously, in the ABC's mind, I know a great deal about sport.'

Then there were the questions about experience in financial management. I had been treasurer of the Law Society of New South Wales, which controls about $60 million. I had been managing partner of a multi-million dollar law firm for a year. Along with my other partners, I had also been responsible for a trust fund of about $15 million in my own small law firm.

I went carefully through the ad and felt I answered all of its requirements. But there were some good lessons in the exercise. As I had never done a CV before, I had forgotten a lot of things I had done. It really was worth spending a lot of time on it and thinking back through my career to get everything right.

So my application didn't look too bad.

I had an interview with Patrica Rochford and Errol Williams, the two people who ran Rochford Williams. At the meeting, Patricia gave me a lot of papers to read. She gave me the report of Bruce Baird's committee on the feasibility of Sydney bidding for the Olympic Games and another paper by John Coates, the president of the Australian Olympic Committee, on the process of bidding for an Olympics. She spent some time explaining what a difficult job it would be — how there was a lot of politics in sport and how much travel would be involved. She asked me if I had thought it all through and if I really wanted to do the job.

Rochford Williams put me on their short list and I was interviewed by a panel that included Ken Baxter, the deputy director of the Premier's Department; John Coates; Greg Daniel, the Sydney boss of advertising agency Clemenger; Ted Harris, the chairman of Australian Airlines and also chairman of the Australian Sports Commission; and Jeremy Bingham, Lord Mayor of Sydney.

I knew John Coates, who was also a lawyer. I had recently been involved in a very large legal matter in which John was acting on the other side. It was a difficult matter but it was always handled with goodwill by both of us. We had became fond of each other in a professional sense. I thought he had a high regard for me as Law Society president and he knew how I worked, and how hard.

I knew Bingham slightly because he was the partner of another law firm.

Greg Daniel knew Deeta because of her public relations business, but not well.

I had never met Baxter or Harris before, although I knew who they were.

I went through the interview and it seemed all right to me. I retired to the anteroom. Errol Williams said, 'That wasn't one of your best interviews'.

I was told I was close to the job and had an interview with Bruce Baird. Bruce was the Minister for Transport but he was soon to be formally appointed as the minister in charge of the bid. By this time I knew he had been making private inquiries about me from a number of my colleagues in the law.

More than 100 people had applied for the job. I found out later that it came down to a short list of three. Much later, after the bid was over, in a speech, Nick Greiner revealed that when they were all discussing the candidates, I was described as a person who not too many people had heard about — and someone who could be a bit abrasive. When Nick heard this, he said, 'I want him.' I suppose it wasn't 100 per cent complimentary to me, but he obviously thought if we were going to win, we needed someone who was not just a nice person, but someone who would take a stand and drive the bid.

One Tuesday late in April, I had a meeting with the Sydney City Council at the Town Hall where all the players were present and I was confirmed as the successful candidate. At this stage it was still very confidential. No announcement was to be made for about three months. I thought that was fine: I would be able to give Corrs' reasonable notice.

There had been a tremendous amount of speculation at the time about who might get the job. Roy Masters wrote a full page article in the *Sydney Morning Herald* which mentioned Nick Whitlam and former Olympic swimmer John Konrads as two possible contenders. But my name was never mentioned. I'm grateful to Rochford Williams that it didn't.

On the Friday morning I got a bit of a shock. I got a phone call to say that the whole thing was going to be announced the following Wednesday. The government was going to sign a contract with the Australian Olympic Committee and my appointment would be announced at the same time.

So I had to break the news to my partners, giving them only a few days' notice. I rang my Alan McDonald, another partner at Corrs and a friend, and told him I planned to take leave from the firm for three years to run the Sydney Olympic bid. He was stunned. Then I spoke to Ron Finlay who was extremely under-standing. We decided that all the partners would be informed by our internal electronic mail half an hour before the press conference. Most of the partners wished me well and gave me great support.

My appointment was announced at the Sydney Olympics 2000 office in the Maritime Services Building in Kent Street, near the southern entrance to the Harbor Bridge, overlooking Darling Harbor.

The news caught everyone by surprise. The *Sydney Morning Herald* carried a story the next day headed:

MEET ROD WHO?

Not knowing this outsider, the press quickly decided to put me to the test at my first press conference:

'What is your favorite Olympic event?'

'The men's 100 metre dash — the race to prove who's the fastest man alive.'

'What was the most memorable Olympic race?'

'The 100 metres at the 1960 Rome Olympics.'

'Who won?'

'The German, Armin Hary.'

'What was his time?'

'10.2 seconds.'

'Who was second?'

'Dave Sime of the US.'

I spent the next few weeks winding up my work at Corrs and getting up to speed on the Olympic movement.

Phil Coles, one of Australia's two members on the International Olympic Committee or IOC, spent hours with me. He really went out of his way to brief me. Coles, 59, had been an IOC member since 1982 and knew a lot about the movement. He had been an Olympic class canoeist. He competed in the Olympics in Rome in 1960, captained the canoeing team in the Tokyo Olympics of 1964 and was a member of the team that went to Mexico in 1968. He had won 25 Australian canoeing championships. In his youth he had been a lifeguard at Bondi and was Australia's national surf lifesaving champion five times. He retired from competitive sport in 1970 and went into sports administration. He was involved in managing the Australian Olympic team which went to Munich in 1972 and Montreal in 1976 and, in 1980, he was general manager of the entire Australian team going to Moscow. He became executive director of the NSW Olympic Council in 1973, the same year he became a board member of the Australian Olympic Federation (as it was then called). He had been secretary-general of the Australian Olympic Committee, the AOC, since 1985.

Coles certainly knew about the business of Australian Olympic sport and the international Olympic movement. Kevan Gosper, Australia's other IOC member, was working in London at the time as a senior executive with Shell. As the only IOC member living in Australia, Coles had obviously decided to help get me up to speed very quickly and he was fantastic. He came up to my office at Corrs and I went down to his. He sent me things to read and things to listen to. He gave me copies of the magazine *Sport Intern*, a German publication which specialises in reporting on the Olympic movement, magazines on the Olympic movement, a casette tape of the Melbourne presentation to the IOC in Tokyo for the decision on the 1996 Games and lots of other papers.

John Coates was also very helpful but he was obviously busy with his own law firm.

Before I started the job, I went to Melbourne for the annual meeting of the Australian Olympic Committee. On the way to the meeting, I shared a cab with John Constantine, the head of Australian soccer, 'football' in the Olympic vernacular. He said to me:

'Of course, you realise, my sport is the most important one in the Olympic movement because Mr Havelange [Joao Havelange, president of the International Federation of Football Associations or FIFA] is a very important IOC member. There are anything between 15 and 20 votes in the control of the football group and you'll need me to think through your football strategy. I'm more than happy to help you with anything I can do.'

I said nothing much at the time, but what he said felt right. The Latin Americans were soccer mad and there were 16 IOC votes there. Europe was pretty much soccer territory and there were 38 votes there. The soccer teams in Africa were steadily improving, gaining a growing amount of public support. There seemed to be no end of the fronts on which the team bidding for the Sydney Olympics would have to fight. But at the same time clever, committed allies of our cause were also emerging.

It was quite a large meeting and I had been asked to say a few words. When I got up to speak, I recounted this conversation as an indication of the immediate help that people had offered me. I told them I needed to be educated about all 25 sports.

In the coffee break, people surrounded me. People like David Prince and Marlene Mathews from track and field, Michael Wenden from swimming, John Whitehouse from water polo and Sasha Dimitric from handball. They were all wishing me well and wanting to help.

The first person I got a proper chance to speak to was Sasha Dimitric. I had to admit that I didn't really know what handball was. I thought it was like racquet ball, something where you hit a ball up against a wall. But it is an Olympic sport played with a ball the size of a volley ball which you throw into a net, like a soccer net, which has a goalie. It's big in Europe and Africa. He gave me the rule book and said, 'You'll need to read that.' All the way through the bid, Sasha never stopped helping and making suggestions and jotting letters to me.

I had my first meeting with Kevan Gosper who had flown out from London especially for the meeting. I already knew of his impressive sporting career. He had been the Australian record holder for the 400 metres from 1955 to 1960. He had won a gold medal for the 400 metres in the Commonwealth Games in Vancouver in 1954 and a bronze in the 4 × 400 metre relay at the Cardiff Games in 1958. He had won a silver in the 4 × 400 metre relay in the Olympic Games in Melbourne in 1956. He was highly respected within the Olympic family. An IOC member since 1977, he was elected a member of the executive board in 1986 and became Australia's first ever IOC vice-president in 1990. He was also a very successful businessman. He had been chairman and CEO of Shell Australia from 1980 to 1991, when he moved to London to be regional coordinator for Shell International. I noticed that the satchels for the delegates to the meeting were sponsored by Shell, so his company was obviously a strong supporter of the Olympic movement.

Gosper, then 57, was a tall man, physically very striking. He was very friendly to me although it was really only a very brief meeting. Someone took some pictures of the two of us together. He had just been given an honorary doctorate from Newcastle University and everyone was calling him 'Doctor Gosper'.

What struck me was how everyone at the meeting wanted to help and be a friend. Ideally, it is what you should expect from Olympians. They were perfect examples of the Olympic charter. In a world where the ideal is seldom realised, this was the single most heartening realisation of the early days: Australian sportsmen and sportwomen were 100 per cent behind me, from all sports and from all states.

They all wanted so badly to win the Olympics for Australia. I felt humbled by that meeting. It gave me the first glimmerings of an idea, an approach to the task, too: if the spirit and will I'd witnessed could be bottled every company in the world would buy it. I came back having enjoyed the day — but realising too, I was carrying a heavy weight on my shoulders. I knew it was going to be a big job to win the Games and that I just couldn't let all these people down.

I was to be employed as a public servant out of the NSW Premier's Department, on loan to the bid office. The bid was actually run by a company called Sydney Olympics 2000 Bid Limited which was jointly owned by the Australian Olympic Committee, the Sydney City Council and the NSW government.

I signed a standard form of contract that was provided to members of the senior executive service. I was to start on Monday, 27 May. I don't know how I got out of my law firm as quickly as I did, but I did.

Over the previous ten years, I had had a wonderful personal assistant, Margaret McLennan. She had dumped me once in our working relationship but I went and found her again, and she came back. She had not enjoyed Corrs at all after having been used to work in a small law firm with me. Outgoing and responsible, she took a high profile role in my practice. Many of the clients dealt with her directly. She said, 'If you think you're going down to that bid office on your own, you've got another thing coming.'

3
Building on the Past

If we go with Sydney, it will be with all guns blazing. It won't be a half-hearted attempt.

John Coates, February 1991

At my first press conference I was asked if I thought Sydney could win the 2000 Games. I said I wouldn't have taken the job if I didn't, and meant it.

I felt it was time for the Games to come to Sydney. If I had a gut feeling Sydney's bid had strength at the time I got that unexpected phone call, I was even more convinced after people like Coles and Coates showed how much work had already been done.

As the new guy on the block who had never even been to an Olympic Games, let alone met any IOC members except Phil Coles, I knew there was already a sound framework in place for the bid. When John Coates stressed the importance of going in with all guns blazing if Sydney were to bid for the Games, he knew exactly what he was talking about.

I believe there has always been a lot to be said in business or any endeavor for recognising the importance of experience and building on the talents already in place. But an unhealthy practice has crept into Australian business from overseas. The idea that a new broom should sweep clean has been taken to manifestly absurd and destructive levels. I believe the new boss who wants to sack the old people left, right and centre; completely overturn every habit or system that was running; re-locate or renovate the place; and generally spurn all that went before his or her arrival, should be regarded with suspicion.

I suspect that I am as ruthless as anybody when it comes to the necessary shake up, but I see no point in unsettling the

28

well-settled, fixing what ain't broke, squashing or sacking the talented along with the talentless, the vigorous as well as the dead wood. Experience is valuable, and radical restarts, while occasionally necessary, are often wasteful. I suspect new bosses in old teams who require such things are insecure or perhaps a bit stupid about coming to grips with the old because, for them, it's new.

From the beginning, I believed my job was not to reinvent the wheel, but to co-ordinate and build on the talent and experience available. Only now do I fully realise how valuable — if not vital — to Sydney's success was all the work that went on before May 1991. No-one will ever know how much that work actually tipped a scale in Monte Carlo in September 1993 but it was certainly extremely valuable for me as the newcomer.

In saying that, I'm not being generous, I'm simply being honest.

Two previous bids for the Games had generated a wealth of knowledge and experience in the Australian Olympic movement about bidding for the Games. The election of a city to host the Games takes place six to seven years before the Games themselves. And the process of bidding can take at least a year — often two. This means any city looking at staging an Olympics has to start preparing to bid about a decade beforehand. To try to sell a city as a host city to the Olympic movement without taking the proper time to prepare a bid is to sell that city short.

Sydney certainly had a long history of interest in hosting an Olympics. In 1970 Nicholas Shehadie, then the deputy Lord Mayor of Sydney, chaired a citizen's committee to look at the possibility of Sydney bidding for the 1988 Games — Australia's bicentenary year.

An initial proposal to develop an Olympic complex at Moore Park was abandoned after strong community resistance, but a subsequent report by Walter Bunning recommended the development of a sports complex at Homebush Bay, in Sydney's inner west, which would be capable of hosting an Olympic Games. In 1978 Neville Wran, the Labor Premier of New South Wales, established an interdepartmental committee to look at the feasibility of Sydney hosting the 1988 Games. The committee's findings were positive, focussing on the idea of having the Games at Homebush. There was a strong belief that the idea of a Sydney bid would have been appealing to the IOC. The fact that 1988 was Australia's bicentenary year would have been a good selling point for us. But there was concern that Sydney did not have the requisite venues and infrastructure. The NSW Treasury was worried that the state might not be able to afford the Games and Wran withdrew his government's support for the idea. Melbourne did actually notify the IOC in late 1980 that it wanted to bid for the 1988 Games, but it withdrew its name several months later. And, of course, those Games went to Seoul.

But there are some people in the Australian Olympic movement who felt we might have won that bid. In the end only Seoul and Nagoya competed for the Games.

Although Sydney didn't go ahead with the bid for the 1988 Games, the NSW government had started to do its homework on what would be needed to bid. This was significant, because one of the strengths of Sydney's ultimate bid was that it had its plan in place very quickly, having started to prepare it way back in the 1970s.

In the mid-1980s Brisbane made a bid for the 1992 Games with the enthusiastic support of its Lord Mayor, Sallyanne Atkinson. About a year before the decision on the Games, which was to take place in October 1986, Sallyanne approached John Coates, a senior member of the AOC, to become chief executive of the bid. He moved from Sydney to Brisbane with a very young family. He worked hard on the bid, which did respectably given the fact that it was up against Barcelona, Paris, Birmingham, Amsterdam and Belgrade. When it came to the vote Brisbane survived into the third round. It ranked third after Barcelona and Paris — well ahead of Belgrade, Birmingham and Amsterdam. It was a good bid as a starting bid, although everyone now concedes it was underfunded and Brisbane was probably too small at the time to host the Games.

But a lot of experience was gained and Sallyanne became a very popular figure in the international Olympic movement. She was an excellent leader of the Brisbane bid and a great lobbyist. She built very good relations with the important people in the movement such as President Samaranch and the IOC members who were royalty, including Princess Nora of Liechtenstein.

When it came to the competition for the 1996 Games, Sydney again seriously looked at bidding. Before a city can bid for the

Olympics, it must have the support of its national Olympic committee — in our case the Australian Olympic Committee. In 1988 there was a three-way contest between Sydney, Melbourne and Brisbane for the right to bid for the 1996 Games. The Australian Olympic Federation decided to support Melbourne.

There is no doubt that Melbourne had by far the best facilities for the Games It already had the main stadium — the Melbourne Cricket Ground, the Tennis Centre and Port Phillip Bay for the yachting. It also had a number of facilities left over from the 1956 Games that could have been used for a second Games. A lot of the venues were very close together which would also appeal to the IOC.

Kevan Gosper was the AOC president at the time. He lived in Melbourne and was very much involved in the bid. Melbourne thought it had a strong chance. But it was up against the sentimental favorite: Athens.

The 1996 Games would be the anniversary of 100 years of the modern Olympics. The Games had been restarted in 1896 as a result of some inspired lobbying by Frenchman, Baron Pierre de Coubertin. The baron was a great believer in the importance of sport and sporting competition as a good means of developing a 'stronger and better individual' and, thereby, a strong vital nation. He was inspired by the recent discoveries of the ruins of ancient Olympia in Greece about the great athletic ideals of the ancient Greeks. They regarded the Games so highly, they would stop their wars to allow them to go ahead. He believed that if the athletes of the modern world could come together and compete against each other and live together in one Olympic village, they would make lasting friendships which would be good for world peace. De Coubertin put his ideas to a meeting of the Athletic Sports Union at the Sorbonne in Paris in 1892 and again at the International Athletic Congress in Paris in 1894 where the decision was finally taken to revive the games of the ancient Greeks.

The first modern Games were not held in Paris, but in Athens. This was partly because of Olympic history and partly because of the financial backing from a wealthy Greek architect, Georgios Averoff. So when it came to the Games of 1996, Athens believed it was in a great position to win the bid.

But bidding against it was an extremely well-run bid out of

Atlanta — and also Toronto, Belgrade, Manchester and Melbourne. Melbourne had a good report from the IOC's Evaluation Commission, which assesses the venues and technical capacity of a city to hold the Games. By the time they got to the IOC session in Tokyo in September 1990, Melbourne was convinced it was going to win.

Melbourne certainly made a very impressive presentation before the IOC members. Their team included Prime Minister Bob Hawke, Kevan Gosper, CRA chief executive John Ralph and a gold medallist in the Commonwealth Games in Auckland, Cathy Freeman.

But when it came to the vote, its performance was disappointing for its team. It started out with only 12 votes. It got 21 votes in the second round. But only 16 in the third. It was then eliminated, with Athens, Atlanta and Toronto still in the race. Effectively it was ranked fourth out of the six contenders. In the final round Atlanta beat Athens by a clear majority — 51 votes to 35.

There were some difficult moments for everybody in the Australian camp immediately after the announcement of the decision to award the Games to Atlanta. There were urgent discussions among Melbourne supporters in Tokyo. There was a public position from the team that Melbourne had put up a very good bid which would be very hard to beat next time. And next time would be for the 2000 Games.

But by this time, NSW Premier Nick Greiner was looking at the feasibility of Sydney hosting the Games. John Coates and Phil Coles both lived in Sydney and were keen to see a Sydney bid. And Coates was becoming increasingly important in the Australian Olympic Committee. Some months after the Tokyo decision, Gosper had planned to move to London to take up his appointment with Shell. Coates had been chosen to succeed him as AOC president.

John Coates was a rowing enthusiast. He was an official at the Moscow Olympics in 1980 where he met his wife, Pauline, who was also a rower there. Coates had the dream of Australia hosting an Olympic Games for years. He was bitterly disappointed when Barcelona beat Brisbane for the 1992 Games — although no-one could have faulted his commitment to the job. Then there was the defeat of the Melbourne bid in 1990. But he was still undeterred by the task, determined to take all the lessons he had learned from the previous bids to push ahead with another three-year campaign to see his home town get the Games. Coates was a man for whom I had great respect and someone who was always going to have a very significant influence on how Sydney would bid for the Games.

Discussions were held between Nick Greiner, Bruce Baird and Coates about a Sydney bid. In October 1990 Greiner formed a special committee to undertake a feasibility study. It was instructed to take a 'pragmatic and hard-headed look'.

Chaired by Bruce Baird, it included Robert Webster, the Minister for Family and Community Services; John Hannaford, Minister for State Development; John Lewis, chairman of Concrete Constructions; David Smithers, a partner at accountants Coopers and Lybrand; Andrew Turnbull, the managing director of Burns Philp; David Hoare, chairman of Bankers Trust Australia; and Nick Whitlam, a merchant banker and Sydney businessman.

The Baird committee was to give the government a report on the financial consequences of the Games to advise whether Sydney could afford it. Because Sydney had been trying to mount a bid for so long, it had a good understanding of the venues — what use could be made of the city's existing facilities and what needed to be built — and all the other technical requirements. There were people in the state government who had considerable experience with the requirements — people like David Churches, an architect in the NSW Department of Public Works, had been working on the project side of a Sydney Games since 1988.

Soon after its team returned from Tokyo, Melbourne sensed that the momentum was moving towards the AOC backing Sydney for 2000. There was a move to try to discourage Greiner from going ahead. John Ralph, a senior member of the Melbourne business community, came up to speak to Greiner. Lots of lobbying was done. But in the end Greiner said it was time for Sydney to bid.

Things quickly came together for Sydney. On 15 November 1990 Nick Greiner wrote to Kevan Gosper, still the head·of the AOC, and said the NSW government was interested in underwriting a bid for 2000, pending a satisfactory outcome of the Baird committee.

On 16 November the AOC made a provisional decision to endorse Sydney as Australia's candidate. One of the conditions of AOC support was that the state government had to build some sporting facilities — specifically, the International Aquatic Centre and the State Athletic Centre at Homebush. The AOC thought it was important for the bid. And if the bid lost, there would still be a good outcome because there would be a new swimming complex and track and field facilities for Sydney.

The Baird report came out in December and said an Olympic Games in 2000 in Sydney was a very bankable proposition. It predicted that the Games could be staged at a profit of $53 million. It noted that AOC officials and others in the Olympic movement were convinced that Sydney had a good chance of beating the two cities which were expected to be its major rivals, Beijing and Berlin. It said it was 'abundantly clear that the contest to host the year 2000 Olympic Games is wide open and unlike 1996, there is no city that can put forward a sentimental or emotional claim to the 2000 Games.'

Another important step forward was taken that month when the Federal government announced it would release 84 hectares of land at Homebush Bay which could be used to build the athletes' village and other Olympic facilities.

In the months after the decision in Tokyo, the AOC took a good, hard look at how Atlanta had won the 1996 Games. When that contest got underway, most people thought Athens unbeatable. There was no doubt that the leadership of the movement wanted Athens to have those Games.

But Billy Payne and Charlie Battle, two Georgia lawyers, also believed that the Olympic Games would be good for Atlanta. They ran the most professional, inspired bid ever made for an Olympic Games. They ran an impressive *marketing campaign* on the international Olympic movement using a wonderful youthful and friendly lobby team. They had no official backing for their bid. Payne and Battle, whose names I was to think of many times during the next two and a half years, raised all the money themselves. They were our inspiration.

Watching that bid, Coates and Coles could see that sentimental favorites and powerful candidates could be beaten using a well thought-out strategy based on building personal relationships with the IOC members. There was a good case that in the race for the Games, a skilful lobby team could beat the power brokers of the Olympic movement.

So my first bid was John Coates' third. Before I joined, he wrote a detailed paper on the process of bidding. It was an approach we were to draw on heavily in preparing our strategy.

Coates argued that a city must really win the bid *before* it gets to the final presentation — in our case Monte Carlo in September 1993. Sure, a great deal of attention needed to be given to the preparation of the presentation — which at that stage was going to be an hour long. But after the outstanding presentation given by Brisbane, and Melbourne's subsequent improvement on that, it was clear the bid needed to be won well before that final day.

Many will find Coates' strategy imperative simple, even self-evident. In the politics of the office most people know that acceptance of the new product, service, administrative restructure or whatever is being proposed will be won in the pre-meeting canvassing or discussions with colleagues. In most cases, final meetings only would represent a ratification of views already formed. But the way the veteran Coates couched it in the paper was new, strongly argued and persuasive. And its detail was impressive.

Coates's paper also helped us shed a complex or two that might have otherwise dogged us. Sydney, with 3.5 million people, looked small alongside Beijing's 14 million; Australia's 17 million was not much compared to China's 1.1 billion. In some people's eyes, a mere anniversary of nationhood — 2000 would be 100 years of Australian federation — paled a bit before the historic re-unification of the long-divided city of Berlin and the political attraction of China as an emerging economic superpower.

But Coates had defined who we were selling to and how it was to be done. He defined the target audience and was never distracted.

For the Sydney bid, the two and a half years of lobbying in the lead up to the Monte Carlo vote would be critical.

The decision on the city to host an Olympic Games is made by all the members of the International Olympic Committee, each having one vote. (The actual number of members changed over the course of the bid as some new positions were created and some existing members died. But in early 1991, when Coates wrote his paper, there were 94.)

All the bidding cities make a final presentation to all the members and then they vote by secret ballot. At the end of each round of voting, the candidate city with the least number of votes is eliminated. The voting continues until one city has a majority — that is, 50 per cent of the votes plus one.

Sway the majority of the 90-odd minds to your product, and the prize was yours, sentiment, history, power, population and whatever else notwithstanding.

As Coates pointed out in his paper, a key part of the lobbying strategy was to get as many IOC members as possible to visit Sydney. Received Olympic wisdom holds that if a member doesn't visit your country, they're probably not going to vote for you. And one ignores received wisdom at peril. For Australia, which is not as well known or as accessible as, say, Europe, getting the members to visit was set as a key part of our strategy. I don't believe anyone can appreciate the true attractions of a city like Sydney until they have seen it. Our critics always argued that Sydney was too far away. I joked that it was only two meals and a movie away, but we knew that the issue of distance and travelling time was a potential problem; jokes helped but mind-sets held.

Again, the previous bids had aided our cause. Melbourne had attracted 65 IOC members — a most respectable hit rate — during its campaign and many had also travelled through Sydney on their visit. Even those who had not, knew that coming to eastern Australia was no great problem. But, as always, nothing stays quite the same. New rules were coming in which would restrict IOC members to making only one official visit to a bidding city per campaign.

Coates said it was also important for members of the bid city's lobby team to attend major international sporting events and meetings where IOC members would be present. This not only showed a city was serious about bidding and provided further opportunities to lobby, but in the final two years, there would often be sessions where bid cities could make short formal presentations. We should also visit IOC members in their countries.

He said it was acceptable for bid cities to use regional specialists as lobbyists who were not necessarily part of the actual bid committee. These were people who either had good contacts with officials from the Olympic movement in a particular region or had a special standing that might appeal to certain IOC members. The Atlanta team had made good use of one: Andrew Young, one of city's foremost black figures. Young had been a mayor of Atlanta and was US ambassador to the United Nations in the Carter Administration. He did a lot of lobbying of black African members. Atlanta had a specialist lobbying team of ten people. Most of them were not paid, but they worked full time on the bid and formed the basis of Atlanta's representation at major sporting events and meetings. They may not have known anyone when they started out, but by the time they got to D-Day in Tokyo in 1990, they knew almost all the members.

He explained the extended nature of the Olympic family. In addition to the IOC members, there were two other arms — the national Olympic committees of each nation or NOCs and the international sporting federations, or IFs. The NOCs had regional associations and meetings (Australia was a member of the Oceania National Olympic Committee) as well as a global umbrella organisation called the Association of National Olympic Committees (ANOC). The IFs actually ran the individual sports at an Olympic Games. There were 25 different federations, or IFs, involved in the summer Games. As if that wasn't enough, the IFs also had their own global umbrella groups: the Association of Summer Olympic International Federations (ASOIF) and of Winter Olympic IFs (AWIF). In a number of cases, key officials of these organisations were also IOC members. But even if they weren't members, the leaders of the NOCs and the IFs had an important influence on the views of the IOC. It was the international federations which declared if venues were suitable for their sports — or what changes needed to be made to bring them up to scratch. In addition to all these, there was also a separate body representing a whole range of Olympic IFs and other international sporting federations called the General Assembly of International Sports Federations or GAISF.

Coates recommended that the Sydney bid team also try to get the support of influential national and regional Olympic committees — particularly the Oceania National Olympic Committee, ONOC, and the Olympic Council of Asia, as well as the Association

of National Olympic Committees, ANOC. We should also lobby
hard to get the support of the 25 summer Olympic IFs. Other
lobbying targets included:

- diplomats, Australian embassies and the Department of Foreign Affairs and Trade
- senior Australian politicians and business leaders
- IOC opinion leaders such as the IOC power brokers and key
  international sporting officials
- the international media, international television networks
  especially
- leading athletes

The bid should have the support of the domestic media and
local community groups. It was important that the bid be managed efficiently, that the IOC was convinced of the overall
financial viability of the Games and the city's ability to cater for
a large contingent of national and international media.

Coates forecast that the two main problems for the Sydney bid
to counter in its communications strategy would be (1) the length
of travel time to Australia and (2) the controversy over Australia's
quarantine laws.

In the Olympic Games in Melbourne in 1956 Australia's tough
quarantine laws had prevented the equestrian events from being
held in Australia. These had since changed and Melbourne's 1996
lobbying effort had, we thought, largely overcome the perceptions of Australia's laws being a problem. But it was something
to keep in mind.

Sydney's strengths included (1) its compact Olympic plan with
minimal travel to the venues for athletes; (2) a government with
a strong commitment to sport — as evidenced by the construction of $300 million of sports facilities during the candidacy of
the Games and the fact that 70 per cent of the sports facilities
would be available by the time of the vote in September 1993;
(3) our good climate, (4) our political stability and security, (5)
community and government support, and (6) the fact that it was
Australia's third consecutive bid.

Our main challenges — so we thought then — would come
from the financial muscle of a Berlin bid and the potential
political power of a bid from Beijing.

As the incoming chief executive, I couldn't have had a better base to start from. When I was handed the baton, our team was already running fast. Sydney already had a very clear idea of what was needed to achieve its goal. It was up to me to capitalise on this momentum.

4

Culture Shock

culture shock *n.* confusion caused by difficulty in getting used
to a culture different from one's own.

Macquarie Dictionary

Corrs had its work culture. The public service had another.
One of a thousand cultural differences I found was the
matter of the bathroom.

My status in the Premier's Department apparently meant I was
entitled to an office of a certain size and a bathroom. When I
saw the plans for the renovations of our offices, I noticed a
bathroom off my office. I had never had a bathroom off my
office. I have never understood why anyone would want one.

I told them I didn't want a bathroom. But they said I had to
have one because I was an SES 7 or 8 or whatever. I couldn't
understand why people were insisting on it. I said:

'I don't want a bathroom. If there's going to be a bathroom
in the office, there's going to be one on the other side that all
the staff can use.'

The public service couldn't understand this attitude and the
plans kept coming back with a bathroom off my office. I was even
told that there couldn't be another bathroom on the other side
for plumbing reasons.

Who was really running the place? I put my foot down.

I didn't have a bathroom off my office, the bathroom was
eventually put on the other side of the bid office for the use of
everybody — and somehow the plumbing all worked.

When I arrived there was already a temporary staff of about
15 in the office made up of public servants from various state
government departments who had been loaned to the office to
get things started. The staff was headed by David O'Connor, a

very experienced public servant. David had been an applicant for my job. He had played a very prominent role on the Bicentennial Authority and had been awarded an AM for his efforts.

It was part of my job to decide which staff should be sent back to their respective departments and what new staff needed to be hired for the office. One early thing I encountered what one might call 'political patronage'. A lot of politicians were suggesting that friends apply for jobs. I was being confronted by people saying Minister-so-and-so said I should come down here and there would be a job.

I kept knocking back people I didn't like and I couldn't work out why I started to have problems. I suppose it was all part of my naivety in dealing with governments and politicians. I had a simple view: if the person was good, they got a job; if they weren't, I didn't care who they knew, they didn't. I stood my ground and people ultimately respected me for that. I was never forced to hire anyone I didn't want to. Eventually the pressure went away — although maybe the memories didn't.

David O'Connor advised me about the rules and regulations of the public service. The issue of the RDO came up. I had to ask him what those initials meant. He told me it meant Rostered Day Off. He explained that if you work half an hour a day extra, the time accumulated over a month into a full day which people could get off to go shopping or see the dentist or whatever. I told him:

'Rod McGeoch would be laughed out of this city if he administered a company with RDOs. David, I can tell you now that if people work hard here they can go to the doctor everyday. Ask my secretary. She's never had to worry about going to the dentist because she works hard. If you always do more than nine to five, the credit is there in the boss's mind and there's no problem. So there won't be any RDOs here.'

I knew there were going to be horrendous hours involved in the job. A Remuneration Committee was trying to sort out salaries and talk about hours and bonuses. Somebody on that committee suggested that we pay a 10 per cent loading and there would be no RDOs and no overtime. That suited me fine and that's what happened. It meant that people were getting a little extra for the big job that was ahead of us. But the message was out. There were going to be no public service style work practices in our office.

I have always believed that the best way to create a culture in an office is by the power of your own example. If a leader sets a certain kind of example, it says everything about their operation. As a partner in a law firm I never took late lunches. I was always at work by 7.30 am and stayed until 7 pm or later. If I was ever anywhere longer than expected, I always rang my secretary and told her what I was doing. It's all part of a sort of efficiency — a diligence and a work ethic. That might sound a bit tough but I have always been a bit of a stickler for getting done what is supposed to be done in an office. On the other hand, if it *is* getting done and done well, I think I'm a very reasonable boss. I believe in a happy working environment. I told even the youngest kids in the office to call me 'Rod', not 'Mr McGeoch'. I used to make my attitude to running the office pretty plain. I told them in our early meetings, 'Nobody's better than anyone else here. I'm not going to ask you to do anything that I'm not going to do. We're all the same here. So, let's get into it.'

My new role was different from that of other chief executives as I had one single goal — winning the Olympics for Sydney — and a specific timetable — by 8.20 pm 23 September 1993. There's nothing like a tough deadline to sharpen the focus and get everybody motivated towards the same goal. But even if there isn't one externally imposed, most successful people in business do set their own deadlines. If you don't have an outside deadline, you should set your own — whether it be to double production in two years' time or improve sales by 30 per cent within 12 months or whatever. And for it to be really effective, it should be known throughout the organisation.

I had a clear view from the start that winning the Games would depend on having a high-quality, highly-motivated team at the bid office. But early on, I felt I was having unexpected difficulties and problems. I didn't feel I was getting the kind of support from the existing staff that was necessary. It was understandable that people were more loyal to David O'Connor than they were to me. He had been around longer. I was from private enterprise; they were from the public service.

On a couple of occasions, David came to me and said, 'Look. You've really got to decide which staff you want and which staff you want to send back to their departments, because people are unsettled.' But it seemed to me that far from being unsettled, most people in the office were very keen to have jobs on the Olympic campaign and were crossing their fingers, hoping I was going to keep them. I didn't think there was any overwhelming need to make quick decisions; it was more important we make the right decisions. I wasn't going to be hurried into either sending people back or committing myself to them.

David gave me a couple of more prods and one day he came in and really put it on me. It was an inconvenient moment, at about ten to one. He said, 'I think you really have to decide who's going back.' I guess he got me slightly agitated. So I said, 'David, I can tell you one person who's going back and that's you.' He was stunned. He said he thought we were getting on well together and he wanted to be my second in command. But I said I was sorry, but I wanted to pick my own 2IC.

As it turned out, it was the right decision in a number of respects. David became the Olympic liaison officer in the Premier's Department and basically took over the protocol area, very important in all our visit programs. Just how important that is will unfold later. Once he and I had rebuilt our relationship, he was very effective in the bid process in representing government. Now, as far as I am concerned, I enjoy a warm relationship with him, and he now has a very high-profile and important job which he does very well.

David's departure meant I was able to get the general manager of my choice. And that decision quickly made itself for me. Early on in the bid, I was accepting every invitation to every sporting engagement I received so I could meet people and understand who was who. On two occasions I had to go out to the State Sports Centre at Homebush. The master of ceremonies on both occasions was a guy called Bob Elphinston, the general manager of the centre. He was wonderfully open, friendly and enthusiastic. He had already made an impression on me, so when I was told by Graham Lovett, one of the members of our board, that he might be available for the job and that he was very good at his paperwork and did a very good job at the State Sports Centre, I telephoned him. Bob shot straight into the office and was prepared to start in the next five minutes. It didn't take long for me to offer him a job as general manager.

Bob had been an 800 metre runner in his younger days and was a sports fanatic. Once a physical education teacher, he had managed the Australian basketball team at the Los Angeles Olympics in 1984. He was on the board of the Sydney Kings basketball team. He would often start his speeches with a cheerful, 'Hello, sports lovers.' He loved red wine and so did I. We both had wives who smoked and we didn't. We quickly struck up a close personal rapport.

Little did I know that my offer to hire Bob was outside public service guidelines. Apparently I was meant to advertise the job. I simply didn't know that at the time I made my commitment to Bob. By the time I found out, he had given up a good job, his long-service leave and assured employment for the rest of his working life to come and work in our office. I got called up to see Premier Greiner and the head of the Premier's Department, Dick Humphry about the whole question of swapping David O'Connor and hiring Bob Elphinston. Humphry wanted to make me advertise the job. But I had already given the job to Bob. Nick Greiner said he thought I should have the general manager I wanted. So I was saved the embarrassment of having to advertise the job, and wasting a lot of applicants' time.

In retrospect, I don't think that there's anybody on the bid board or anywhere else who doesn't think Bob went on to do a remarkable job. He was an excellent administrator. I never had any secrets from Bob. I said, 'Bob, I'm working on the theory that I'm going to be hit by a bus, so you must know everything.' It was the kind of frank, open management style I often used and, with Bob and I, it worked well.

Bob had tremendous energy and enthusiasm and was a wonderful staff communicator. Because I was travelling so much, it was very reassuring to me that I had such a phenomenal 2IC. The staff loved him. We tried to have a rule that one of us always had to be in the office at any time. We broke it twice, I think; but we did try.

Bob and I began to put in place the organisational structure of the office and the early plans for the bid. Like the ultimate goal and the timetable, the corporate structure for the Sydney Olympics Bid 2000 was already set out before I arrived. Sydney

Olympics 2000 Bid Limited had been established as a public company incorporated in NSW with the capacity to draw funds from the private and public sectors. There was to be an executive board of 15 directors (later expanded to 16) with the premier as the president. These board members and another 30 members of the company made up a bid committee which represented a cross section of community, government, business and sporting interests. But it was the executive board which was the main supervising force.

When we started out, Jeremy Bingham, the Lord Mayor of Sydney, was the chairman. But there was always going to be a problem with having the Lord Mayor in such an important position in our team because of the high turnover in that office. We knew it wouldn't go down well if we kept changing key people during the bid and had to keep introducing the new person to the IOC members. It had been a problem in the Melbourne bid where the mayor changes every year and Coates and Coles were very sensitive about it. So when Jeremy Bingham lost his position as Lord Mayor, Nick Greiner said he would take on the job of both president and chairman which meant that the Premier was a very important player in the team.

Under the president was the chief executive who reported to the board and then Bob, who reported to me. Also reporting to the board were to be five commissions — on sport, building, culture, communications and finance — and a strategy committee. Our office structure was basically divided into these areas.

The Sports Commission was chaired by Graham Lovett. Lovett has described himself as 'a businessman in the world of sport'. He was the chairman of the NSW International Sports Council, a government-sponsored organisation which aimed to attract prestige sporting events to the State and was the head of the marketing division of the NSW Rugby League. Graham was an outstanding tennis player who reached seventh in the Australian rankings in his day. He became a marketing executive with Dunlop/Slazenger before leaving in 1983 to start his own company, Sport Australia. He was on the board of the Association of Tennis Professionals, which organised many of the men's tournaments around the world, and had been on the board of Basketball Australia. He was the promoter of the Australian Indoor Tennis championships and a similar annual tennis tournament in Brisbane. He certainly knew a lot about sport and administration.

The Building Commission was chaired by Ted Harris. Harris, who had been chief executive of Ampol for many years, was chairman of Australian Airlines and the Australian Sports Commission and, from 1992, Australian National Industries. He was an excellent tennis player and a former tennis commentator. Harris was also chairman of Arena Meetings Conventions and Exhibitions, the operator of the Entertainment Centre, and on the board of the State Sports Centre Trust which administers all operations at the Homebush complex. He was familiar with the demands of keeping to a budget and construction timetables. Lovett and Harris were both pretty obvious choices for their respective commissions.

David Smithers, from Coopers and Lybrand, was in charge of the Finance Commission and Greg Daniel, from advertising agency Clemenger, was in charge of the Communications Commission. I was put in charge of the Strategy Committee and we appointed the general manager of the Australian Opera Company, Donald McDonald, as chairman of the Cultural Commission. Donald was one of the leading people in Australia who could straddle both the world of business and arts. He was very professional and commercial in his outlook, very familiar with fund raising at the same time as being very sensitive to questions concerning the arts. I knew he would be ideal for the job. He also became a very important part of the lobbying team. Many people involved in the Olympic movement are very keen about the arts. Donald and his wife Janet were a very engaging couple and they got on well with many IOC members.

We had to create a whole structure in the office. My philosophy was keep things small and enthusiastic. I was determined that we were not going to get bureaucratic. The Australian Olympic Committee was on the floor below us in the Maritime Services Board Building, with its own staff and it was always going to provide some support.

But it was critical to fill the top spots. We didn't have an office manager but soon found a good one. John Shirley, who was in the public service, came to our office to sort out our computers. He was a very competent operator so we asked him to stay on to run the office. John was very familiar with the public service as well as being very good with computers and office equipment. He was also very loyal to me. We had to create a whole financial division. David Smithers said he would send us one of the top guys from Coopers and Lybrand, Bob Prater, to be our chief accountant. His services were paid for by Coopers as part of their contribution to the bid.

David Churches, the architect from the Public Works Department who had a long experience in planning the venues was already in the office and he stayed to head up our planning and design section.

But there was nobody in marketing and communications. We had to create a whole division for that. We knew there would be merchandising and needed to produce videos and brochures and to deal with the press.

We had no corporate support program.

We knew we would have to create a whole cultural program to run during the Games at the same time as the sporting events.

Morgan and Banks, the employment agency, offered their services to us free of charge. So I used them to help find a head of our communications division. But I had also got a suggestion that Susan Hunt from the Federal government's Tourism Task Force would be an excellent choice. I interviewed Susan as well as some people suggested by Morgan and Banks and appointed her. Susan was a triathlete who was very health conscious and keen on sport. She introduced environmental sensitivity into all aspects of our bid and correctly predicted the environment would become an important issue for us. Our first fact sheets, brochures and give-away pads were printed on recycled paper and we had a note on the back to that effect. Susan was a very capable, attractive woman who could talk sport with the experts. In the early days we were also looking upon her as a potential lobbyist.

Alan Hoskins, who had been Bruce Baird's principal policy adviser, became our manager of government relations. For all the right reasons, Bruce wanted one of his people in our office and it was Alan. A well-educated guy, he could speak French and Spanish, which also gave us some extra multi-lingual skills. He knew all about government relations: how to deal with the bureaucracy and the politicians; when something would be politically sensitive and when it wasn't; what had to be done to look after Premiers and Lord Mayors when they were travelling. Alan and Margaret McLennan would always go to major international events and he became an integral part of the backup for our lobby team.

Alan's presence in our office also gave Bruce Baird another person, apart from Bob Elphinston, he could talk to find out what was going on if I wasn't there. I had a standing instruction with Alan that there was to be nothing in my office that he couldn't tell Bruce. I think it gave Bruce tremendous comfort that he had a close confidant in our office and I welcomed it.

In August, when we visited Atlanta, we learned a few other things about running a bid. Ginger Watkins from the Atlanta bid team told me it was important to have the switchboard manned 24 hours a day. She said people would ring the office when it was convenient for them and they wanted to be able to speak to someone. So we put on a professional answering service out-of-hours and used pagers so that anyone could get us. They also showed us their photo albums of fun runs, days for the handi-capped and other events they used to raise money and keep the local community enthusiastic about the bid.

The Atlanta people strongly recommended we have a full-time person to manage the hospitality program for the IOC members and other VIPs. So, in November, Sue Bushby joined our team as our manager of hospitality. I had met her at university and known her for 25 years. She was a very elegant woman and a very tough, determined organiser. She had been president of the Asthma Foundation and had been in charge of the arts exhibition at my children's school. I knew she was looking for work. When I asked her if she was interested in the job, she couldn't start quick enough. She did a lot of work organising all the gifts for the IOC members whenever we travelled and she organised all their visits to Sydney. When she travelled overseas with us she would sit down with members and their wives and ask them what they would like to see when they came to Sydney.

Bob and I roughly divided up the work between us. There were certain things that I wanted to be directly involved in. Lawyers are not known to be great at public relations and marketing, but having been president of the Law Society and having done a lot of media and public relations work for it, I felt I had a natural nose for that area, and I liked being in it. So I made the Communications Department directly accountable to me. I took charge of communications, culture and strategy. Bob looked after finance, sport and building.

We had our work cut out for us. We had to prepare detailed plans for the board on how we were going to carry out the bid by September 1991. This was to include a business plan, a communications plan, a financial plan and a strategy plan.

We had a number of sessions locked in a room with a white board working through these plans. These included John Coates, Phil Coles, Peter Montgomery, another member of the AOC board and a member of the Athletes' Commission of the IOC, and myself. We talked through everything we would have to do to achieve our goal. Our strategy had two major arms — preparing our Olympic plan and selling the bid. Our first goal was to submit to the IOC what would be the best bid proposal of all the competing cities. For Sydney that was a necessary condition for achieving our ultimate goal of winning the Games.

We had to make sure we got our product right; then we had to sell it to a majority of IOC members.

Of course, we focussed on the need to have top-class facilities, but out of our discussions came another important point — the importance of looking after the official members of the Olympic family themselves. The IOC members were our customers and we had to put up a plan which would make them want to come to Sydney in 2000. They had to be assured they would be looked after at a high standard as well as the athletes, officials and visitors.

So we listed four essential elements of Sydney's Olympic plan. These were:

1 world-class and convenient facilities
2 a demonstrable capacity for Sydney to manage and host the Games
3 an exciting and caring plan to take care of the Olympic family (athletes, officials and the media)
4 a hospitality plan for the members of the IOC and other VIPs during the Games.

When it came to the selling of the bid, we identified three essential components of our marketing strategy:

1 communicating Sydney's ability to host the Games
2 communicating a commitment to Olympism
3 a marketing strategy with a number of innovative incentives such as travel subsidisation.

We identified three unique strengths of our bid which we needed to capitalise on and communicate:

1 the proximity of our facilities: the compact area, how the athletes' village meant that athletes could walk to many of the events
2 Australia's telecommunications expertise and capacity, where we knew Beijing would be weak
3 The integration of the Australian Olympic Committee with the bid office which would show the IOC that the Australian Olympic movement was firmly behind us.

Our primary target market was clear — it was the IOC members. We identified our secondary market as the international sporting federations, the national Olympic committees, the Olympic media, athletes and other members of the Olympic family. The third was the Sydney business and political community, the Australian community, and NSW and national sporting federations.

We spent many hours at the white boards thinking through all our plans, setting out our goals and the steps we needed to get there. We also put a lot of work into our financial plan — estimating every item of cost and what we would need in terms of revenue and corporate support. It was a very demanding task. I was travelling a lot as well. At one point Ken Baxter from the Premier's Department started to worry that we were never going to get these plans *finished!* He sent out a signal that maybe I should stop travelling until I got it all under control. I could see I was going to get myself in trouble unless I got them done, so I put in long hours. We all did. It was seven-days-a-week stuff until they were finished.

But Ken Baxter was absolutely right about the importance of getting them done. All the plans were finalised two years before the decision. They proved to be fantastic documents. They were very good plans and, for the most part, we never deviated from any of them. It was like building the right foundations for a house. If you don't build them properly, the house will eventually fall down. But if you do it all correctly, you have a sound basis to work from. I'm a great advocate of that style of management. It's a winning strategy. If you put the effort into working out a solid plan and then execute that plan correctly, you'll be very hard to beat.

There was a very clear timetable of activities ahead of us over the next two years. We knew that we would have to make an appearance — and often a presentation — at all the major international sporting events until the decision in September 1993. This would include the Winter Olympics in Albertville, France, in February 1992 and the summer Olympics in Barcelona in July 1992, as well as a whole host of regional sporting meetings and IOC sessions.

The deadline for bidding cities to register their interest with the IOC was in April 1992. But the really big task was the preparation of a detailed presentation books, commonly known as 'bid books', which outlined how Sydney proposed to run an Olympics. This was due to be delivered at IOC headquarters in Lausanne in Switzerland in February 1993. In March 1993 we would be getting a visit from the IOC's Evaluation Commission to inspect our facilities. We knew this would be critical. Two of our major selling points were that we would be holding 'The Athletes' Games' — the Games that were designed with the best interest of the athletes in mind — and that we were well advanced with our construction work. The contents of the bid books and the evaluation visit would be important in communicating both to the IOC.

Then there was the big day: presentation day and voting day at Monte Carlo on 23 September 1993. Our presentation would have to be superb and it would take some organising. And on top of all this, of course, was an intensive international lobbying campaign.

The biggest single marketing exercise for Sydney in the immediate future would be in October 1991 when there was to be the annual meeting of the General Assembly of International Sports Federations, known by its acronym GAISF (pronounced 'gafe'), at Darling Harbor. This was a great opportunity for us. The annual GAISF conferences bring together all the sporting federations of the world. There were about 70 sports which were members of GAISF, including all the Olympic sports. Some 20 IOC members were due to attend the conference, an excellent chance for lobbying.

This was important for the Sydney bid. As a result of complaints about the high cost of previous bidding exercises, the IOC was planning to tighten up the rules on a what could be done in the course of lobbying. The aim was to cut down the lavish parties, the expensive gift giving and prevent the occasional incidences of too many trips to bidding cities by members.

The visits of the 20-odd IOC members to the GAISF conference would be in addition to the one official visit per campaign allowed each IOC member. There were a few lawyers on this bid. We argued that the new rule did not really come into force until everyone had registered their intention to bid in February 1992. We also argued that Sydney had been awarded the right to host the conference before the IOC proposed changing the rules. So we were in the fortunate position where at least 20 IOC members were really going to be entitled to come to Sydney twice.

It was John Coates in particular who had the foresight to lobby for the right for Sydney to host the conference back in 1990. The NSW Government also realised its importance and Bruce Baird went to the GAISF meeting in Monte Carlo in 1990 to give a presentation to convince the organisation to have its next meeting in Sydney. The State government also agreed to underwrite additional logistical support and entertainment to make it outstanding. It was important that the conference went off well. We knew we would also have to be ready to give a high-class presentation to it. So Susan Hunt and others in the office became heavily involved in the preparation for the GAISF meeting.

Sometimes it seemed things were running smoothly, then I would get another lesson about what a different world I was operating in. I had a big lesson on the political sensitivities involved in being a public servant. In July 1991 Bruce Baird spoke at a business lunch and made some critical comments about Berlin and Beijing. It was the sort of thing that a bidding city just couldn't say publicly — whatever it thought privately. Coles and Coates got on the phone to him to make sure he wouldn't say them again. When I was asked about Bruce's comments in a television interview later, I said, he had used 'words I would have preferred he did not use. I don't think you will hear him say them again.' I had no idea of the impact *my* words would have. Here was a public servant effectively ticking off a minister. Bruce was very upset about it. He rang me several times as the news broke that evening on television and said, 'You've really hurt me politically.' I tried to play it down.

The next day I was called into his office where I was told in no uncertain terms that the paid public servant does not say those things about their minister. Nick Greiner had been away on holidays when it happened. When he came back, he carpeted me too. He said if he hadn't been on the ski slopes when it happened, I wouldn't have been working for the government today. I was reminded that I was paid by the government and did not tell government ministers what to do or say. They were the boss and I was their employee.

They made their point, loud and clear. But it was hard. One minute I was being told, 'You're in charge. You pick the team. You handle it all.' Then when I said one small thing out of line, I was hit with a tonne of bricks! I don't think it did hurt Bruce Baird. We found we often said things in the media during the bid we wished we hadn't and got terribly worried about it all, but in the end they were often great storms in teacups. But, nevertheless, it was another lesson for me in the protocol of public service. I was a public figure — that went with the territory — but I always had to remember that I was also a public servant whose responsibility it was to make sure that I did not embarrass my minister.

It was a long way from my old life at Corrs.

Within a few months I had put together my own team to run the bid and was starting to focus on our first big meeting with IOC members. Over the next two and a half years, I was to lead a dual life — one running an office in Sydney and another lobbying IOC members around the world with a hectic schedule of international travel. There wasn't much time to think about it all. From here on in, life was to be a series of deadlines. I had plenty of advice and support, but I still had to make a lot of the big decisions and lead the team. Everyone seemed to have a view on how we should go about our job, but I had to sort out the real 'experts' from the big talkers. Sometime I felt like a duck on a pond — on the surface the duck looked calm gliding along, but underneath paddling furiously.

From Sydney, State highways radiate to regional cities and towns.

The major highways to Canberra, Newcastle and Wollongong have been constantly upgraded over recent decades to freeway standard for most of their length.

The Federal Government recently announced network extensions which will significantly benefit Sydney.

10.1.2 Planned improvements

Sydney's existing road system is capable of handling an Olympic Games now and the necessary traffic management systems have already been implemented.

No major road infrastructure developments are required for the Olympics, but improvements to the road system are planned as part of the State's continuing transport infrastructure program.

New roadworks totalling US$ 570 million will further enhance Sydney's capacity to stage the Olympic Games by 2000. Major projects include the East-West Corridor (City/Homebush Bay/Penrith), US$ 92.4 million; the City West Link (Darling Harbour to Rozelle Bay), US$ 86 million; the F4 Westward extension to Lapstone, US$ 23 million.

The Sydney Harbour Tunnel, completed in August 1992 at a cost of US$ 511 million, has significantly improved city traffic flow.

The Roads and Traffic Authority of NSW states that:

'The road improvement projects outlined in the Candidature File have been planned by this Authority as part of an overall masterplan for the transport infrastructure of Sydney and NSW to the year 2000 and will be beneficial to the City of Sydney.'

'I confirm the matters contained in the above statement by the Roads and Traffic Authority of NSW.'

The Hon John Fahey
Premier of New South Wales

10.1.3 International links

From around the world, 45 airlines from 56 major cities in 41 countries fly to Sydney. As well, Sydney Airport has provided access for charter flights from all countries competing in the Olympic Games.

The nations and cities linked to Sydney are:

Country	City
Argentina	Buenos Aires
Austria	Vienna
Bahrain	
Canada	Toronto/Vancouver
China	Beijing
England	London/Manchester
Fiji	Nadi
France	Paris
Germany	Frankfurt
Greece	Athens
Guam	
Holland	Amsterdam
Hong Kong	
Indonesia	Bali-Denpasar/Jakarta
Italy	Rome
Japan	*Chitosi (Sapporo) Fukuoka/Nagoya/Osaka/Tokyo
Lebanon	*Beirut
Malaysia	Kuala Lumpur
Nauru	
New Caledonia	Noumea
New Zealand	Auckland/Christchurch Wellington
Norfolk Island	
Papua New Guinea	Port Moresby
Philippines	Manila
Poland	*Warsaw
Rarotonga	
Russia	Moscow
Singapore	
Solomon Islands	Honiara
South Korea	Seoul
South Africa	Johannesburg
Sri Lanka	Colombo
Taiwan	Taipei
Thailand	Bangkok
Tahiti	Papeete
USA	Chicago/Honolulu/Los Angeles New York/San Francisco
Vanuatu	Port Vila
Vietnam	*Ho Chi Minh City
Western Samoa	Apia
Yugoslavia	Belgrade
Zimbabwe	Harare

*Linked by charter flights.

The Bid Books: sample pages showing technical complexity (and the data kept changing everytime airlines put on a new connection for example, and the government had to sign every promise off) and inspired design. There were over 500 pages like these.

Sydney, Melbourne et Brisbane, respectivement deuxième et troisième villes d'Australie.

Des trains ultramodernes à grande vitesse seront introduits dès 1993 et réduiront considérablement les temps de voyage entre les grandes villes et les centres de province.

Route

Le réseau de routes nationales relie Sydney à toutes les capitales des Etats et Territoires d'Australie.

Au départ de Sydney, les routes de l'Etat rayonnent vers les villes régionales.

Les routes principales reliant Canberra, Newcastle et Wollongong ont été améliorées au cours des dernières décennies, atteignant le standard d'auto-route sur la plupart de leur longueur.

Sydney bénéficiera grandement des extensions du réseau récemment annoncées par le gouvernement fédéral.

10.1.2 Améliorations prévues

Le réseau routier de Sydney est en mesure de recevoir les Jeux Olympiques dès à présent et les systèmes de gestion du trafic ont déjà été mis en place.

Aucun développement majeur de l'infrastructure ne sera nécessaire pour les Jeux mais des améliorations du système routier sont prévues dans le cadre du programme continu concernant l'infrastructure des transports de la Nouvelle-Galles du Sud.

De nouveaux travaux routiers s'élevant à 570 M $US amélioreront encore la capacité de Sydney d'organiser les Jeux Olympiques d'ici l'an 2000. Parmi ces grands projets, on compte: le corridor est-ouest (Centre ville/ Homebush Bay/Penrith), 92,4 M $US; la liaison "City West" (entre Darling Harbour et Rozelle Bay), 86 M $US ; l'extension Ouest de la F4 vers Lapstone, 23 M $US.

Le tunnel de la baie de Sydney, achevé en août 1992 pour un coût de 511 M $US, a nettement amélioré la circulation dans la ville.

L'Administration des routes et du trafic de NSW a fait la déclaration suivante:

'Les projets d'aménagements routiers décrits dans le Dossier de candidature ont été planifiés par cette administration dans le cadre d'un grand projet d'ensemble concernant l'infrastructure des transports de Sydney et de NSW jusqu'à l'an 2000 et seront bénéfiques à la ville de Sydney.'

'Je ratifie les points contenus dans la déclaration ci-dessus de l'Administration des routes et du trafic de NSW'.

M. John Fahey
Premier de Nouvelle-Galles du Sud

10.1.3 Liaisons internationales

Au niveau mondial, Sydney est desservie par 45 compagnies aériennes au départ de 56 grandes villes de 41 pays. De plus, l'aéroport de Sydney a prévu l'accès aux vols charters venant de tous les pays participant aux Jeux Olympiques.

Les nations et villes reliées à Sydney sont:

Pays	Ville
Argentine	Buenos Aires
Autriche	Vienne
Bahreïn	
Canada	Toronto/Vancouver
Chine	Beijing
Angleterre	Londres/Manchester
Fiji	Nadi
France	Paris
Allemagne	Frankfort
Grèce	Athènes
Guam	
Hollande	Amsterdam
Hong-Kong	
Indonésie	Bali-Denpasar/Jakarta
Italie	Rome
Japon	*Chitosi (Sapporo)
	Fukuoka/Nagoya/Osaka/Tokyo
Liban	*Beyrouth
Malaisie	Kuala Lumpur
Nauru	
Nouvelle-Calédonie	Nouméa
Nouvelle-Zélande	Auckland/Christchurch/ Wellington
Ile de Norfolk	
Papouasie-Nouvelle-Guinée	Port Moresby
Philippines	Manille
Pologne	*Varsovie
Rarotonga	
Russie	*Moscou
Singapour	

5
The Winter Draw

You can see a lot by observing

Yogi Berra

It was not long before I got my first real taste of what the Olympic movement was about. In June 1991 we went to Britain's second city, Birmingham, for the IOC's 97th annual meeting. The session would also choose the city to host the 1998 winter Olympics. We would be able to see first hand what it was like, right at the death, when cities were in their final throes of lobbying and the decision-makers gathered to pass their verdict on the candidates who were trying so earnestly to get them to buy their product.

Our lobby team included Bruce Baird, Graham Lovett, Phil Coles, John Coates and Peter Montgomery. Kevan Gosper came up from London and Alan Hoskins came along to help with the organisation. Because it was an IOC session and the IOC members would be taking their spouses, our lobby team also took their spouses and I took Deeta. It was the first trip away for all of us as part of the Sydney bid team.

One of the first things we noticed was the degree of formality and ceremony which surrounded these big IOC meetings. The IOC takes them very seriously and everything is organised — or supposed to be organised — down to the last detail. IOC members and important guests are always very well looked after.

When we got off the plane in Birmingham we were met at the steps of the aircraft by some shiny new Rover cars. That surprised us. And then, as we got into the terminal, every woman was presented with a large spray of flowers. The Rover company had donated four or five hundred courtesy cars for the occasion. The drivers were all very smartly dressed, all stunningly attractive young women. But when I asked our driver what our hotel was like — we were staying at The Albany — she said, 'I don't know, I've never been there.'

'Is it where the Olympic family stay?'

'I don't know, I don't come from Birmingham.'

And then we got lost. It was the first of a repeating problem I found at some of these big IOC events. Volunteer drivers and hire-car drivers never seemed to be properly trained. The drivers looked terrific, but they had trouble getting people where they wanted to go. It was the same all week.

It started to give us an idea of the logistical arrangements that would be needed to host a Games. We only had to be told once: if Sydney had the 2000 Games, the town would have to have drivers who knew where they were going.

Security was tight at the five-star Hyatt Regency where the officials and the IOC members were staying, opposite the city's new International Convention Centre. The entire hotel was booked for the use of the Olympic family. Princess Anne, the president of the International Equestrian Federation and one of Britain's two IOC members was there, as was Prince Albert of Monaco, Princess Nora of Liechtenstein and Grand-Duc Jean de Luxembourg. Prince Faisal, the IOC member from Saudi Arabia, was there as well as the young Sheik Ahmad from Kuwait, who was head of Kuwait's national Olympic committee and soon to become an IOC member. No-one could enter the hotel without a full search.

Birmingham had unsuccessfully bid for the right to hold the Olympic Games in 1992. Manchester had nudged it out of the way as Britain's candidate for 1996 and the British Olympic Association had recently decided that Manchester should be the one to try again for 2000. Of course this meeting was not in Manchester, but because Manchester was bidding, but the meeting was a chance for a would-be host *country* to impress the members with its capacity to stage an event. Just as we planned to do with the GAISF conference in Sydney in October.

When the Brits really put their mind to a bit of pomp and circumstance, they can be hard to beat. They put on a stunning opening cermony. The session was opened by Queen Elizabeth in the new convention centre. Then there was a great pageant.

Called 'A Taste of Britain', it had singing and music from Wales, Ireland, Scotland and England. They had Irish 'little people' — children dressed up as leprechauns, English Beefeaters and a marching band, and Scots Guards with their pipes and kilts. It ended with the full Welsh choir singing.

Birmingham provided the first opportunity for me to get to know IOC members. At first it was a matter of putting names and faces together. Having Phil Coles and John Coates, who was also well known to the Olympic family, certainly helped us to meet people.

Coles continued to go out of his way to help me. His attitude was: stick with me and I'll introduce you to everybody. We soon met the IOC members who were good friends of the Sydney bid like Dr Nat Indrapana from Thailand and Kevin O'Flanagan from Ireland. Phil and John would always have breakfast or lunch with them.

In fact we found there was a lot of having breakfasts and lunches and dinners and waiting around hotel lobbies to meet IOC members. I remember meeting Vitaly Smirnov, the member from Russia. He was one of those men who is a lovely, soft man underneath but has a pretty gruff exterior. I forget who introduced me, probably Coates or Coles. But he said, 'Beijing. Sydney. The battle of the giants, eh?' That was the race as he saw it — the battle of the giants.

Our efforts in Birmingham were later to receive a passing mention in the controversial book, *The Lords of the Rings*, which was published in 1992 in the lead up to Barcelona. The authors, Vyv Simson and Andrew Jennings, noted that: 'Large Australian gentlemen, who weren't even bidding for the winter Olympics, were walking around with handfuls of free ties to publicise Sydney's bid for the year 2000.' The Sydney bid didn't have ties in those days. The Australian Olympic Committee did, but I can't remember giving out any.

We were all well aware of John Coates' advice about the need to get as many IOC members to visit Sydney as possible. We spent a good deal of time — particularly in that first year — carrying around our diaries and asking IOC members, 'When are you coming to Sydney? How does your year look?', trying to get commitments on exactly when they would make their visit. We asked the Australian Immigration Department to send a visa officer to Birmingham with us. She stayed at the Albany with us, but we arranged a desk for her in the foyer of the Hyatt. John Coates and other members of our team targetted about 30 IOC members who we hoped would come to the GAISF conference in Sydney and offered to arrange visas for them. In many countries of the world people have to make a special trip to another city to get a visa, or send their passport off in the mail and wait two weeks. To be able to go down to a hotel lobby with a passport and have a visa put in straight away was a great help for many of the members.

We all got swept up in the competition for the 1998 Games. Who was going to win?

There were five cities bidding for the right to host the winter Games in 1998 — the Japanese city of Nagano; Salt Lake City, the capital of Utah; the small town of Jaca in the Spanish Pyrenees; Aosta in Italy; and the Swedish town of Ostersund.

We felt for the first time what it was like to be right at the *end* of the bidding process. It was very intense and it dominated the week. Nothing else was on anybody's mind.

It was fascinating to watch the lengths to which each city went to impress the members. Members of the Nagano team appeared in a new uniform and were all over the IOC members all the time — shaking their hands at breakfast and all that sort of thing. Each of the bids had dancers and musical groups which played outside the Hyatt.

It was the last of the bids before the new rules came out, tightening up on gifts and entertainment. Nagano rented a nearby mansion called Highbury House and brought over Japanese chefs. It invited IOC members out to the house and wined and dined them. But even in the Hyatt itself, the bidding cities had very extravagantly decorated hospitality suites. The team from Ostersund had built a complete Swedish home in light pine timber and furniture. You went in and sat down in their lounge room and ate Swedish food.

When it came to the presentations by the cities bidding for the winter Olympics, Deeta — who is very experienced in staging events — and I independently noticed that there was a lack of real sophistication. I didn't see anything at Birmingham that frightened me; Sydney could do just as well, if not better.

The quality of the field varied dramatically. Sweden had a long history of interest in the winter Olympics. Salt Lake City had by far the best bid. It only had to build one more venue and it had bid before for the winter Games of 1972 and 1976. Nagano in Japan was bidding for the first time and had no facilities at all. Aosta in Italy had never bid before and didn't seem to be terribly well organised. Jaca from Spain hardly had any venues either.

There was intense debate on how the voting would go. In the past, many people assumed that members from the 'Latin' countries — Latin America, Spain, Italy and Portugal — always voted as a bloc, backing their own interests ahead of any others. They had good reason to. In his book, *Olympic Politics*, Christopher Hill notes how the Latin American vote was important in the 1980s in the campaign to get Barcelona the 1992 Games. He explains that, '[Spain's] relationship to those countries is regarded by Spaniards as similar to that between the United Kingdom and the rest of the Commonwealth, without the structure but with more affection'. During that campaign, Italian Dr Primo Nebiolo, president of the International Amateur Athletic Federation, from Italy; Brazilian Joao Havelange, the president of the international soccer federations, FIFA; and Mexican Mario Vazquez Rana from Mexico, the president of the Association of National Olympic Committees, were strong supporters of Barcelona. Of the three, only Havelange was an IOC member at the time, but together they were influential in helping the Spanish city get the Games.

The Birmingham vote would be a real test of Latin solidarity in the Olympic movement. We were all wondering if the Latins would stick with the Spanish candidate, Jaca, although it had never bid before and had no real facilities or the Italian city of Aosta which was also not particularly advanced in its preparations. Would the Latins vote in a bloc? What would be the effect on Salt Lake City of Atlanta having just won the right to stage the 1996 summer Games? If Salt Lake City won, it would mean having the summer Games and the winter Games in the one country only two years apart. Was it time for a winter games back in Asia, and hence Nagano? The winter Games had only been in Asia once, in 1972. Who had the best bid? Who lobbied best?

Alan Hoskins said, 'It's got to be Nagano. It can't go to Salt Lake City because Atlanta have the summer Games and you can't give the US both. And the Albertville Games are coming up in France next year so you can't give the winter Games to Europe. That knocks out Ostersund, Aosta and Jaca. So it's got to be Japan.' Deeta agreed with him.

I said, 'It's got to be Salt Lake City because they've got the best bid and they're nice guys and they've bid before.'

But Alan and Deeta were right: Nagano won. For me, it was a very important lesson about regional sharing of a Games. It reinforced in my mind the lesson that the IOC would not put a Games back in a region where they'd just had one.

There are five official regions in the Olympic movement as signified by the five Olympic rings — Europe, Africa, Asia, the Americas and our region, Oceania. With the 1992 summer Games to be held in Barcelona, I thought it would be difficult for the IOC to give the 2000 Games back to another European city such as Berlin or Manchester or Milan — and maybe even Istanbul. It was good for Sydney, but it was also good for Beijing.

It taught me another important selling point for the Sydney bid. Australia could never really host a winter Games; our alpine climates are just not reliable enough. We would always make the point that the summer was our only chance to host an Olympics. So if the IOC was really interested in sharing the Games around, it had to take a good look at our bid for the 2000 Games.

The Birmingham vote also highlighted the sort of erratic voting patterns you could get with IOC decisions under the old voting rules. Some members had got into the habit of giving a first vote to a candidate that they felt had nice people or deserved a bit of encouragement along the way. Only when it came to the later rounds, would they get serious and vote for the city which they really thought should win. This was becoming an increasing occurrence and it had the potential to create some real problems.

The power of the Latin votes meant that in the first ballot Aosta from Italy got 15 votes — the same as Salt Lake City, the city with by far the best technical bid. Aosta had no facilities but obviously the Latins had decided to vote for their Italian friends. And it had nearly thrown Salt Lake City out of the race. Because there was a tie, they had to have another vote between Aosta and Salt Lake. Salt Lake won that vote — as it should have — and Aosta was eliminated. In the end, Salt Lake was beaten by Nagano by four votes — 46 to 42. Nevertheless, in the first round, the city which had by far the best technical bid nearly disappeared.

People realised things were getting out of hand. Flor Isava, the IOC member from Venezuela and the first woman member of the IOC executive board, told me later that she and Agustin Arroyo from Ecuador always voted together. They were going to vote for Jaca because of the Latin connection, but right at the end — on the steps going into the session — Arroyo said to Flor, 'We're voting for Salt Lake City.' And Flor said, 'I thought we were going to help Jaca first.' But Arroyo said, 'No, we're going to vote for Salt Lake.' And she did. If she hadn't voted for Salt Lake City it probably would have been eliminated in the first round. That scared her forever. She said there was going to be no more capricious voting. From then on, Flor became a very strong advocate of the need for members to vote for a city on its merits; for members to cast their votes properly and not to hand out any misguided favors to another city they really didn't want to win.

She was not the only one to be alarmed. The Birmingham vote caused enough concern among all the IOC executive for them to decide on changing the rules to make the voting numbers secret between rounds. They thought if the members didn't know how many votes each city got in each round, they would have to be more serious about their first votes. The changes were formalised by the IOC in early 1992 and the vote in September 1993 for the summer Games was to be the first time the new system operated. It was good for Sydney because it meant that the members would have to cast their first vote on the city they really thought should win rather than give some sort of sympathy vote to a city that was backed by an IOC powerbroker or was not well prepared.

The Birmingham IOC meeting also showed me something of the power of President Samaranch. It was the occasion on which Mario Vazquez Rana was elected an IOC member. Rana was one of the wealthiest men in Mexico, president of the Mexican Editorial Organisation which published more than 70 newspapers and has various radio and television stations. In 1986 he bought the financially troubled US news agency, United Press International, which he presided over until 1988. Rana had been president of the Association of National Olympic Committees from the time it started in 1979.

Rana had quite a reputation. Peter Ueberroth, the businessman who ran the 1984 Games in Los Angeles, told some interesting stories about him in his book, *Made in America*. Ueberroth and his wife flew down to Rana's estate in Mexico for a wedding party for his daughter. It was a gathering of some 1600 people. Ueberroth recalled:

> While showing us the sumptuous grounds, he led us past his own private soccer field and tennis courts toward a large, caged area. Inside we were shocked to see a huge bear.
>
> 'A gift from the Moscow Organising Committee,' Rana had explained nonchalantly. Suddenly my gift of a handcrafted Weatherby rifle to the father of the bride seemed less impressive.

Ueberroth also recalled another story about Rana:

> He always travels with a large entourage and picks up all expenses. On one occasion, at a Pan-American Sports Organisation meeting in Los Angeles in 1982, Rana's retinue panicked when the peso plummeted overnight and the hotel management called for immediate payment. Rana took it in stride, however, and persuaded the hotel to give him a day's grace. The next day, one of Rana's assistants presented a suitcase filled with American dollars to the manager of the hotel as collateral. He'd had the money flown in from his bank in Mexico by his pilot.

These stories were subsequently retold in *The Lords of the Rings* — as if to imply that Rana was not quite the right type of person to be an IOC member. He may have been something of a controversial figure — but in all my dealings with Rana, he was always very friendly and never acted with anything but propriety. He gave me a tremendously warm welcome when I visited Mexico City and when I met him at meetings in Acapulco and Mar del Plata in Argentina. He couldn't have been kinder. He *was* very generous to the Olympic movement and I think that was a very positive thing. He flew 70 IOC members to the ANOC meeting at Acapulco in 1992 from all over the world at his own expense. There could be no doubt that he was a man who had a keen interest in sports administration and was very committed to advancing the Olympic movement. I have a view in life that I take people as they come and don't listen to all the gossip. And I can only say that I found Rana a hospitable and impressive man.

Rana had the strong backing of President Samaranch, but when it came to the election, some 60 members abstained from voting and ten actually voted against him. Six out of the seven women IOC members — including Princess Anne — stood up and voted against him. The seventh, Flor Isava, only abstained because she was on the IOC executive. Prince Albert of Monaco voted against him, as did 'Tay' Wilson from New Zealand. Even his own countryman, Pedro Ramirez Vazquez, voted against him. He was elected as an IOC member with only 13 votes!

There were very good reasons why he should have been a member. He was long-time president of ANOC, long-time president of PASO and president of the Mexican Olympic Committee. President Samaranch prefers presidents of regional NOC organisations be also IOC members, and I agree with him.

But I was staggered that somebody that the president was promoting could have 60 votes abstaining and ten actually voting against him. In other words, 72 people didn't want him in there and yet he still got elected! It showed me the power of the president within the IOC. The president wanted Rana in, and in he went. When push comes to shove, the president generally got what he wanted.

But then again the powerbrokers of the IOC had also wanted Athens for the 1996 Games and Atlanta won. In IOC politics, it seemed, nothing could ever be taken for granted.

6
Sharing the Spirit

Share your hopes
Share your dreams
Share the spirit of the Games

From Share the Spirit,
Sydney Olympics 2000 Bid theme song

When you got down to it, the Sydney bid was a sophisticated international marketing exercise. The 90-odd IOC members were our customers. We were marketing Sydney's competence to hold the Games — the facilities, the venues, the fact that athletes could walk to many of the events from the village, the good weather and the safe environment. We were also marketing the very spirit of Sydney and Australia as a young, colorful, friendly, modern and informal place. It was a city and a nation where people loved sport and loved competing — but they also believed in the Olympic spirit of 'friendship, solidarity and fair play'.

In any marketing exercise — be it for soft drinks or cars or a city — the sales team needs to have a clear vision of the image and the message they want to convey to the customer. It may be an intangible, but for anybody involved in marketing it is an important issue that needs to be addressed. The style and tone of the product as presented and the sales pitch needs to be considered at the top level of the company to give a clear direction to everyone on the team.

It affects everything you do from your letterheads, brochures and publications to your advertising campaign, your team's dress and the whole tone you strike in dealing with customers.

When James Strong merged our law firms at Corrs and our names changed, all our letterheads and stationery had to be changed. Strong was meticulous about what the new livery would look like. He spent a lot of time getting it right. Most of us couldn't understand why he took it so seriously, but now I do. It goes to the whole image of your brand, your image and your product positioning.

Great marketing companies such as Coca-Cola and American Express have taken years to create corporate images and develop their brands. They count their brand and their corporate image as assets worth millions of dollars. I'm always amazed how people who don't have much experience with marketing and the development of branding don't seem to understand the importance of this.

These days many products available to a consumer are of a high standard. Take cars for example. The quality of most cars available on the Australian market today is a lot higher and a lot more consistent, no matter where they have been built. The modern marketing edge is gained by trying to convince the customer that your product and the company behind it stands for something more than just a consumer item — that the company has a higher mission than just putting its hands in customers' pockets.

That was the way I approached the selling of the bid. In the beginning I read a lot about the founding of the modern Olympics and came to admire the energetic, forward-thinking Baron de Coubertin and his high-minded ideals which saw sport both as an essential part of the education of a well-rounded human being and an instrument for improving understanding and friendship around the world. I was no marketing expert, but I knew the image I wanted our bid to have. IOC members, our customers, were charged with the responsibility of upholding the ideals and traditions of the Olympic Charter. I knew the image I wanted our bid to have would somehow have to be linked to those ideals.

The theme, Share the Spirit, didn't come up until 1992 when we started to think about our advertising campaign — but when I heard it, it sounded so *right* because it was the essence of the image I had been trying to fashion for the bid from the beginning.

The first step in the creation of our image was the selection of our logo. By the time I arrived at the Olympic bid office, a competition for the logo was underway. About eight firms had been invited to send in an entry. Some companies sent in three or four entries and others not on the list sent one anyway. We ended up with about 50 or 60.

As the new chief executive, I was added to the judging panel which included Leo Schofield, Greg Daniel, Andrew Andersons and David Churches. Famous people like Ken Done, Ken Cato and Michael Bryce had all submitted entries. But when they were shown, we weren't told who did them so we could judge the designs on their merits, not on the name of their creator. When I looked at them all I was bewildered. There seemed to be about 20 winning entries. I sat in the judging panel meeting thinking, 'I hope they don't ask me.'

There was a lot of deep consideration and milling around. All of a sudden Leo Schofield said, 'It isn't here. It simply isn't here. Tell them to do it again.' There were discussions about how there was no Aboriginality in the designs and that nothing just jumped off the page.

So the firms were asked to resubmit designs by the end of the week. We gave a few hints such as the importance of including something with Aboriginality but left it open. As a result Michael Bryce from the Brisbane firm of Minale Tatterfield Bryce and Partners, assisted by Aboriginal artist Ron Hurley, sent in the design below. It depicted the sails of the Opera House in a line drawn in the five colors of the Olympic rings.

It is difficult to show the virtues of the logo in black and white but it still works. But one of its great strengths is the way the five Olympic colors merge from one into the other. This allows it to be set against different colored backgrounds. So if there was a blue background, the blue could be taken out of the logo and substituted with white. That meant we could have tee-shirts and ties and scarves and banners and other promotional products in a range of different colors. The versatility of the design kept it surprising and fresh. The logo was further developed by our own in-house design people and the ISIS/FHA Design company which we used.

When we saw it, we didn't need to look any further. It was the unanimous choice of the judges.

After he won, Bryce explained he wanted a design that you could draw in the sand with your finger. It was to be a design that involved 'no slide rules, no set squares, no computers. If it can't be drawn by your fingers in the sand, then it's no good.'

The logo was given an official explanation on our fact sheets which I thought summed up its relevance to the bid:

> The design is the spirit of an ancient and colorful land. One vigorous line progressing in a fusion of Olympic colors. It is a cultural message of the union of nations expressing the freedom of the Olympic movement and the informal vitality of the city of Sydney.

During the bid, the bold colorful Sydney 2000 logo was seen all over the city as an expression of our enthusiasm and excitement at the prospect of holding the 2000 Games. But the selection of the logo was important as it did a lot to set the creative tone of what the Sydney bid was all about; in essence, the message about the Sydney bid that we were trying to communicate to the Olympic family, an image that said our bid was colorful, vibrant, youthful and energetic.

On the road, our merchandise was envied by everybody for its great color and variety. The Berlin logo was plain yellow with a black bear on it. They could never change it to anything else. We had five colors all the time and our merchandising gave the impression that everyone associated with our bid was a bright, upbeat person with a youthful outlook.

Nick Greiner launched the logo at the Ramada Renaissance hotel in August. We put up an exhibition of all the entries in the hotel so people could see the creative range of ideas that had been submitted.

One of the first tests of our image and approach was our presentation to the GAISF conference in October — our first ever to the Olympic family.

Phil Coles wanted to have Vivaldi as the backdrop music for our video. He had seen Atlanta make skilful use of classical music in its final presentation in Tokyo and it had gone down well. But I wanted something more in keeping with the youth image we were trying to create. So I pushed for John Farnham's *The Voice*, which I thought captured some of the messages we were trying to convey. It was an upbeat, fast paced song with moving lyrics ('We're all someone's daughter, we're all someone's son. . .')

We were able to put the video together quite cheaply using a lot of existing film. We used visuals from tourist promotional videos and shots of the women rowers from a television commercial. We wanted to convey something of Australia's excellent record of sporting achievements, so we included shots of the world boxing championships, the world equestrian and world football championships and any other major sporting event that Australia had staged or would be staging over the next few years.

We had some fun making the video. It was decided that there should be a shot of me walking up the stairs that trace the arc of the Harbor Bridge. On the day of the shoot, it was incredibly windy. I walked briskly up the stairs. But the producers wanted me to walk up again. And again. And again. I had walked up and down about five times before the work supervisor on the bridge said it was too dangerous and ordered everybody down. If it wasn't for him, I don't know how many times I would have had to walk up that bridge.

Practising my speech in the hall at Darling Harbor, I learned an important lesson. Susan Hunt was listening to me. She interrupted me several times with suggestions on how I could improve it. I was a bit irritated at first. I had always prided myself on being a good public speaker and I had lots of experience in public presentations. But as I listened to her I realised her suggestions were good ones. I took them into account and felt it improved the speech. It was an important presentation for the bid and we needed to get it right. I learned that no matter how good you think you are, you can always benefit from taking some advice. You should always be prepared to listen to an independent comment, particularly if it comes from a professional or an expert on the subject.

My speech was an important step for me in deciding how I would present myself to the IOC. There were certain rules of conduct when speaking at these events. You never criticised the other bids. You never said, 'We're the best.' So what did that leave us? Plenty. I had always thought it would be a strong part of our campaign if we took an unashamedly lofty, even idealistic stance on Olympic matters, the Olympic family, the Olympic spirit and the competition for the Olympics. As the representative of the host city, I thought I should deliberately set a high-minded tone. I wanted to acknowledge that the other cities were also great cities and tell the audience that the winner of the whole contest had to be the Olympic movement itself; that the Olympic movement was lucky that it had such a great choice. I wanted to finish my speech saying that the Olympic movement would have an undertaking from Sydney that, whichever city won, that city would have our unstinting support because we support the Olympic movement. I was advised not to say it, but decided to anyway.

While we were checking out the systems and acoustics in the hall before the conference began, we noted there were three screens that could be used to show a film. Most of the time, people only used one.

So when the actual day came we let all our opponents make their presentations first, as protocol demanded. As host, we went last.

I made my speech and then we played the video. Suddenly, people were seeing color and movement across all three screens and hearing John Farhnam's powerful, emotional song. It was an absolute knockout. The audience couldn't believe it. The combination of the speech and the impact of the video went down really well. There were 21 IOC members there, all the sporting federations and all the staff from our office. Deeta felt it was such an important occasion that she came along with our two daughters, which was unusual. They loved it. To have made a really huge impact with our first presentation was really important. A quarter of the voters saw it. All the sporting federations saw it. Our own people — and that's important to morale — saw it. We knew it looked good and that felt good.

The next day I saw Les McDonald, the head of the International Triathlon Union, who said he had tingles down his spine over the speech — exactly the impact that I was striving for. I wanted people to go away thinking that whenever they saw the Sydney bid it was not just about saying Sydney's the best — we were all there for a greater cause. It was the kind of thing I kept saying in my presentations throughout the campaign, appealing to the higher aims and lofty ideals of the Olympic movement.

It was part of my belief that in marketing — whether you are trying to convince a crowd or convince a customer — there's a lot to be said for rising above the ruck and standing for worthy principles. If you have a quality product, you've got to stand for something more than just making a sale or turning a dollar.

The GAISF presentations also provided another small but important lesson in presenting to an international audience. Never tell jokes. John Coates and Phil Coles had warned me and I didn't include any. But it didn't really hit home to me until I saw Manchester's presentation.

It was about the time of the final games of the World Cup Rugby series. Western Samoa was the big surprise in the competition. Rank outsiders, they kept beating people. Someone from the Manchester bid joked about Western Samoa beating Wales. He said it was lucky that Wales didn't play the whole of Samoa; that they only had to play Western Samoa. I thought it was quite funny, partly because I love rugby. But in an international audience, it just didn't work; it fell flatter than a tack.

Throughout the bid, I was adamant that we set the right tone and that everyone should be quite clear what sort of image we were presenting. But it took some doing. As the bid progressed, I found there was some confusion within the organisation about our creative approach. This was making life difficult for people down the line — particularly in our communications department. I decided it was so important that in early 1992 I prepared a paper for the board setting out the creative outline of our bid. In it, I tried to set out just what the Sydney bid was and what it wasn't, in point form and in plain language.

I wrote that we were:

- organised (as to venues, our office, the city and the government)
- youthful
- vibrant
- business-like but fun
- friendly to both visitors and new settlers
- casual
- proud and independent
- fair-minded
- aware of the Olympic ideal and the honor of hosting the Games
- prepared to share the spirit

We were not:

- European or British
- aggressive
- manipulative
- xenophobic
- impatient for the Games
- unaware of the importance of the Games

I stressed to the board the importance of agreeing at the highest level of our organisation on the creative tone we wanted to set and noted that the logo was the one item of artwork which was integral to our bid.

I told them that everybody was entitled to their opinion but once we agreed everyone had to support our style and image. The board backed me and that set the tone. Of course I knew a board decision would not solve everything but it was important to have the matter formally agreed upon from the top. It was then up to me as chief executive to make sure that what we did conformed to that creative outline.

It was that basic approach which helped shape our advertising campaign. Susan Hunt wrote the full creative brief for the advertising agency which drew on ideas from my paper. A day was set down and several agencies pitched for the business. I had never seen a pitch by an advertising agency and it was a fascinating exercise for me. Three firms had chosen, as a sort of knock-out blow, the dressing up of the Centrepoint Tower to look like the Olympic torch, an idea that had also emerged in some of the designs in the logo competition.

Clemenger and George Patterson gave the two best presentations.

Pattersons came in last and gave an extraordinary presentation, full of vigor, creativity and enthusiasm. They had a team of five or six people. Their equipment was all organised and they were a very happy lot. They had brought in name tags to put in front of everyone on our team who was in the room — and they had their people watching all our reactions. They had a theme, 'We're Ready'. They had a highly impressive presentation of music and posters and brochures, all based on this theme.

Clemenger brought two people — Mike Thomas and Guy Abrahams. They were an interesting duo who bounced off each other. Their theme was 'Share the Spirit'. It was a slogan which recognised the importance in the Olympic Charter of an Olympic spirit. In some ways it was a play on words — we were asking the Olympic movement to *share* the Olympic spirit with us by giving us the right to *host* the Games. We were saying that Sydney had that spirit. I thought they really had something there. Share the Spirit was something I had been searching for ever since those early days. It fitted in with my views on aspiring to noble ideals and not boasting that Sydney was the best. I believed if our bid was seen as putting something *back* into the Olympic movement, we would get full marks for being idealistic but not naive, generous of spirit, globally aware and not parochial. Share the Spirit seemed to be something that was particularly apposite for what we were trying to do.

There was a lot of support on the committee for the team from George Patterson because of the way they presented. They were very polished and enthusiastic. Clemenger was not as impressive in presentation but their two-man team had what I thought might be the creative nub. We couldn't decide between the two of them so the committee decided that, since I was the one who had to work with the agency, I should make the decision. So we asked for another briefing from both agencies.

I am now cautious about rebriefing any consultant pitching for business. The trap is that in the rebriefing process, you tend to give them a lot more of your ideas. Then they can just feed your ideas back to you in a different form, instead of giving you something creative or original which may have been better for you. It's something you have to be careful about. But the choice of an advertising agency was important to us and we needed to be able to work closely with them. In the end, it's more important to get the agency right and to put the work in at the beginning of the relationship, no matter how long the process takes.

Pattersons took me out to their offices in North Sydney. I went through this extraordinary day of meeting everybody in the office, five floors with every single one of them primed to say, 'I'm ready, Rod. We're ready'. When I got up to the top floor there was a staff gym and everyone who was working out said, 'We're ready'. Then we got to the roof of the building and they had some Olympic music and a flag and a new song, *We're Ready*. It was quite an experience for me.

George Patts may have been excellent presenters and have an incredibly enthusiastic team, but it was the theme which was the core of what we were looking for in choosing our agency. And a creative image has to be an accurate reflection of the facts. We couldn't, for example, pretend that Sydney was a bright, vibrant, friendly city if it wasn't. To do that would be to invite danger and leave one's product open to ridicule as opponents point out the difference between the image and the reality. And the one thing that was wrong with the theme of 'We're ready' was the fact that we weren't. Although Sydney was well down the track in terms of its facilities, they were not all completed and would not be by September 1993. 'We're Ready' could expose us to criticism that we had a misleading or thoughtless campaign slogan.

I had to make a decision. I was privately learning towards Share the Spirit and Clemenger. But I was also really taken with Ian Elliott from Pattersons as a man with a lot of get-up-and-go. Greg Daniel, who ran Clemenger's Sydney office and was on our board suggested that both agencies be appointed and we have a joint committee that worked for the bid. It was a very magnanimous gesture but Ian Elliott didn't like the idea. He said, 'Rod, your problem is that somebody has to come first and somebody has to come second and you are trying to make us both come first. You can't do that.' He also said he thought that a committee of advertising agencies would be difficult to work in practice.

But I was convinced that Share the Spirit was the right theme, so I appointed Clemenger. When we advised Ian Elliott he was very disappointed but he quickly said that although we had not chosen George Patterson, his agency would do anything we needed — for nothing — if we wanted. It was a great testimony to Pattersons that they presented so well and took the loss in great spirit.

Of course Clemenger didn't charge us for their services either. They gave us hundreds of hours of their time in what turned out to be the very successful Share the Spirit campaign. The original Clemenger presentation actually took the Share the Spirit theme a step further. They had obviously studied the Olympic Charter. Their campaign theme also talked about 'one Olympic village — the Olympic ideal. All the athletes can walk to the Games — the Olympic ideal.' But when we thought about it, the blatant 'Olympic ideal' reference didn't really catch our fancy. It's not that we didn't believe it was important but we needed something that was simple and said it all. So we decided to go with the Share the Spirit theme, period.

I suppose my selection showed something about the importance of understanding the themes which appeal to the customer. Clemenger had taken the trouble to read the Olympic Charter and realised how important it was in our thinking.

But I found people at both agencies pretty extraordinary. They didn't know anything about the Olympic movement initially but they had to come to grips with it and given a sophisticated presentation on it. There was a lot of creativity and lateral thinking there which was great to see.

Having decided on that theme, Clemenger then worked with songwriter John Gillard to produce a campaign song. The music was uplifting, the words moving:

We want to share the century's dawn
A golden age will reign
Where the spirit of competition
Burns so bright in the eternal flame
Share your hopes
Share your dreams
Share the spirit of the Games

We all share the same sun
The same dream, the same earth, the same air

The spirit is the one
The spirit's you and me
The spirit of the dream that we all share
The spirit of the dream that we all share

The spirit of sport, the spirit of sharing
The spirit of striving, the spirit of daring
The spirit of hope, of woman, of man
The spirit of clasping a rival's hand
The spirit of challenge, the spirit of a smile,
The spirit of going that extra mile

We want to share the winner's joy
Share the glory and the fame
Not only in the victory
But share the spirit of the Games
Come share our hopes
Share our dreams
Share the spirit of the flame

We all share the same sun
The same dream, the same earth, the same air
The spirit is the one
The spirit's you and me
The spirit of the dream that we all share
The spirit of the dream that we all share

Now we had it all. The combination of our theme and our logo was just magnificent. I found if we were worrying about what to say in a speech or a presentation, they always gave us the answer. When we were trying to draw out the themes and images for the big presentation in Monte Carlo, I remember saying one day, 'Why are we leaving what our theme and logo says? It has been with us all the way. We want to share the spirit; we want to be young and colorful and idealistic.'

We found ourselves drawing on those simple themes all the time. It taught me the importance of thinking through your themes and your public image; getting the right logo and the right campaign slogan. It forces you to decide just what it is you are trying to say to the market. Having done that, you invest in your image and you work hard to maintain it. It provides the discipline of consistency. And it becomes a major asset in the way you present yourself to the world.

7

Making Friends and Influencing People

> All things being equal, people will buy from a friend. All things
> being not quite so equal, people will *still* buy from a friend. Make
> friends.
>
> *Mark McCormack,* What They Don't Teach
> You at Harvard Business School

Atlanta had set new standards on how to bid for the right to
host an Olympic Games in the modern era. Up against
favorite Athens, Billy Payne and his team set out with a simple
but powerful strategy of forging good personal relationships with
all 90 plus members of the IOC.

Payne argued that most modern cities of the world probably
had the capacity to host an Olympic Games. The art was to win
the hearts and minds of the people who would make the decision
— the IOC members.

'We could only do it by making friends,' Billy Payne told
Sydney's *Daily Telegraph-Mirror* in 1991. 'And those 92 people
are still our best friends.'

It was one of those disarmingly simple marketing concepts —
powerful if done properly — to make friends with the people you
want to be your customers. People don't want to do business with
people they don't like, or don't feel comfortable with. If they like
you, it's a great start to making a deal. If they *really* like you, they
may even be prepared to overlook a few shortcomings in your
product.

Payne had an enthusiastic team of people marketing the
Atlanta bid. He was backed up by another lawyer, Charlie Battle;
former UN Ambassador Andrew Young; an enthusiastic house-
wife, Ginger Watkins; Linda Stephenson; Bobby Reardon; and a
team of eager young volunteers. Their lobbying was simply
brilliant. For two years, the Atlanta team toured the world
making friends. When IOC members visited Atlanta, they were

treated to large helpings of good ol'fashioned Southern hospitality. They always entertained at home. They always put a person's
national flag in the front yard of their home if someone was
visiting from overseas. They were professional and very well
organised.

David Miller's biography of President Samaranch, *Olympic
Revolution*, describes the Atlanta team as being 'the essence of
courtesy, modesty and efficiency'. They set about becoming
everyone's first or second favorites. And the Greeks, who had
been so confident that their place in Olympic history would give
them the Centenary Games, were overtaken by the sheer power
of Atlanta's ability to win the confidence of the IOC members.

The whole business of trying to win the right to stage an
Olympic Games had changed dramatically in the 1980s. By the
late 1970s, the Games had got to the point where no city wanted
to host them. The 1972 Munich Games were overshadowed by
the massacre of the Israeli athletes, then there was the crippling
municipal cost of the big spending on infrastructure for the 1976
Montreal Games and all sorts of politically-inspired boycotts, like
the Moscow debacle. Los Angles won the right to host the 1984
Games on its own more commercial terms because nobody else
wanted them. It was the financial success of the 1984 Games run
by Los Angeles businessman Peter Ueberroth, who relied heavily
on private-sector funding, which gradually turned around the
fortunes of the modern Olympic movement. Two cities bid for
the 1988 Games — Seoul and Nagoya. But there were six bidding
for the 1992 Games and six again for 1996. In the early years of
our bid, there were eight cities vying for the right to host the
2000 Games. The competition for the favorable attention of the
IOC members had become intense. The Atlanta team worked out
exactly what was needed in this new environment. And, the
Sydney team, like any sensible people in business, studied how
the experts had done it before us.

Phil Coles and John Coates had got very close to the Atlanta
people and they came back from the Tokyo session with the
message that the key to winning was to get the kind of lobby
team that gets on well with IOC members — people who were
hospitable and friendly, able and successful. And that set the tone
for the kind of chief executive that they were looking for. That
was why they were open minded about using an 'outsider' to the

Olympic movement to fill the job — provided he or she had the broad qualities they were looking for.

But, as I learned early on, it was not just a matter of making friends with the members — if we wanted to win their vote, we would have to build really strong bonds with them.

One of the problems with the Melbourne bid was that it started much later than we did and their lobby team didn't have as much time to build the really solid relationships with the IOC members that were necessary.

I was reminded of this one day when there was a ceremony to launch a River Cat at Darling Harbor. An IOC member from one of the South American countries spotted Sir Laurence Muir, who had been very involved in the Melbourne bid. There was an immediate recognition and happiness; a coming together and a great bear hug. But I knew that IOC member did not vote for Melbourne. I thought: there's a lesson in that. We've got to do more than have great times together with the members. We've got to get closer and closer to these people and become very good friends with them.

I saw my father do it. He was a stock and station agent. If he wanted to get business, he needed to be able to do all sorts of things for his customers. If somebody wanted front seats at the Davis Cup at White City or a good table at Romano's Restaurant, he had to be able to get it for them. And he always brought people home. He always had us kids serving the drinks and taking the plates off the table. We were all a part of the process. He always wrote regularly to his contacts and sent Christmas cards. And whenever he travelled, it was always to see all his old friends again.

That's always been my approach. You can't run a business where you're trying to sell something and stay at your desk from nine to five with your head down. You don't just hire a public relations company and an advertising agency and hope for the best. You'll come second. You have to do it yourself, you have to set about making genuine, long-term friendships. It makes sense. People *do* want to do business with people they like.

That's why sometimes it's sensible for business people to get out on the golf course between Monday and Friday. It's all part of relationship building, making business contacts and, ultimately, sales.

I never had any worries about this side of the job. I've always found that given enough time in a building of a relationship where people get to know me and I get to know them, people have generally ended up supporting me.

But solid relationships do take time to build. Nobody's good enough to say: 'G'day, G'day, G'day. I'm a good bloke' and expect somebody will vote for them.

I had a long talk with Billy Payne when we invited him out to Sydney to address a corporate supporters' dinner in October 1991. Billy was a great guy and I grew to like him a lot. He was quite a big fellow who had been a pretty good American footballer in his day. We had much in common, both lawyers who have been fairly successful in our careers. Like me, he wasn't a fellow that you'd ever see roll around having an extraordinarily good time. He was very determined but also quite understated in his own way, not the sort of guy who draws attention to himself. But when you met him, you could tell he had a feeling of great inner strength, that 'I'm not going to be beaten' feeling. And he had a great reputation. I had been going to Atlanta since 1976 for legal conventions and people had told me that Payne was the sort of guy that always gets the job done.

Billy told me how he got involved in the Games. He had raised a lot of money for his church and had put together a group of volunteer workers around him. 'So I thought to myself, what else can I do with my group? It's such a great group. What about the Olympic Games? And I said to my wife, Martha: "We're going to bid for the Olympic Games." And she said: "We are, Billy?" And I said: "We are." And from then on, Rod, we were bidding for the Games.' In the process he had become a good friend of President Samaranch and very well connected in the Olympic movement.

He also gave me two very important pieces of advice:

'You must use Sallyanne Atkinson. She's absolutely formidable in the Olympic movement. She's very popular. In our bid we couldn't believe it when Melbourne didn't use her.'

But the most important comment he made was on my personal style:

'Rod. You've got to be humble,' he insisted. 'Everybody knows your bid's the best. You've got a great team. You can see it. You're young and you know what you're doing. Your videos are always the best. Your exhibition stand is always the best. Your brochures are the best. But you've got to be careful. If they already know you're the best, you don't need to overdo it.'

Being seen to be too competitive, overconfident or arrogant in the race for the Games does not go down well with the members. He told me how he coped with it: 'I'm not a humble man, Rod. Nor are you. I can tell. But I am very sentimental and I kind of translated my sentimentality across in a way that they accepted I was humble enough.'

I had to pinch myself because this was contrary to the attitude I had taken until then. When I first started out in the bid, I went out of my way to foster a very competitive attitude among the staff. I used to tell them that if we were going to win, every single person on our bid had to know they had beaten the other bids every day. They were not to put their head on the pillow at night unless they were sure they had beaten their counterparts in Manchester, Beijing, Berlin and all the other cities for the day. I remembered going into the office one day when something had upset me about the China bid — some violation of human rights. I took off my coat and threw it over the table and I said to Bob Elphinston, 'Those Chinese are *not* going to beat us'.

Australians are a very competitive group of people and it's easy for us to take a very competitive approach to things. Give Australians a race and they like to win. But I took Billy Payne's advice and tried for more humility when I was with the Olympic family. Even though I was always confident we had the best bid and the best team, if anyone asked me about how it was going, I always said it was going to be tough. And no-one on our team would ever say, 'We're the best and we're going to win.' I feel there are lessons in this for all sales people: there are few long-term friends in highly aggressive selling.

But it's more subtle than that. You can't even say it privately among the members. And so it became part of my psyche. And even now, to everyone who says, 'Rod, you've done a fantastic job', I always say, 'I had a great team.' And we did.

As the newcomer, I was keen to learn about the politics of IOC voting. So I asked a few questions about this when I visited Atlanta in the early days. I met Charlie Battle, the joint leader of their lobby team. He was a wonderful, friendly, open fellow who would always come up to people and say, 'Hi, I'm Charlie Battle. How're you doing?'

If anybody knew who voted for Atlanta, Charlie did.

I asked Charlie if all the black Africans voted together. He said, 'Absolutely not. You've got the English-speaking and the French-speaking countries. They're all over the place.'

So I took notes.

Then Bobby Reardon came in. He also lobbied the African members. Battle was out of the room. And I said, 'Bobby are there voting blocs in Africa? Do all the black Africans vote together?'

'Absolutely, they do.'

That's when I realised nobody, but nobody, really knows.

The voting for an Olympic Games is done by secret ballot. So, unless a member actually tells you that they did or didn't vote for you, you never really know what happened. And even then you can't be 100 per cent sure unless you know the member well. As the bid went on, I found that there were always so-called experts who would confidently tell you exactly how a particular member had voted or was going to vote — but you had to assess their intelligence, filter it through what you already knew and then make up your own mind.

It was up to me to choose our lobbying team. The two pillars were John Coates and Phil Coles.

Coates really knew the bidding process — he'd run the Brisbane bid and he was involved in the Melbourne bid. Coles was an experienced Olympic sportsman and team leader and had been an IOC member for about ten years.

Coles was 100 per cent behind the bid and was always travelling — either with us or for us. And that was very important. Often people from the other bids would say, 'Do you realise how lucky you are, having your IOC member travelling with you?' Bob Scott from Manchester didn't have this kind of support available. Britain's two IOC members were Mary Glen-Haig, who was 73 when the campaign got underway, and Princess Anne. He could hardly ask them to travel around the world and wait around in hotel lobbies.

Coles and Coates had a remarkable relationship. They had known each other for years and frequently travelled together overseas. Phil was almost 20 years older than John but he had a lot of respect for what John had done for the Australian Olympic movement. John was a brilliant guy and responsible for a lot of the financial strength of the AOC. I think John saw himself as being responsible for looking after Phil when they were on the road together. There was always a lot of kidding around between the two of them.

Coles and Coates were very useful in helping me get to know the members, particularly at the beginning. I'd ask Phil or John if they could invite a few of their colleagues for me to meet. Meanwhile, the people from the other bids were standing around and hoping to meet the members.

It wasn't quick. The first couple of times, the members wouldn't remember you. But it got us a start. A lot of it was just, 'Hello. How are you? When did you arrive?' and other pleasantries. When you got to know them better you'd ask after each other's families and talk about sport and things would develop from there. Most of them were not big drinkers or *bon vivants*. You didn't often sit down and discuss Shakespeare with them: more likely Carl Lewis. We backed up the personal contact by sending the monthly newsletter of the Sydney 2000 bid, *Share The Spirit*, to all the members. We also sent personal letters, Christmas cards and birthday cards. When I would give presentations they'd remember the tall dark man from Sydney. Then the name 'McGeoch' began to stick.

Kevan Gosper was in London with Shell, but he was an important member of our lobby team. He would often help us at international events or even fly out to Australia for important visits. In the last six to nine months of the bid he travelled extensively for us.

Lobbying was greatly assisted by having the headquarters of the Australian Olympic Committee in the same city. In fact it was not only in the same city as us, but six months after the bid got going, the AOC moved into offices a floor below us in the Maritime Services Board Building. We knew the importance of showing the IOC how our national Olympic committee was committed to the Sydney bid. It was one of the strengths we had identified in our early strategy papers. Many bid cities didn't have their NOCs near them. Atlanta was in Georgia but the US Olympic Committee was based in Colorado. The British Olympic Association was in London, not Manchester. We had the president of our Olympic Committee and our IOC member as part of our front line lobby team. Manchester never had that, neither did Berlin, Milan or Brasilia.

I asked Bruce Baird to help us because I thought he would be an excellent lobbyist. I picked Graham Lovett because he obviously was very knowledgable on sport and well-connected at high levels of sport and sports television. The idea at the start was to take a core group of people which would go everywhere together. That core team was Coates, Coles, Baird, Lovett and myself. We were a close group and we did a lot of work on the road. Baird couldn't travel as much because of his ministerial duties — but he was a very good lobbyist.

We would take my assistant, Margaret, if we needed administrative backup or someone to run a desk or a hospitality suite. And at the really big meetings we would take Sallyanne Atkinson and other specialists. Sallyanne was very good with the more senior members. She really knows the top end of the Olympic movement. If President Samaranch saw her, he would always come over and kiss her and ask her how she was.

Our official lobby team was boosted by the appointment of several regional specialists.

We hired Gabor Komyathy to help us with eastern Europe. He was born in Hungary. He had hotel management qualifications. He ran the Beverly Hills Hilton in Los Angeles and did some administrative work at the Olympic village in the 1984 Games. He was brought out to Australia by the Hilton group and ended up staying in Melbourne. Gabor was a good athlete, a keen swimmer and tennis player, and had very strong language skills. He could speak Hungarian, German, Czech, Italian, Spanish and French and could get by in Russian. He had worked on the Melbourne bid and Coles and Coates said we *had* to have him. Billy Payne and Charlie Battle also thought very highly of him. (So highly that they later hired him to be director of national Olympic committee services in the athletes' village for the Atlanta Games.) We engaged him as a consultant to the bid and soon placed him in Hungary full time. He lived with his mother in Budapest and worked the Europeans from there. He was already good friends with Pal Schmitt, the IOC member in Hungary. Whenever we went to major meetings, he would fly over from Budapest. He was also very good with ideas about how to appeal to particular members, particularly the eastern European members. He would often remind me of their birthdays or the anniversary of their membership of the IOC and arrange small dinner parties with key people. I sent him a detailed fax once or twice a month to keep him up to speed on what we were doing in Sydney.

There was an initial concern about the language problem in South America. People who had worked on the Melbourne bid said the region would be difficult for us and we needed Spanish speakers travelling with us. In my legal career I had acted for Mrs Elizabeth Fox for some time. She was born in Colombia, fluent in Spanish, and very elegant. She had married an Australian and settled in Sydney. At Nick Greiner's suggestion we gradually introduced her into the scene and people liked her, so we added her to the team when dealing with South American members. When anyone from South America visited Sydney she and her husband would entertain them at their harborside home, among their South American artefacts.

Our Arab specialist was Mahmoud Elfarnawani, who was based in Toronto. We got onto him by sheer force of people's recommendations. A couple of the Arab members said to Phil Coles, 'You must contact my colleague, Mahmoud.' His name kept coming up. Then, at the winter Games in Albertville in February 1992, I met a woman called Julie Osborne who had been involved in Toronto's bid for the 1996 Games and she recommended Elfarnawani. She said he had worked on the Toronto bid and knew all the Arab members. Elfarnawani was born in Egypt and was a world class volleyball player. He become an international volleyball coach. He was revered in North Africa. He went to live in Toronto to coach the Canadian volleyball team. When Toronto decided to bid for the 1996 Games they used him as a lobbyist. I asked Julie to set up a meeting with him when I went to Toronto in April to learn about their bid. Then I brought him out to Sydney to meet the others. We engaged him and he became part of the team, travelling with us to all the major meetings.

When it came to black Africa, there was some debate about whether we should take an Aboriginal lobbyist with us. But we were advised by black African supporters, such as Sam Ramsamy, the president of the South African Olympic Committee, that it would make more sense to have an eminent person who was a respected figure on the international political stage. We were told that two former Prime Ministers, Malcolm Fraser and Gough Whitlam, were two of the most highly regarded international politicians among Africans. At one stage we thought of using both, but then we thought it might be a bit too heavy-handed.

Gough lives in Sydney and both he and Margaret speak French, which would be useful with the French-speaking African members. They had lived in Paris when Gough was the Australian ambassador to UNESCO. Many black African leaders pass through Paris and the Whitlams had met a lot of them during their stay there. We had seen how useful Andrew Young had been in lobbying black African members in the Atlanta bid. Gough may not have been black, but we thought he was the closest thing we had in Australia to Andrew Young when it came to someone with strong credentials on the African stage. So we asked Gough and Margaret to help us with South and Central Africa. They were both into their late seventies at the time but they were excellent. With the help of their son Nick and his wife Judy, they entertained almost every black African IOC member that came to Sydney during the bid. To meet Gough Whitlam was regarded as a great honor by most of these members. As far as they were concerned, he was as important as any current Prime Minister. In the final months, the Whitlams made a major lobbying trip for us through Africa.

Sam Ramsamy was another important friend of the Sydney bid in black Africa. Ramsamy had been exiled in London during much of the struggle against apartheid and was the leader of the South African Non-Racial Olympic Committee. Kevan Gosper was a member of the IOC's Apartheid and Olympism Commission and was one of a group of IOC members who had gone to South Africa to tell them they could rejoin the Olympic family if they got rid of some final pieces of discriminatory legislation. They did and in July 1991 the IOC readmitted South Africa. It had been 31 years since their last participation in an Olympic Games — the Rome Olympics of 1960.

Suddenly, the South African Olympic Committee and its team were able to go to the Barcelona Games. But they had done no preparation. So John Coates immediately promised Ramsamy that the Australian Olympic Committee would help them. He flew over to South Africa to see what was needed. He lobbied the organising committee in Barcelona to put the South African team next to the Australian team in the athletes' village and we shared our physiotherapists and doctors and training equipment and whatever.

This helped build a strong bond between Coates and Ramsamy. Ramsamy was a very popular figure among the black Africans and happy to help us. So we had him providing advice and contacts in the region. He was not an IOC member and he was new back in the official Olympic movement, but he was a very useful supporter for us.

The regional breakup worked well in most cases but where a team member had a particular connection with a member, we would use them.

In North America, for example, there were only three IOC members — Anita DeFrantz from the US and Carol Anne Letheren and Dick Pound from Canada. Phil Coles and Gabor Komyathy were appointed to look after their close friend Anita; Phil, John Coates and myself focussed on Carol; and John Coates and myself focussed on fellow laywer, Dick Pound. I was appointed to handle Mongolia because I always got on well with its member, Shagdarjav Magvan.

As the bid progressed and our lobbyists started to head off in different directions around the world, we needed to add to our team.

Geoff Wild, who was a vice president of the Sydney 2000 bid company and chairman of the NSW Tourism Commission, was a very charming fellow. His wife, Barbara, was a wonderful woman. Geoff had some experience in the Melbourne bid when he was the Sydney boss of the advertising agency, Clemenger. Peter Clemenger, the chairman based in Melbourne, had been very involved in the Melbourne bid and when IOC members were transiting through Sydney, he asked Geoff to look after them for the day. This had given Geoff some insight into who was who in the IOC. He was a great networker, well travelled and very relaxed in the company of foreigners. He had retired from the advertising business; chairmanship of the NSW Tourism Commission was not a full-time job. I asked him if he could do some travelling and come to some meetings with me, which he did. He and Barbara lived down the road from our house and I invited him to most of my dinner parties with IOC members. Barbara and Deeta became good friends. We got very close to the Wilds and they were great on the travel circuit.

Peter Montgomery also did some travelling for us because he was well known in the Olympic movement. Peter had been in four Olympics for water polo and captained the Australian water polo team. He was on the Athletes' Commission of the IOC, the board of the Australian Olympic Committee and was a member of our strategy committee.

Towards the end of the bid, when we needed even more people, we used Doug Donoghue who used to work for Ted Harris at Ampol. He was well connected in sports circles — president of the Carbine Club, a club of prominent sports people which raises money for charity, and is on the State Sport Centre Trust. He had been very involved in the Melbourne bid and had lived in Paris during its final months to lobby the European members. We had already decided to send Phil Coles to Paris for the last six months of our bid, but decided it was a two-person job. We wanted to focus on the sporting federations, the IFs, as well and a lot of them were based in Europe.

The international lobbying exercise involved attending most of the big international sports meetings which attracted a reasonable number of IOC members. There's a whole calendar of events set down years in advance.

Each of the five regions in the Olympic movement have an annual meeting and most an annual games. So the Association of National Olympic Committees of Africa (ANOCA) would have a games and an annual meeting. The Americas are run by the Pan-American Sports Organisation (PASO). They have games and an annual meeting. And then there's the Asian Games and the Olympic Council of Asia annual meeting and the Mediterranean Games. And, of course, there's the summer and winter Olympics every four years, and the annual GAISF meetings and the World Track and Field Championships. And the IOC board meets quarterly, so we had to be at their meetings. It was hectic. You could spend your whole life going to them if you wanted. We weren't going to go that far, but we ruled that if there was going to be three or more IOC members attending a meeting, we had to be there.

We would all sit down with our diaries at our strategy meetings and decide which meetings each of us would go to. It took some organisation. And if we were planning to take a minister and a premier and an ex-prime minister, we had to make sure it was done very efficiently. Margaret would come to the meetings where we were working it all out. Once we had decided who was going where she would go straight back to her office, get all the applications for accreditation, send the photos off, get the visas fixed, make the bookings and put all the other logistical arrangements in place.

As I began to travel and meet the members, it didn't take long for me to realise that these people were ordinary, and generally very pleasant, people. I suppose I should have realised it before we started, but you hear all sorts of gossip and assume things. They weren't politicians, most had little connection with their own governments. By and large, members were not pressured by their governments and the IOC works hard to keep it that way.

IOC members are selected from any of the countries which are officially part of the Olympic movement, although not all countries who participate in the Games have members. Officially, you can't run for the office. Names are put forward — usually by the president. The person has usually been a good athlete and very involved in the Olympic movement in their home country. There was originally only one member per country but, in the 1920s, the Olympic movement decided that there were some regions which were so large that there was a need for more than one member to represent it in the area. That's why Australia, Brazil and India have two members. Members are supposed to be representatives of the IOC *in* their country — they are not supposed to be representatives *of* their country or their government within the IOC. Thus Phil Coles and Kevan Gosper would be the IOC members *in* Australia, not the IOC members *from* Australia. It is an important distinction which underlines the high regard the IOC has for its independence from governments and political interference.

When the modern Olympics began last century members were appointed for life to help protect them from political and other outside interference. The rules have since been modified although the commitment to independence from politicians has never waned. There are still about 14 life members but new members must now retire at age 75. After that they remain as honorary members and can attend meetings but they cannot vote. Most of the members are male — there are only seven women members. The average age is over 60, but the actual ages ranged from late thirties to the late eighties.

I found lobbying these people strange at first. When we went to these big events, the aim was to make informal contact with the IOC members and other influential figures in the Olympic family. We would go to all the official functions, but a large part of what we did was actually wait around hotel lobbies where members were staying or attending meetings to catch them for a chat. It is a difficult to sit in the lobby of a hotel, do nothing and look busy, especially for people like Bruce Baird and myself and my wife Deeta, who has a busy career of her own. John Fahey was never able to handle it.

We would take a strategic position in a room where we could see everybody — and who was chatting to whom. Then we would order coffee. We were virtually running continuous coffee meetings.

When we were overseas with a group, I would say, 'If you're not doing anything, a few of you should go up and sit in the lobby of the hotel for an hour or two.' That was part of our strategy, and as the time to the decision got closer, it became a very important part of our strategy. I'd insist we had a roster of people to wait around the lobbies. When our wives travelled with us, they too would be rostered. We used to call ourselves 'lobby lizards'. Often I'd say, 'I'm going off to do a bit of lobby lizarding.' It was the only way to be visible in the early days when people didn't know us.

We had seen how it happened in Birmingham. We'd always go to breakfast. We'd try to get the best table — right in the centre of the room. We didn't push ourselves at anybody. We wouldn't sit ourselves down next to someone who was eating unless they asked. But we were visible. Coates would generally meet someone he knew and bring them over.

After breakfast we would break up. But often we'd make sure a few members of our team were in the coffee shop for the morning and a few for the afternoon. It seemed weird not to be writing something or on the phone, but we got used to it in the end. After a while I'd just sit there and actually enjoy myself. People would come up to chat — and I was being paid to do it.

We decided early on that we wouldn't chase people into lifts or across hotel lobbies. We had a good group; it was cohesive and focussed. And it had enough sense to be patient about building relationships. I think the members appreciated this.

I remember one international sporting event later in the campaign, I had had a tough night. There were IOC members all over the place and I knew them all by then. I actually hid in a corner of a lounge behind a screen to read the paper. Two IOC members saw me and asked me what I was doing.

'I've had it with all this. I'm just reading the paper.'

And they said, 'Can we sit with you?'

That was how we built those relationships.

I remember at the Mediterranean Games in Montpelier in 1993 there was a cocktail party to which I wasn't invited, so I waited around the hotel lobby. President Samaranch left early. He came over and said, 'Come with me. I want to have a talk to you.' And all of a sudden I was sitting with the president. He ordered two jambon rolls and we were talking away, eating our rolls. It was a big break through. Gabor Komyathy said to me afterwards, 'That was the most important moment of the whole trip.'

You never knew when the opportunity would come up to meet a member. The key was to be available. There was not much point sitting in your room at these events. To be available you had to be out and about.

Gosper, Coates and Coles helped to break the barriers for us.

It was up to us to translate them into successful relationships. But we did it slowly, with good manners.

Our first big exercise in lobbying IOC members was at the GAISF conference in October 1991 in Sydney.

The General Assembly of International Sports Federations, which has its headquarters in Monte Carlo, is an association of some 70 international sporting associations, everything from ballroom dancing to tug-of-war. Not all are recognised as Olympic sports but the 25 summer Olympic federations are all members and would be represented there as well as 21 IOC members, so the conference was critical. Prince Albert of Monaco would be there, as would the head of FIFA, Joao Havelange, a life member regarded as one of the power brokers of the IOC and the president of GAISF; and Dr Un Yong Kim, from Korea, who was a member of the IOC executive board. Kim had been instrumental in Seoul winning the 1988 Games and was highly respected within the IOC. But it was also important for us to make contacts with the leaders of the sporting federations who would be there. Bob Elphinston and Graham Lovett were specifically charged with the responsibilities of trying to win the endorsement of the 25 summer IFs before we prepared our bid books.

The work of organising the conference was largely done in our office. All the preparations were well underway and everything was on schedule. I was up at the Sanctuary Cove resort near the Queensland Gold Coast being trained to drive for a celebrity car race for the Adelaide Grand Prix.

Sometime before, the NSW Labour Council had planned a general strike to protest against the state government's new industrial legislation. The strike had been scheduled for 15 October to co-incide with the introduction of the legislation into state parliament. This just happened to be the day when 21 IOC members were due to visit.

At first I didn't know much about it. But as soon as it looked like becoming an issue, Bruce Baird and John Coates got straight onto it. They called Michael Easson, the head of the NSW Labour Council. Easson was on the bid committee and his wife,

Mary, who has since become a federal politician, was on our Communications Commission.

As it turned out, neither Easson nor the leader of the Opposition, Bob Carr, had realised that the strike co-incided with the GAISF conference. We feared that a general strike in the state could have turned it into a disaster. So they all went to work quickly to try and fix it.

Michael Easson, John Coates and I held a press conference at the airport after I flew in from Queensland and it was announced that the strike would be deferred. The Australian Olympic Committee said it was grateful to the union movement and the problem was solved. The union movement made it clear that it was in full support of the bid, something we were to make much of later.

Coates and Coles had stressed the importance of making sure the IOC members were well looked after. Coates told us it was normal for a member attending such an event to have a minder throughout the entire visit — a local person to look after them, handle transport, restaurant bookings, advise on any side trips, help their spouse, let them know where they had to be next and interpret for those who couldn't speak English.

Before the conference the government came up with the idea of getting people in the public service to volunteer for the job. They were given leave from their job but they didn't get any extra pay for it. We were particularly looking for people who could speak foreign languages. These visit officers, as they were called, were matched with IOC members based on their language and interests. Phil Coles and I briefed them on what was required. The system worked well and some good relations were built between the visit officers and the IOC members and their spouses.

The conference went off very smoothly. The opening ceremony was at the Opera House. There were some problems with one of the acts but I think the members just thought that was the way Australians did their music. There were fireworks over the harbor. The NSW Government put on a magnificent dinner under a marquee down at the harbor foreshore point known as Lady Macquarie's Chair. There was another one at the Art

Gallery of NSW, sponsored by Caltex. Before that dinner there were cocktails and a showing of the Guggenheim collection which was on tour in the gallery. We deliberately selected the venue to emphasise the cultural side of our bid. It was a real coup for the NSW Art Gallery to get the Guggenheim exhibition — only two other cities in the world had been able to show it and we regarded the dinner as a very important one for the bid.

Luis Morales, who was representing Brasilia's bid, came to Sydney make a presentation but he didn't speak much English. At one of the dinners I sat him next to Deeta and asked her to look after him. I had to move someone off the table to do it. He was a really nice fellow and had played tennis in the Brazilian Davis Cup team. He was very grateful we looked after him and I had a friend for life. Over the next two and a half years he couldn't do enough for me although we were supposed to be rivals.

David O'Connor was in the Premier's Department at the time and was very involved in the organisation and protocol. Our early clashes were buried and his professionalism and dedication manifest. He and Kevin Simmonds in our office handled logistics. Nick Greiner was available for everything. Government cars were provided for the IOC members. We gave people tours of Taronga Park Zoo and the art gallery. Sydney's Carnivale, the annual festival of all the ethnic cultures in the city, which was usually in September was deferred to co-incide with the conference.

There were some fun times as well. We were really building relationships nicely with the IOC members. Coates realised that two of the members were Olympic yachtsmen — Peter Tallberg from Finland and Jacques Rogge from Belgium. Tallberg had sailed in five Olympics and was president of the International Yachting Union. So Coates, who can organise just about anything, rang up Peter Gilmore and Iain Murray, the skippers of our 12-metre yachts, and asked them if they could put both of the *Kookaburras* out on the harbor.

Rogge sailed one and Tallberg sailed the other and other IOC members and ourselves crewed. Gilmore and Murray stood behind them just to make sure everything went all right. Jack Pinkerton, one of the technical directors of the Atlanta bid was there, as was Alex Gilady, a senior executive of NBC Television in the US, the network's expert on the Olympics. He was a very close friend of President Samaranch and was at every major Olympic meeting. He was clearly an experienced sailor and he called out a lot of instructions to everyone. I had never been sailing and I ended up on the coffee grinder with Anita DeFrantz, the IOC member from the US. Anita was the first black woman member of the IOC. She won a bronze medal for rowing at the Montreal Games in 1976 and was also a talented lawyer. She was a big strong woman and I was worried that I might have to give up working on the coffee grinder before she did. I knew I had to keep going. Fortunately it didn't happen. We were on Rogge's boat and we won two races out of three. It was fun to sail with these kind of people in world class 12-metre yachts. We finished up with a barbecue at the Cruising Yacht Club at Rushcutter's Bay, all in our yachting gear. There was a lot of sheer hard work in the bid, but that day out on the harbor was one of those times when my job was just plain good fun — even though my back and arms ached from keeping up with Anita.

8
Our Man in Havana and Elsewhere

Rod, I don't think it's a good idea for a bid city to have a chauffeur-driven Mercedes while IOC people are being driven around in old taxis.

François Carrad

One great friend I made was Paul Wallwork, the IOC member in Western Samoa. Both he and his wife Julia are very important and influential in Western Samoa. Western Samoa receives a lot of foreign aid — including aid from China.

Paul did an arts degree at the University of Sydney and got a Bachelor of Education in New Zealand. He was a teacher before becoming permanent secretary to the Ministry of Youth, Sports and Cultural Affairs in Western Samoa in 1982. He had a remarkable sporting career. He was a great all-round sportsman with interests in weightlifting, tennis, boxing, rugby and athletics. In 1959 he was badly injured in a sporting accident but worked on his strength and built his body up again through weight lifting. He went on to win the Auckland Senior Weightlifting Championship in 1964 and a gold medal in the South Pacific Games in 1966. He was Australian weightlifting champion in 1972 and a silver medallist at the 1974 Commonwealth Games. He was only about five foot six but he had a strong neck and very big shoulders: you wouldn't mistake him for anything but a weight lifter. His son Gerry was also a weight lifter and had lived in Australia for a while. They were a very close family.

Paul was a very sensitive man and we knew he had one memory of his ties with Australia which may have been painful for him. In 1972, after he won the Australian Championships, the International Weightlifting Federation said he could go to the Munich Olympics that year as a member of the Australian team. But the Australian organisation said he couldn't go because he wasn't an

Australian. So his only chance to compete at the Olympics was denied to him by Australians. We were always conscious that it must have been a disappointment for him. But I never heard him refer to it and he was always a great supporter of ours.

When I visited him in Apia, we went down to his favorite beach with his daughter, Helena, and had lunch. He asked me if I had seen the film, *Return to Paradise*, with Gary Cooper. I hadn't. I thought Gary Cooper only made westerns and war movies. He said it was made on the beach we were on. I asked him if there were any videos of it, and he told me an interesting story.

'It went out of production and you can never see it. But on the morning of the vote in Tokyo for the 1996 Games, Charlie Battle from Atlanta gave me a copy. He said Ted Turner had got a copy for him. Now that's not bad.'

I put that in the back of my head. It was going to be a hard act to follow.

Over the next 48 hours Paul and I had a great time. We found we both enjoyed the same sort of music, and we were both nuts about rugby. We went to watch a game and Bob Dwyer, the coach of the Australian Rugby team, the Wallabies was there. I had asked Bob to go to Western Samoa to speak at a sports night there.

I was listening to Paul's music which was a lot of 1950s and 1960s stuff I like and somebody said something about Ray Connif. I had found a musical soul mate. I had a great compact disc with all the old greats of the 1950s at home and Ray Connif was on it.

So as soon as I got home, I got a copy of this CD and sent it across to Paul and signed the letter, 'Ray Connif'. Now I sign everything I send to Paul, 'Ray Connif'.

Then I went to Channel 10 in Sydney which covers rugby union games. I asked them if they could give me a video tape of the weekly games — without the commercials — of whatever they were covering and also any international matches. We sent them off each week to Paul. Julia later complained that Paul was always sitting up in bed at night watching the rugby!

Paul came up to me on a later occasion. He looked at me for a moment with a wry smile and delivered the ultimate compliment: 'I can't decide whether you're worse than Charlie Battle or not.'

Deeta and I also became very fond of Mohamed Mzali, the IOC member from Tunisia. His dignity and the way he kept his intelligent idealism intact humbled and inspired us. Mr Mzali was the prime minister of Tunisia from 1980 to 1986 but was later exiled and went to live in Paris. His wife and children had been imprisoned at times and their passports confiscated; they were still in Tunis. At the Mediterranean Games in Athens in June 1991 we dropped a letter under the door of the hotel rooms of the IOC members to invite them for a drink or dinner. Mzali sent word that he would like to see me. I knocked on his door.

'*Bonjour.*'

'*Bonjour, monsieur. Parlez-vous Anglais?*'

'*Non, Francais.*'

He couldn't speak any English but told me to come in. I saw he was reading some interesting political books. I sat down and spent an hour with him. Even though we couldn't speak each other's language, we somehow managed to communicate. He had actually written many works on politics, history and Olympism. We struggled through, both wanting to take the time to understand each other. We formed a special friendship. I went out of my way to meet up with him later. When Deeta was there we had no language problem because she could speak French.

Mzali was a fascinating man, extraordinarily intelligent and politically aware. He made me more appreciative of the rights and privileges of our own system by telling me of the extreme difficulties he and his family suffered. When Deeta went to Paris on business she would always look him up and have lunch. He was lonely without his family and I think he enjoyed our company.

Mzali gave some interesting speeches during his later visit to Australia. He was taken with the way the different ethnic communities in Australia were all living together. He talked about how good it was that people from all these different countries had come to Australia and were 'living beyond their differences', a very perceptive remark.

The lobbying for the 2000 Games was affected by the new rules brought in by the IOC to cut down the amount of spending in the bidding process. The IOC had become increasingly concerned at the lavish parties, expensive gifts and the frequent travel some IOC members took from bidding countries. In a few cases, there were reports of members taking first class tickets, cashing them in and going economy or business class instead.

In their book *The Lords of the Rings* Andrew Jennings and Vyv Simson, talked of the 'shocking truth behind the organisation of the Olympics' and criticised the largesse of the bidding process. But well before the publication of the book, President Samaranch and other key IOC members were already taking action to limit spending by the bidding cities. It was only in the highly competitive bidding for the 1992 and the 1996 Olympics that this became a problem. By the time of the Tokyo decision in 1990 the IOC was already signalling plans to crack down on it. By the time I joined the Sydney bid in early 1991 the IOC was already working on new guidelines for bidding. Draft guidelines were issued in August 1991 and came into effect on 7 February 1992.

I thought the authors of that book were trying to cash in on the Barcelona Olympics, taking a cheap shot at the Olympic movement by picking out six or eight people — out of more than 90 — and about ten or 15 incidents where there were problems, and implying that this was what the whole Olympic movement was all about. It was like criticising the entire legal profession because of the actions of one or two solicitors. There was a lot of breathless sensation. One of the examples they used of how out of control things apparently were was a party thrown by the Brisbane bid for IOC members at the 90th IOC session in East Berlin in 1985, where Rupert Murdoch had specially flown in a lot of fresh Australian seafood. Sure it happened and it was an expensive party, but it was hardly an example of wholesale bribery and corruption.

I found the Olympic movement had a lot of thoughtful, high-calibre people who are very committed to the Olympic ideals. Many members had been world class athletes and had a high record of achievement in their own countries. And Baron de Coubertin's goals of giving youth a broad education and using the Games to encourage better world understanding seemed to me very admirable goals for a city and a country to be committed to.

No organisation is perfect and international organisations always have their own particular stresses, bringing together people from such different backgrounds. Even democracy has its flaws and wayward politicians, but the system sure beats the alternatives. For these writers to bash the whole Olympic movement and IOC members because of the actions of a few is, to say the least, to be totally ignorant of what they were is all about. If anyone really wants to understand what motivates these people they should study why the Olympic movement started, read its history and read the Charter. It is only after understanding its context that you can really pass judgement. In my personal and intimate experience of the organisation and its people, Jennings and Simson are way off.

We felt we could live comfortably within the new rules — with a bit of give and take. IOC members could not make more than one official visit to a candidate city during the course of a campaign. In most cases they could only stay for three days — but in the event of long trips they could stay for five. They tried to limit the number of people from a bidding city who could go as part of a delegation to the official Olympic meetings to six — but for some of the big meetings, it was hard to keep to this rule and it was never rigidly enforced.

There was a strict ban on any lavish exhibitions, receptions or expensive entertaining of IOC members. Gone were the big receptions, cocktail parties and dinners for IOC members at the major international sporting events. Bidding cities could no longer use boats, yachts, club houses and villas to entertain members.

Candidate cities were supposed to be banned from sending delegations to visit IOC members in their home countries. But we found this did not mean it was *impossible* for us to visit a member in their own country; if there was a valid reason to be in a country, one could hardly not see the local IOC members. And we could always find a valid reason to be in a country if we needed one. But it certainly did cut down the old practice of frequent visits by bidding cities to members in their home countries.

Overall we liked the new guidelines; if anything they favored us. Anything that cut down the cost of bidding and caused people to vote on the merits of a candidate city helped us. The restrictions on spending helped to put a city from a small country like Australia on a more even footing with one from a wealthier country such as Germany which could easily outspend us. Cutting back on the parties and the travel brought the whole process back on an even playing field. Before the new rules, it would have been very easy for representatives from a European city such as Berlin or Manchester or Milan or Istanbul to make frequent visits to IOC members in Europe. There were 38 IOC members in Europe, the most concentrated area of members. If it was open slather, there was no way people from the Sydney bid could make as many trips to Europe as people from the Manchester bid. The rule on long-distance travel also favored us. If members could stay for five days rather than three, we had time to show them Sydney. But the travel restrictions did set a premium on us having good representation at the big international sporting events which attracted a significant number of IOC members.

The IOC initially set a limit of $US200 on any gifts that could be given by candidate cities to members or their relatives and companions. In the IOC session before the Barcelona Olympics, it went further, declaring that there were to be no gifts at all apart from souvenirs.

Again we didn't mind.

We put together a range of typically Australian souvenirs which would appeal to each IOC member. We developed an interesting collection of knick-knacks and gifts. Sue Bushby was the expert at it. We had Akubra hats, Drizabone raincoats, special interest books and Australian coins. When it came to the big week at Monte Carlo we took cricket lovers books signed by Don Bradman, golf lovers autographed photos of Greg Norman. Gifts had to be individual and creative, not merely expensive or have prestigious brand names. The trick was to find out something simple that they would really like such as Paul Wallwork's CD of Ray Connif and the rugby tapes. They didn't cost much but to the individual they meant a lot.

Whenever I went on a big international trip, Margaret would

work out my itinerary, go into our communications section and work out what sort of knick-knacks and brochures we needed for the members I would be meeting. They would all be packed into a big red wheelie bin, like those big garbage bins. The packing was done in order of my itinerary. So if I was meeting with Mr and Mrs Dibos from Peru, I would just get out the gifts we had for the Dibos and the fact sheets and everything on the Peruvian Olympic Committee from the wheelie bin. At the next city I would open it up again and out would come the gifts and the brochures, all in order. One trip I did was so long I had to take two bins. It all had to be very carefully thought out and planned in advance.

Because the tighter rules on spending were new, there was some testing of the limits of interpretation — and how vigilant the IOC would be in policing them and how far one could push their interpretation.

The city that always seemed to test the new limits was Milan. In the early stages they got into trouble. They wanted a much more relaxed bidding process. They brought a yacht for entertaining into the harbor during the Barcelona Games and were told by IOC officials to take it away. Watching Milan helped the rest of us sort out the rules. We would see what they did, see the response from the IOC and then judge how far we could go if we wanted to stay on side with the IOC.

One element of our international lobbying strategy was to tap into the Australian diplomatic network around the world.

Dick Woolcott, the former Australian Ambassador to the United Nations and head of the Department of Foreign Affairs, was on the overall bid committee. We had some private meetings about how to take advantage of Australia's foreign affairs network around the world. I regarded it as so important that I allocated one full-time staff member to dealing with the diplomats.

Dick's son Peter was on staff in the first part of the bid to help set up the program. We sent the embassies regular reports on what we were doing. We sent them our newsletters, our videos and regular correspondence, so they felt they were a part of our team.

They were specifically asked *not* to do any lobbying of IOC members. We wanted to keep that for our lobbying team. But we wanted them to generally promote the bid and make contacts with friends of the Olympic family; to be our eyes and ears overseas; collect newspaper articles; and feed information back to us.

Whenever diplomats came back home, on holidays or for consultations or for a change of post, we had them in our office for a briefing. Every ambassador and every consul who came back to Australia came into our office. We wanted to make sure they were up to speed on the bid all the time.

The diplomats became increasingly important as we travelled and the international lobbying campaign intensified. As the person in the lobby team charged with looking after South America, I found the Australian ambassadors there particularly helpful. There was Hugh Wyndam in Argentina, Dominque de Stoop in Venezuela and Matthew Peake in Chile. They were all fantastic. They fed back information. They called on people. They suggested people I should meet on my visits. Hugh Wyndham and his wife were particularly kind in looking after Margaret McLennan when she got very sick at a meeting in Argentina. My lack of Spanish was not a real problem; I could generally call on the ambassador or someone from the embassy who could translate. Hugh's wife was Venezuelan and she was always ready to help.

Our first trip to Latin America was quite an experience.

We went to Cuba for the Pan-American Sports Organisation Games in July 1991. We went a few days early because there weren't many flights in and out of the country. When I arrived at the airport in Havana and showed the immigration guy my official green passport I was told to stand aside and wait. Margaret and Graham Lovett were with me. They had no problem because they had ordinary passports. I kept waiting but nothing happened. After a while I thought I'd try another line. Then they really got annoyed with me. Armed guards came and pushed me back and made me wait under guard. I could see Margaret and Graham on the other side and some semi-official people with them, all getting annoyed about what was happening to me. Eventually I was allowed through. The problem was that we had arrived two days earlier than the official guests. The officials were not ready to greet us and they were ordering a VIP vehicle to 'welcome' us. They had impounded me until they could get everything organised.

We eventually got out of the airport and were told to wait for this official vehicle. We were waiting for ages. By this time I was getting annoyed and wanted to get a taxi. But people kept insisting we wait. When it finally came, the 'official vehicle' was a 1940s bus painted bright red with no windows in it. We had been booked to stay in a protocol house but it wasn't ready so we had to stay in a dreadful hotel for two nights.

Havana was a depressing town. Ironically, the road system in the country was very good. It often is in Soviet-dominated countries for defence purposes. But everything else was broken down. Things were not painted, windows were cracked, there weren't many shops, people were queuing for food and restaurants were grubby. I got a bit sick there — the only tummy wog I had in two and a half years of travelling. It was hot and the house we were assigned was isolated. It was very hard to ring home. There were armed guards everywhere. We were cautioned about taking photographs. Graham Lovett took one while we were at the beach and he was confronted by soldiers telling him to stop. There was an atmosphere of unease about the place.

There were still touches of Ernest Hemingway. We went to the restaurant where he had signed his name on the wall and La Floridita nightclub where he often went. It was dusty, dowdy and poorly lit, but the waiters still wore tails and the silverware was out. We went to the famous outdoor Tropicana nightclub. There were colored lights and the entertainers had brightly colored outfits. The stage was created around the trees. Suddenly a light would flash on and somebody would be singing, sitting in the fork of a tree.

They had built a new hotel and a new village for the Games by the sea which was impressive. That was where the IOC members stayed. They had also built a new stadium — but it wasn't quite finished. We sat on the concrete steps. Fidel Castro came to the opening ceremony. When he arrived, the crowd went wild and cheered him for ages. I met Alberto Juantorena, the great Cuban athlete — the only man to win a gold medal for the 400 metres and the 800 metres in the same Games, in

Montreal in 1976. He was an extraordinary athlete and we got on very well. I also met Mario Vazquez Rana and other IOC members from the Americas.

We were invited to the presidential palace for a reception and met Fidel Castro. The palace was a very big building with lots of polished marble. A very big man, Castro walked around, accompanied by about four bodyguards who stood all around him. There was just an opening to his front where you could talk to him. Representatives from all the bid cities were invited. There was great food that night — no expense had been spared. Outside there was tremendous poverty.

Our bookings had been made by the government. We couldn't book accommodation in Cuba directly from Australia. We had to go through the Cuban consul. He had booked us the protocol house, which was obviously the house of some wealthy person, and the government provided us with a car. All of which we had to pay for, of course. We had a black Mercedes, quite an old model, and a driver. I had never been to Cuba before but I thought: if this is the deal, this is the deal. One day the three of us were driving to the stadium in our chauffeur-driven black Mercedes. We were caught in traffic next to one of the old Cuban taxis. In it was the director-general of the IOC, François Carrard, and Anne Beddow, a member of his staff. They just stared at us. Our Mercedes was not exactly flash, but it sure looked a lot better than their beat up old taxi. Carrard came over to me later and said, 'Rod, I don't think its a good idea for a bid city to have a chauffeur-driven Mercedes while IOC people are being driven around in old taxis. It's not a good idea for a bid city to look too flashy.'

I told him I had nothing to do with it and that my government had made all the arrangements. We couldn't get rid of the Mercedes because it was our only way of getting around and our house was a long way from anything. Even so, we felt very self-conscious about it after that.

But it was a little lesson in lobbying; don't *look* as if you've got more money than the people who vote. You've always got to be careful what sort of image you are presenting to the customer — even if part of that image at first appears to be out of your control. In most cases in business no-one will come up to you — as M. Carrard did to me — and gently point out the problem.

You have to be aware of the image you present. If it is distinctly more affluent than that of the customer, that customer may quietly decide that he has been upstaged and is more comfortable with someone else.

We had one moment of real fear during the lobbying.

We heard a lot about the Berlin bid in the early stages and we thought the power of German funding could be something to watch. But the Berlin bid suffered throughout from vigorous local protests. The protests seemed well funded and they became semi-violent.

In December 1991, after the GAISF conference in Sydney, John Coates and I went to Berlin for a meeting of the IOC executive board.

At Berlin airport, we were impressed with the Berlin 2000 signs. But when we arrived in the city, the hotel where we and the other IOC members were staying at was barricaded off. There were signs on the building opposite the hotel saying:

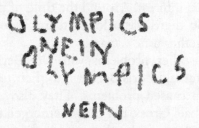

Driving back to the hotel after watching the Australian women's hockey team beat The Netherlands in the Champions Trophy tournament, John and I were in a line of traffic. There was a large bus in front of us. We couldn't see everything that was coming towards us, and the people on the other side of the bus couldn't see us. There seemed to be some sort of strange activity on the other side of the bus but nothing to alarm us.

But then it emerged that it was a protest. Most protestors were on push bikes, and they didn't see us until they got past the bus. But when they saw the Olympic rings on the side of the car, they headed for us. Coates and I were in the back and there was the driver and another person in the front. The protesters tore the aerial off the roof. They kicked the car as they rode past. Our driver got annoyed because his aerial was broken and he wanted to get out of the car. I wanted to get out and flatten somebody. But Coates said we should lock the doors and not go anywhere. So I locked my door. Just afterwards, someone sprayed red paint on the outside of the window right next to my face. It looked like blood, and I suppose it was meant to.

We didn't realise how frightened we had been until they had gone past. What if they had picked up the car and tipped it over or something? It really shook us.

Early on Berlin had been a sentimental favorite. There was a lot of emotional talk about The Wall coming down and how good it would be to mark this by giving Germany the millennium Games. I never really understood it. It seemed to me that by 2000 The Wall would have been well and truly down and the memory would have faded.

The Berlin bid seemed to be beset with problems. They started off with two guys who were a bit stand-offish. They were both ex-IBM employees. There was criticism that one of them had placed US$2 million worth of advertising with an agency in which he had an interest. Around the time of this board meeting, he resigned. So there was a lot of turmoil going on and Berlin had to put together a new team.

There were other problems with the Berlin bid. They co-opted Steffi Graf and Boris Becker into their team without asking them — which caused problems. They also co-opted the great swimmer, Michael Gross, but then it emerged that he was getting $2,000 a day whenever he did anything for the bid. They just kept making mistakes and hitting hurdles.

Then there was the scandal that broke on German television about some very personal profiles of all the IOC members which fell off the back of a truck. The secret files apparently listed their sexual tastes, their interest in drugs or alcohol and how open they were supposed to be to financial inducements. The Berlin bid ended up having to write a letter of apology to every IOC member and tell them they had destroyed the files. They said they had been created by a public relations company that was out of control. They never seemed to be in control.

And there always seemed to be more protests.

Local support just wasn't there. Chancellor Kohl took ages to say he supported the bid. And for a long time there seemed to be a question mark about whether the German National Olympic Committee would support them. Gradually they got it all together. But it was a strain for them. They never really looked strong in our eyes.

If there was going to be anyone who could offer us a serious challenge on lobbying, it would have been Manchester. Bob Scott, its leader, was an outgoing man and well connected in the Olympic movement. But after a few months in the job I was never in any doubt that my earliest intuition was right. The real battle would be with Beijing.

So, for more than two years, there were representatives of eight different cities (the number came down to five in the end) travelling the world; all trying to make 90 new friends; each of us in our own way, each having their own experiences and making particular friends, each of us convinced that our product was the best.

9
Value for Money: a World for our Sponsors

Some see private enterprise as the predatory cow to be shot, others as a cow to be milked, but few are those who see it as a sturdy horse pulling the wagon

Sir Winston Churchill

John Valder and I were at a fund-raising lunch in the board room of SA Brewing in Adelaide with representatives of some of the city's top companies. We were being questioned closely about what benefits there were for companies who donated money to help the Sydney bid. Many Sydney-based companies were willing to give money or other support because they really wanted Sydney to get the Games. But for some companies interstate, the decision was more difficult.

Their questions highlighted one of our problems in trying to drum up dollars from the private sector to fund our bid. We had to explain that we were only a *bid* company — we couldn't promise that anyone would be the official airline for the Games, offer them the official hot dog franchise or be The Official Anything. We couldn't promise contracts, business contacts, or any other spin-offs from the Games themselves. We couldn't even promise tickets.

All we could promise is that we wouldn't forget the people who helped us.

One man listened to it all and didn't say too much. He was different from the other executive types — very much a self-made man. He was a big man with broad hands. At first I thought he may have been a builder. I found out a little more about him after the lunch. Bob Gerard, the chief executive of Gerard Industries, one of Australia's largest electrical accessory makers, ran a business that had been in his family for more than 70 years. He sent us a cheque for $100,000. It was a donation I never forgot. Many executives donated money on behalf of big public companies — the money he gave was from his family company, effectively his own.

The fund raising for the bid was always going to be important. By and large it was an exercise which ran very smoothly. It may well have been a testimony to the amount of public support there was for Sydney getting the Games. We never knew where the money would come from tomorrow, but it kept coming.

Peter Ueberroth's book on the Los Angeles Olympics, *Made in America*, begins with a quote from Winston Churchill: 'Some see private enterprise as the predatory cow to be shot, others as a cow to be milked, but few are those who see it as a sturdy horse pulling the wagon.' He was among those few, and I agree with him.

It was Ueberroth's ability to harness the financial support of the private sector in America which quite literally helped to save the Olympic Games. Since then, the private sector has taken a much higher profile. Television networks provide a big part of the funding with payments for broadcasting rights. After Los Angeles, the IOC also developed a sophisticated international sponsorship program known as The Olympic Program or TOP, where companies could bid to become the official international sponsor for each product range over the course of the Olympiad. Long time TOP sponsors included Visa, Brother, Philips, Kodak, Time Inc and Coca-Cola. At the local level companies play a key role in helping out in all kinds of ways when a city hosts the Games.

The Australian economy has always been more of a mix between private and public enterprise than the United States'. The Sydney Olympic bid was Made in Australia. And it became an excellent example of how effectively the public and private sectors in Australia can work together if they set their minds to it.

When we started, Nick Greiner said the NSW government would guarantee us up to $10 million to finance the bid. At first we thought we could do it for about $20 million. But as we began to do our sums for the budget in some detail, the cost looked more like $25 million.

The state government was prepared to help out with an Olympic Lottery. There was also talk that we could raise money from a series of Sunday horse race meetings. Sunday races had not been held in Sydney before and there were people keen to try it out. The government would contribute the betting revenue it made from the TAB. We estimated we could raise about $8 to $9 million from the lottery and the races, which meant we had to raise about $6 million from the corporate sector.

John Valder was the powerhouse of our fund-raising effort. Well known in business and political circles in NSW, he was a director of Email and deputy chairman of the State Bank of NSW. He had been a prominent Sydney stockbroker, founding the firm of Valder Elmslie in 1967 (which later became Jardine Fleming Australia Securities). He was chairman of the Sydney Stock Exchange from 1973 to 1976. He later became very involved with the Liberal Party, and was a major force in its fund raising. He was president of the NSW branch of the party from 1982 to 1985 and federal president from 1985 to 1987. When Nick Greiner put him on our board he knew what a good fund raiser he was.

Valder headed up our Corporate Support Committee. It included Bevan Bradbury, the former chief executive of Coles, who was the NSW president of the Liberal Party at the time, also well known as a fund raiser. (Sadly, Bevan died in late 1993.) There was also Steve Rattray who had just finished raising money for the 12-metre yacht challenge; Bob Prater, from Coopers and Lybrand who was our finance manager, and David Smithers, the chairman of our Finance Commission.

We started out by trying to generate lists of all the companies we could approach, as well as their chief executives and chief financial officers. We collected all the lists we had from our involvement in charities. I had been heavily involved with the Salvation Army's Red Shield Appeal and John Valder was head of the Australia Day Council. We put all this into a computer and came out with a master list of companies.

We also looked at how Melbourne had raised the money for its bid. Advertising man Peter Clemenger came to Sydney to take us through the concept of Melbourne's 100 Club. Their strategy was to approach 100 companies and ask for $100,000 to raise the $10 million. It was an interesting concept, effectively a club with a $100,000 subscription. But if a company offered $50,000 or $200,000, they rejected it. We listened, but with Australia in the middle of recession, we didn't think we could knock back any money. But we did take their advice on dividing up companies into their industry categories — such as advertising, banking, computing, property development, retailing etc — and allocating them by category to each of the members of the fund-raising committee.

We eventually adopted a three-tiered system of corporate supporters. Top level sponsors we called Gold Supporters. They contributed over $150,000 — there ended up being 25 of those. Then there were Proud Supporters who gave more than $50,000 and Friends of the Bid who gave what they could. (See full list in Appendix 3.)

We got a lot of good help and advice from Coca-Cola, which is a very sophisticated company when it comes to marketing and sponsorship. It had been associated with the Olympics in one form or another since 1928 and had been a member of TOP since it started. The company put together a package of suggested money raising activities for the Sydney bid. I had a meeting with Ron Pugsley and Peter Trives from Coke and they asked if there was anything else I needed. I told them I was short of someone who really understood the business of looking after corporate sponsors. They immediately offered the services of a Coke employee, George Mellick. Not only did they let him work full-time on the bid, but they agreed to pay his salary. Mellick joined us and become heavily involved in all the fund-raising activities. He was responsible for the administration of the entire corporate support program and was John Valder's right hand man. He kept in contact with the corporate supporters — sending them newsletters, fact sheets and videos, and organising the scheme for companies to use Sydney 2000 merchandise. It was such an important service that in October 1992 we hired Peter Wejbora, who had been with the Festival of Sydney, to help him.

I was always very conscious of the fact that we weren't able to offer our sponsors anything specific in return for their support. As those executives in Adelaide found out, the obvious way of raising money by doing deals was just not available to us. I wanted to make sure that the Sydney bid was never criticised if we lost; that no-one could say we didn't look after the people who had given us money. So I worked hard at trying to give all our sponsors value for their money.

We wanted to kick off with a big, high-profile corporate dinner to generate some impact around the corporate community as we started our fund-raising campaign. We decided the GAISF conference would be a good time to do something and we invited Billy Payne out from Atlanta as our guest speaker. Everyone loved him. The dinner was sponsored by the Hilton Hotel and the Catering Institute of Australia, an organisation whose head, Bill Galvin, throughout the entire bid period provided tourism and hospitality staff in a generous, sustained and enthusiastic manner. Nick Greiner and John Valder spoke. They began to encourage companies to be prepared to give if they wanted Sydney to win. It was the start of a number of fund-raising functions.

We had many lunches for corporate supporters in our board-room. John Valder would speak and either I or Bob Elphinston would give a run down on the bid. We always had a VIP guest — either the Premier, first Nick Greiner and later John Fahey, Bruce Baird, George Souris, the NSW Minister for Sport, Recreation and Racing (who later became the Minister for Finance), or the Lord Mayor, Frank Sartor or sometimes John Coates. We would always hand out a kit and fact sheets. Sue Bushby did the hospitality side of it and George Mellick the paperwork and the follow-up.

As I got to know our corporate supporters, I became even more determined to give them proper recognition. We started at home. On the wall facing the major bank of lifts in our office we put up all the names and the corporate logos of the sponsoring companies. Everyone coming into the bid office was immediately met with a wall of names and corporate logos at eye level. It was very effective. Any visitor coming out of the lift could see that a large part of corporate Australia was backing us.

We also developed very sophisticated corporate supporters' kits which were designed by our communications division. Special black satchels with information on the bid. Flags. Videos. The right to buy our merchandise at a discount. The right to put the Sydney 2000 logo on their merchandise for the course of the bid.

I thought most companies did not make the best use of the right to use our logo. They could have made more use of it in their marketing — have it as a badge of honor against their competitors. There didn't seem to be much follow on from the senior executives who made the decision to contribute, and the marketing people who could use it in their promotions. Perhaps it was fear of, say, association with a failed bid if Beijing had got it. Maybe that's something companies will need to look at in more detail if they donate to the Games themselves. But it was all there for them to use.

We negotiated a lot of benefits in kind. Qantas gave us several millions in airfares; its sponsorship was absolutely vital. We were given a 40 per cent discount off airfares. It was a difficult deal to negotiate. Everyone asks Qantas for free tickets and it quite rightly looks for proper recompense. At times we needed Premier Greiner to make a phone call to Qantas chairman Bill Dix to push things along. But eventually we signed a deal. And Qantas were tremendously helpful to us wherever they could.

Wolfgang Grimm at the Inter-Continental Hotel, and many of Sydney hotels including The Regent, gave us accommodation. Wolfgang was a bundle of energy and a good supporter of our bid. He took great pride in having lots of functions for the bid at his hotel. He renamed the bar on the top floor The Sydney 2000 Bar. He was a key figure in the Australian Hotels Association, which gave us $1 million worth of accommodation in a number of Sydney hotels. We had about 170 official visits throughout the bid and we never paid for a night's accommodation anywhere in Sydney.

Telecom completely fitted us out with phones. IBM with computers. Philips were just magnificent with televisions and monitors and VCRs. Fashion designer Trent Nathan kitted us out with our corporate wear for travelling in the final months. It was very distinctive, coming in colours of navy blue and dark grey and was to attract a lot of positive comment wherever we went.

We found companies couldn't do enough for us. And if anyone from our office ever rang up a government department and said they needed something for the bid, it was always given, lent or done.

John Valder reported regularly on progress. Money flowed in and our concern about being able to raise enough money in a recession waned.

But there was more to it than money. The corporate supporters program actually created another group of people with a real interest in the bid. The need to raise funds meant we had to work to create a new tier of supporters in the community. We had to keep them informed, but they were also useful in providing feedback on public opinion about the bid. John Valder would often report back intelligence from the sponsors about what the corporate world was thinking about us — if people thought things were a bit extravagant maybe, or we were not doing enough in certain areas. It was a helpful barometer along the way. It helped ensure we did not get too far out of touch with public thinking.

The Sunday race meetings also turned out to be a great success. Our bid provided a good opportunity for the government, the Australian Jockey Club and the Sydney Turf Club to experiment with having Sunday meetings — as well as raising money to limit the amount of money the state government would have to pay for the bid. We eventually had eight race meetings over the life of the bid. The first race day was at Randwick in March 1992, starting with the Herb Elliott handicap. The last race was on Boxing Day 1993. Each race meeting raised at least $1 million, our biggest single source of cash funding.

The Olympic lottery was one of only a few revenue-specific lotteries ever held in the history of New South Wales. NSW had a Harbor Bridge Lottery and then there were the famous Opera House lotteries which helped finance the construction of that great building. The lottery was launched in August 1992 with 230 000 tickets of $20 each and closed in July 1993. It had a record $2 million first prize and netted us about $1 million.

Overall, raising funds went smoothly. But there were a few problems.

While we were out in the market raising money for our bid, the Australian Olympic Committee was also trying to raise funds to send Australian teams to the winter Games in Albertville in February 1992 and the summer Games in Barcelona in August later that year.

It created some tensions for the AOC and the Sydney 2000 bid. Many companies which were approached by both of us decided they would only give to one. The AOC also had a traditional number of corporate supporters who sign up for the four-year Olympiad which gave them the right to use the Olympic rings with the Australian symbol. It could involve big money: Telecom had paid $1.5 million to be an Australian Olympic sponsor. Some of these thought they had already bought the rights to Olympism in Australia and didn't want to give any money to the bid itself. Toyota was a sponsor of the AOC and it knocked us back. So we approached other car companies. We got $100,000 from Mercedes Benz and a similar amount from Honda.

But more serious tensions soon emerged about the bid having sponsors that were not consistent with AOC sponsors. We got caught up in the beer wars. Tooheys were a major AOC sponsor. Tooheys' arch rival, Carlton and United, which brews Foster's, made a direct approach and offered us $900,000. This raised questions about whether CUB could *be* a sponsor of the Sydney bid while Tooheys was an AOC sponsor. The AOC was not happy. Tooheys was given a chance to match the offer but they didn't come anywhere near it. In the end John Coates just had to accept that we couldn't pass up that kind of money. So CUB became a major sponsor of our bid.

CUB also helped out in other ways. At the beginning of the bid I got a call from John Fitzgerald in Melbourne who ran International Public Relations which did the public relations for Foster's. He said Foster's wanted to give us some free signs on the Grand Prix motor racing circuit in Europe. This was unbelievably generous. Millions watched those Grand Prix races and it was worth a lot to have our signs appearing on television around the world.

But another dispute did not go in our favor. That was between Visa and American Express. Visa is a TOP sponsor *and* an AOC sponsor. John Coates had discussions with American Express about making a contribution to the bid. Coates was well aware of Visa's support for the AOC, and I don't know why he allowed the discussions with Amex to progress as far as they did. They were successful and Amex decided to give us $500,000 cash, a major contribution! Fortunately, in our letter of acceptance in principle to Amex, we qualified it by saying that we could only take the money if the IOC said that it was all right to do so.

Visa Australia found out and was furious. They raised the matter with the IOC in Lausanne. They spoke to Dick Pound, the

IOC member in Canada who heads up the finance commission of the IOC. They raised hell with Coates and complained bitterly to Valder. So here we were, in the difficult position of not wanting to reject the $500,000 but being told that if we took the money it could prejudice our bid. We talked to Dick Pound and he said it definitely could prejudice the bid if we took money from Amex. So we decided that we just couldn't do it. We had to turn our back on $500,000.

John Valder then pushed Visa for some support. But the company only gave us a nominal amount — despite the fact that it had stopped us taking $500,000.

It has to be acknowledged that there have been long time tensions between American Express and Visa over the Olympics. Amex was a sponsor of the Los Angles Games in 1984, but refused to pay the kind of money necessary to be a TOP sponsor. Visa did and the two have been skirmishing over sponsorship of sport and the Olympics ever since.

Two incidents during the bid showed the competitiveness of it all. At the winter Games in Albertville in February 1992 Amex put up signs and advertising which said that the Amex card could be used at the Games. Visa sued and won. I thought it was a strange result because the Amex card *could* be used at the Games and I didn't think Amex were misrepresenting themselves.

But the ambush marketing, as it was called, continued. In Barcelona we stayed at the Princesa Sofia Hotel. It was a big hotel which was block-booked by the IOC for the Olympic family. Each guest was given a plastic card as their key. In the lead up to the Games that key had Amex stamped all over it. Then, all of a sudden, all keys were withdrawn and all guests got back a key that had *no* sponsorship on it.

There was another funny twist in the Visa/Amex battle. There was a major Olympic fund-raising event in Melbourne to raise money for the Australian Olympic team. Ford donated a Capri car to be auctioned on the night. Guess who bought it? Amex. Amex got great publicity at the function and, naturally, Visa's temperature went up. But the patient was made worse when Amex then donated the vehicle to the Sydney Olympic bid and got even more publicity.

These were interesting little battles in a marketing war — and an example of the sensitivities of Olympic sponsorship that we all had to come to grips with and will have to learn even more about as we head towards the 2000 Games.

We decided to spread our fund raising efforts beyond Sydney and Australia. New Zealand had quickly become conscious that there were real spinoffs for them if Sydney won. A third of all international tourists who go to Australia also go to New Zealand. That meant about 400,000 extra tourists would visit their country over the decade from 1994 if Sydney won. So the New Zealanders wanted to be really helpful.

The president of the New Zealand Olympic Committee, Sir David Beattie, a former governor-general and a former chief justice, had helped the IOC with the establishment of the Pierre de Coubertin Institute in New Zealand. He was keenly aware of the value a Sydney Olympics would mean for his country and the region. We sought Sir David's support in lobbying for us in the Olympic family in the South-East Asian region.

As it happened, Sir David's son was head of corporate affairs in Sir Ron Brierley's company, Brierley Investments Limited. He became involved and had some very imaginative ideas about raising money. John Valder's friend, Colin Gibbs, was also a successful New Zealander and Valder went to New Zealand a few times on fund-raising visits. So with the help of Valder, Sir David and his son, Brierley Investments and Colin Gibbs we had some very successful functions there. We regarded New Zealand as so important that Premier John Fahey did a fund-raising trip there in 1993.

The process of getting support from the Melbourne business community had its complications.

In the early days I got into tremendous trouble with Melbourne people. I had no idea of the politics or the players in the city. As soon as I took over the bid, I was being asked things like: 'Why would Sydney win if Melbourne couldn't? What will you do differently from the Melbourne bid? Why are Sydney's chances greater than Melbourne's?' Comparisons with the Melbourne bid were a favorite media question. I suppose it was only natural, given that Melbourne had just lost. I could hardly refuse to answer them. But things have a way of being distorted when the media focuses on them. And what I didn't appreciate was how sensitive people in Melbourne felt about their loss to Atlanta, and about any perceived criticism of the way the bid was run — particularly by anyone from Sydney. The corporate community of Melbourne had been very closely involved in the bid and for anyone associated with the Sydney bid to raise any questions about the way it had been carried out was seen by some as a direct criticism of some of its senior members.

I think Melbourne did not get the 1996 Games because they had them in 1956. Only three cities have had the Games twice — Paris, Los Angeles and London — and each time nobody else was bidding. Melbourne came up against very strong competition: Athens as sentimental favorite, a superb campaign from Atlanta and Toronto, which had never had the Games before.

But we also believed we should learn some lessons from the Melbourne bid about the lobbying process. There was a feeling that while a lot of money had been spent in lobbying, not all of it had been well spent. Had Sydney bid for the 1996 Games, it may well have made the same mistakes. But it was precisely because we did have the experience of two previous bids, that we could learn from what happened in the past, building on the strengths of previous campaigns and trying to avoid their mistakes. Our bid represented the sum total of experience that Australia had learned about this unique process. So when I was first interviewed on radio and television, I would say that we were going to lobby in a different way to Melbourne and mention other things we planned to do differently.

John Ralph, who had been very closely involved in the Melbourne bid, took huge exception to this and took it as a personal insult. So did John Gough and Peter Clemenger, although Peter was gracious about it. There were some pretty stiff letters written and it all got very tense. One of the women who had been involved in the Melbourne bid gave me and the Sydney bid a real bucketing in the Melbourne Sunday papers.

I wasn't really the main culprit, but I had said enough. So I went to Melbourne and saw John Ralph and he said: 'Now Rod, I don't want you to make those kind of comments again. I know you're new and you don't know the scene, so I'm excusing you.

But we in Melbourne don't appreciate it and you can let anybody else up there know as well.'

Unfortunately things continued for a while, which was basically inelegance on my part. In reality no offence was ever intended. I am a partner of a law firm with its biggest office in Melbourne. We were really getting ourselves into trouble. When John Valder wanted to hold a lunch in Melbourne in Sir James Balderstone's boardroom at the AMP as a part of his fund-raising campaign, he was told that it would all be fine as long as Rod McGeoch didn't come. Nick Greiner tried to solve it personally a couple of times and other senior people who knew me argued that I wasn't meaning to criticise them or the Melbourne bid. But it wasn't working.

I had to fix it myself. I offered John Ralph a letter of apology which he could have and show it to whosoever he wanted. I told him, 'If I've upset people, I don't like doing that and I'll apologise.'

From the day I apologised, I never had another problem. And I got nothing but support and friendship from the key people in Melbourne all the way. When the lunch came up, I was actually overseas and couldn't go anyway. But I was invited. Having got that apology out of the way, Valder raised big money in Melbourne. National Australia Bank and the ANZ each gave $100,000. Other big Melbourne-based companies such as BHP, National Mutual, Colonial Mutual, Coles Myer, CRA and Western Mining all gave between $50,000 and $150,000.

Melbourne might be prickly, but it is a city with a big, warm generous heart.

From the beginning, the bid had been NSW government backed. In the state, of course, the conservative Liberal-National coalition was in power throughout our campaign while in Canberra, their opponents, the Labor Party, ran the federal government. The federal government was initially very cautious about committing money to the bid.

But after we had been going a little while, the bid attracted the attention of the new Prime Minister, Paul Keating. This seemed odd: Bob Hawke loved the horses, cricket, golf, football and sport generally; Keating played a bit of tennis but was hardly a sports lover. Yet he was soon captured by the Olympic spirit. In May 1992 we had a big fund-raising breakfast in the ballroom of Sydney's Sheraton-Wentworth which was attended by about 400 people. Alan Jones, then 2UE's morning radio host, broadcast his program live from the breakfast. Paul Keating was invited as the official patron of the bid. He sat next to Nick Greiner, both eating their croissants and jam. It was the first Sydney Olympics 2000 function Keating had attended as prime minister.

Greiner was urging Keating to get behind the bid and give some money. Greiner spoke first, saying that the Olympics was a 'glittering prize' and predicting that Sydney would win, despite the growing attention to the Beijing bid.

When Keating got up to speak, he astonished us all:

'I'll probably get baked for this when I get back, but we'll put in $5 million.' It took my breath away. To get $5 million in a budget of $25 million was a huge bonus. There was a full 30-second applause. The money was much appreciated. Keating may not be a great sportsman, but he was an internationalist and could see a Sydney Olympics would be important for Australia's national pride.

This was the first of a number of bi-partisan occasions in the Sydney bid when the emotion of the Games brought together state and federal politicians of different political parties. Bruce Baird was elated with Keating's unexpected announcement:

'I'm absolutely delighted,' he said. 'It's the first time I've felt like embracing a Labor politician.'

As Keating was leaving, John Valder told him he 'could come back any day'.

Simon Balderstone, Paul Keating's representative on the Board, later told me that he and Keating had a brief discussion before the breakfast about a possible Federal Government donation for the Bid. Keating asked Balderstone how well it would go down. Balderstone replied: 'Not too well in Finance, but very well elsewhere, I can assure you'.

In the end, every single company that made a promise to donate, came up with the money. Not one promise in the whole time of the bid failed to be fulfilled. Not one.

The whole process was a financial success. We raised about

$6.8 million from the private sector in cash — and even more than than in terms of support in kind. It was far above our $6 million budget. We got $8.8 million from the Sunday race days and another $1.25 million from the lottery. With the $5 million from the federal government, the state government only had to contribute $2.9 million to our final budget of $25.2 million — far less than the $10 million they had initially budgeted. (Interest and some other smaller items made up the difference.) This meant they had extra money to help fund the Games themselves.

The whole exercise was a good lesson in fund-raising for a non-profit operation. To do it well, you've got to have people who have experience, good information and a first-class list of companies and the names of people to approach in those companies. You have to have well-connected fund raisers who can talk to chief executives and their offsiders. Your fund raisers must be excellent door openers who will not be put off by an early rebuff: Peter Clemenger told me that in the fund raising for the Melbourne bid he went to one company ten times before he finally got his $100,000.

You've got to have a person who's prepared to carry a lot of the load — who's prepared to do the work and has the time to do it. John Valder was perfect. He was well connected and very hands-on. He would come into the office and prepare lists and sign letters and get on the phone. He was prepared to travel anywhere — across the Harbor Bridge or across the Tasman — to raise money. And then you've also got to have the backup and the follow-up. George Mellick would always follow up after the fund raisers and the promises.

But it's not a one way street. You have to be prepared to give sponsors something in return. It's important that they feel a part of the organisation and that they can use the association in their own marketing, to generate a sense of support and endeavor among their customer and employees. You need to consider them as part of your support team.

Before we went to Monte Carlo many of our sponsor companies wrote to us and said how well they thought the bid had been prepared and how professional the whole thing was. Whether we won or lost, they reckoned they had really got their money's

worth. They were very satisfying letters to get. I was being paid
by the state government, but I was also working to give all our
supporters value for their money.

10
Fast Forward

'You make sure you vote for Sydney'
3000 Arab Australians to Mohammed Mzali

By the beginning of 1992 the pace began to heat up, at home and abroad.

The year's first major lobbying exercise was the XVI winter Olympics in Albertville, France, in February. It was to be the last time that winter and summer Olympics were to be staged in the same year. After that they would be held two years apart: the summer Games in Barcelona in 1992; winter in Lillehammer, Norway, in 1994; summer in Atlanta in 1996; winter in Nagano in 1998; and summer of 2000 — hopefully in Sydney.

Albertville was the main town at the foothills of the Savoie Alps in the south-east of France, near the Italian border, an upmarket ski area with a number of different resort villages scattered throughout the mountains.

The winter Olympics is a big event on the Olympic family's calendar. Before the Games there was to be an IOC executive meeting and a full session of all members. Many would stay on for the Games. It was one of the few times in our campaign that there would be so many IOC members in the one place, so we had to have a significant presence. It was the biggest logistical exercise we had undertaken so far. Because it was an IOC session, the IOC members took their spouses so we took ours. There were the Greiners, the Bairds, the Lovetts, the Coates and Deeta and I. Kevan Gosper and Phil Coles were there in their capacity as IOC members. Sallyanne Atkinson and Geoff Wild came and Gabor Komyathy flew across from Budapest. Peter Woolcott, Alan Hoskins and Margaret also came.

We all had to get ourselves equipped with ski gear. We weren't going there to ski, but we needed the clothes to rug us up for the cold weather. We did a deal with a helpful local ski-hire company, Inski.

We stayed in the resort area of Courchevel in the mountains, some miles from Albertville, which was where the ski-jumping was held. There are a number of villages in the area which were named by their height up the mountain. President Samaranch and other IOC board members stayed in the Byblos hotel, which was at Courchevel 1850, at the top of the mountain. It was a very comfortable hotel with wooden beams and white walls and a recreation area with lots of glass to catch the sun. Our hotel was the Carlina which was also at Courchevel 1850. Margaret and Alan stayed down the mountain at Courchevel 1650.

Deeta went skiing within 32 hours of us getting there, but, after that, I banned her from the slopes. I told her we were there to work, not ski. She was very put out by it. Nick and Kathryn Greiner were there on vacation. They had given up their holidays to come over. Nick got a bit of flak from our television for going skiing. The reports implied he should have been spending all his time on the bid. But he was on holidays, so he was entitled to some time off, and it was very helpful for our bid that he came. He stayed for the IOC sessions — which were the important events for us — and left after the opening ceremony of the Games. Many of the IOC members who had been at the GAISF conference remembered the Greiners and their presence was a reminder of the NSW government's commitment to the bid. Kevan Gosper arranged for Greiner to have dinner with some members of the executive board.

Albertville was where I had my first formal meeting with President Samaranch. I had seen him in 1991 at the Mediterranean Games and the African Games, but it was just a quick shake of the hands. I asked Kevan Gosper to arrange a private meeting with the president for Nick Greiner and I went along. It was not a long meeting but the president handled it well and the contact was established. Samaranch is a very worldly man. Always gracious and properly dressed, he was a businessman and had been the Spanish ambassador to Moscow before being elected IOC president. He was used to dealing with politicians and world leaders and soon put everyone at their ease.

I had planned something for him to remember me by, in the hope we would be able to arrange such a meeting. I had taken a bottle of my own wine with me, made from the grapes from our vineyard in Pokolbin in the Hunter Valley. As we were all filing out, Samaranch was standing at the door, shaking people's hands. I was the last in line, as the most junior member of the squad. When it was my turn, I spoke to him with one hand behind my back: 'Mr President, I have something for you.'

'Yes?'

'I've brought you a bottle of wine from my own vineyard.'

It was something no-one else there could do.

'You have a vineyard. How are the grapes?'

He was a gracious man and known to appreciate good wine. It gave him a point of reference on me for the future. I had tried something to make him take notice of me, and it worked.

As always, there were lessons to be learned at these big events on the problems of staging a Games.

At the foot of the mountains in Albertville, a big warehouse had been converted into the accreditation centre. This was where the athletes, the members and everyone else arrived, had their photo taken and got their passes. It was somewhat disorganised. It was our first experience of how Sydney might have to handle a mass arrival of people. It started us thinking about what could happen if plane loads of people suddenly arrived, all wanting Olympic accreditation. In retrospect the problem seems obvious enough, but before Albertville none of us had really thought through what happens when so many people arrive at such a centre at once, wanting instant attention. It was another thing we would have to get right if we won the 2000 Games.

As in Birmingham, a lot of drivers didn't know the way. We discovered most of them had come from Paris and they had never been to Albertville before. Nick Greiner got lost for two hours on the way to his hotel. Kathryn was furious. It was happening all the time and you kept saying to yourself, 'Sydney will do better than this.'

With so many IOC members present, we decided we should

write a letter to all of them, officially inviting them to visit to Sydney. As a matter of strategy, we also decided to immediately register our acceptance of the new bidding rules which were issued at the session before the Games. Bob Scott from Manchester had been saying that the new rules were inadequate and difficult. We wanted to send a quick message to the members that we would be complying with them. We wanted to have the letter delivered to their rooms before the opening ceremony, because many would be leaving straight afterwards. We stayed up late the night before, working on it. It had to be written in three languages — English, French and Spanish. Deeta and Alan helped with the French and Alan also worked on the Spanish translation. We finished it around midnight. Then Margaret went back to her room and worked all night producing the letters and delivered them to all the IOC hotels first thing the next morning. She did a fantastic job.

The opening ceremony was staggering. I had never seen anything like it. It was out on the ice in Albertville with the Savoie mountains lit up in the background. Each team was led by a mascot wearing a clear plastic bubble shaped like an apple. Inside was artificial snow which looked like the snow you see in those plastic snow making toys. When they moved their arms it created a snowstorm in the bubble. Then the pageant began. There was lots of color and movement. It looked like a circus. There were acrobats on trapezes and swings and court jesters and people in costume with winged feet jumping down — almost bungee jumping — from a central structure. There were stiltmen in red suits with big white balloon hats, jugglers and dancers. It was all fun and good times and dancing. The ice was like one big playground. The message was that we were all going to have a good time at the Games. We just thought it was fantastic.

Then my feet froze.

I got the impression that not all the members were comfortable at the winter Games. There were members from Africa and other very hot climates who hated the snow and the cold. Many of them stayed in the hotels because they were not interested in the events or they were too hard to get to. Some people got altitude sickness. There were also a lot of murmurs about the athletes' village not working well and people having to travel for hours to see events which were scattered over five different areas of the mountain range.

There was no major hotel in Courchevel 1850, the village where the IOC members were staying. The members were split up into five different hotels which they didn't like because it was one of the few times in the year they could catch up with each other.

But the fact that many of them spent a lot of time in their hotels was good for our lobbying. We worked out a plan to keep lobby-lizarding in all the hotels. Fortunately, Mercedes and Toyota had donated two cars to the bid for the session, which helped us to get around. We worked the lobbies and the breakfast rooms of all the hotels and met over 80 members.

Sallyanne Atkinson was in her element there. She could really work a room. She knew many of the older members and helped me with the ones I didn't know. She was also popular with the women members and her presence underlined the fact that this was Australia's third bid.

One of the incidents that struck me was a meeting between two guys from Salt Lake City and an IOC member. The guys were part of the team which had lost the bid to hold the winter Olympics in 1998 to the Japanese city of Nagano. They were back on the road, lobbying for the next winter Olympics in 2002. The two guys and the IOC member had an extremely warm relationship. I knew this member too, but only to say hello. I wondered if I would ever get the same sort of relationship with him. But when I talked to the two Americans later, they told me their IOC friend had voted for Nagano. They had a warm relationship with him but they still didn't get his vote.

It confirmed my thinking that the whole matrix of getting a vote is having a very close personal relationship, having a good bid and many other factors. (In the end we did get close to this particular IOC member and I'm sure he *did* vote for us.)

I watched Bob Scott, our rival from Manchester, work the crowd. Or his version of it. In all my time lobbying the members, I never went over to someone who was eating and sat down at their table. If a member came to sit with me, that was fine. But Bob used to go up to them at their table and say, 'Do you mind?' and sit down beside them. Phil Coles would say, 'Rod, that's exactly what you shouldn't do. The man's obviously having a quiet breakfast; don't intrude, don't press yourself on them.' I wouldn't have anyway, but Phil was always warning us.

I remember one of the Scandinavian members was sitting peacefully on his own, having breakfast in the Byblos, really enjoying the morning sun coming in through the window. Suddenly Bob was next to him. The member was charming and friendly — they always were — but it was the sort of thing we wouldn't do. These were some of the little lessons in people skills that we learned. It takes time to get to know the members and sometimes you had to work to their timetables, not yours. If they were slow in getting to know you, there was no point trying to hurry them. I suppose you could draw a graph of the process — it takes all the time in the world to make a friend but when someone finally does become your friend the amount of effort and sensitivity you have to put into the relationship is not nearly as much.

By this time we were all closely watching the IOC's deliberations to see how they might affect our bid. It was in Albertville that the IOC executive board formally issued the new rules for candidate cities as part of its attempt to cut the cost of bidding. We had seen the draft guidelines issued in August 1991. The IOC used this session to issue the final ones which were pretty much as we expected.

But we were all sensitive about them, particularly in the beginning. When the Australian Olympic Committee held a reception for the Australian team at Albertville, we had to be careful that we did not officially invite any IOC members so it wouldn't put the bid in breach of the new rules banning special receptions for IOC members. It was probably erring on the side of caution on our side, but we were not sure at that stage how strictly the rules would be interpreted.

The big issue was the move by President Samaranch to get Dr Primo Nebiolo, the president of the International Amateur Athletics Federation (IAAF), appointed as an IOC member. As head of world track and field, there was a good argument for having him on the IOC. Track and field, after all, is considered the jewel in the crown of the Olympics. But Nebiolo was from Italy and Italy already had two IOC members. The President put up a proposal that he be able to appoint some members at large. Some people in our group were worried about this: they thought Samaranch was trying to put power brokers on the IOC who might not favor Sydney.

In the lead up to the vote, every member I talked to was saying: 'We can't let this sort of thing happen.' In the end the President was allowed to appoint two more members of his own choosing, without election. Weeks later, Nebiolo was confirmed as one of those members.

It was another demonstration of the power of the president.

Major events such as these gave us a chance to check out how we were going against the other bids. We always watched them closely.

Manchester had a lobby team of 22 people. Bob Scott was very active, but he left fairly early and after that their lobbying effort seemed to flounder. Clive Lloyd was there as part of the UK lobby team but he looked a little ill at ease around the snowfields and no-one seemed to recognise him apart from our team.

The six-person delegation from Brasilia was relatively active among the Latin American members. On their return to Brazil, the delegation put out press releases talking about having a core Latin American and football vote of some 35 to 40 votes. Anyone that really had that many votes to start with was virtually assured of winning. Their press releases also suggested that arrangements had already been reached for Brasilia and Beijing to swap preferences.

Istanbul had a low key presence.

The Milan bid had put up posters in the IOC hotels and many of the shops around the Courchevel area but we didn't see much of their lobbying effort.

The Berlin bid seemed to be floundering and we saw little of their members.

Beijing had a small team which were accredited as government officials. This gave them good access to the VIP areas during the sporting events — far better access than we had. The officials were very tough on people having proper accreditation to each venue. We couldn't get into any of the VIP areas but all the Beijing people did. We were a bit upset about this. Because the

members of the Chinese bid were all national government officials they were always able to get much better access than we did.
Bob Scott was occasionally able to go to the VIP events as Mary
Glen-Haig's partner but, throughout the bid, we found the
members of the Chinese bid were always able to get into the
restricted areas and have more opportunity to talk with the
members.

Assessing the Beijing position in a report to the board when
we got home, I wrote: 'Indications prior to the Games that
Beijing is emerging as a formidable competitor were largely
confirmed. Their bid made progress in Albertville and many of
the IOC now talk about it as a race between Sydney and Beijing.'

I was happy with our lobbying effort at Albertville. Our team
was well known, our professionalism acknowledged. We were
making substantial inroads into most regional groups, except the
Latin American members.

After Albertville, we did a preliminary estimate of the way we
thought the votes would fall. We were on track for a core vote
of at least 25 members. This was coming from North America,
Oceania, parts of Asia, Eastern Europe and Western Europe. I
felt we had been helped in Europe by Berlin's poor start.

But the message was clear — if anyone had any doubt about
our early assessment of Beijing as the most formidable challenger,
it was dispelled at Albertville. The idea of Beijing being a strong
candidate was now gaining currency within the broader Olympic
movement. I told the press in an interview when we got home:

'Beijing is a very serious contender. We always knew it was.
But now it is more widely recognised.'

In 15 April 1992 we formally registered with the IOC as a
candidate for the 2000 Games. Then the key office work began.

For the Sydney bid office 1992 was to be dominated by the
preparation of the 'bid books' or 'candidature files' in official IOC
terminology. They were essentially a detailed report to the IOC
on how Sydney planned to hold the Games. We had to reply to
a series of questionnaires from the IOC on a large range of topics
— the proposed venues, the athletes' village, how we planned to
finance the bid, what the weather was likely to be, how we were
going to sell tickets and a whole lot more.

Atlanta had set a high standard for bid books as it had done with all of its bid. As part of our basic research, we had put together a collection of bid books from previous Olympics bids, including Atlanta's, to see how they were done. We had talked to the guy that had overseen the preparation of their volumes, Jack Pinkerton, on a visit to Atlanta in 1991. We invited him to the GAISF Conference in Sydney later that year. Bob Elphinston and I spent some time with him going through what was needed for the books, what we had to do to finalise our venue plans to the standard needed for these reports.

The requirements for the bid books could be modified from Games to Games so we had to pay close attention to what the IOC wanted this time around. In May 1992 all the bidding cities were called to IOC headquarters in Lausanne, in Switzerland, for a briefing on what was required.

The IOC headquarters were in a large stately house called Chateau de Vidy, on the shores of Lake Geneva. While it was called a chateau, it wasn't particularly glamorous. It was really a private home with a new wing attached to it. The extension was designed by Pedro Ramirez Vazquez, a Mexican IOC member and internationally acclaimed architect, and built at a cost of about $US13 million. There was a lot of glass in the new building, called Olympic House, and a connecting glass tunnel to the chateau because the city was covered in heavy snow in the winter.

President Samaranch's predecessor, Lord Killanin, had remained in his native Ireland while the IOC was administered from Lausanne. But after Samaranch took over the job in 1980 he surprised the Olympic movement by moving to Lausanne permanently, living in a suite at the Lausanne Palace Hotel, high up on the ridge, with a wonderful view of the lake. The president had his office in the Chateau, about a mile away from his hotel, along with the director-general, François Carrard. The staff worked in the extension which was built around an atrium with the offices around the sides. The staff offices were upstairs and there was a public exhibition area downstairs. It was all set on beautiful parklands which featured sporting sculptures donated to the IOC.

We were briefed in the Lausanne Palace Hotel on what the IOC wanted in the bid books. We were told we had to provide information on 23 separate themes of our proposal to stage the Games. These were:

- the characteristics of Australia
- details about Sydney
- customs and immigration
- weather conditions
- environmental protection measures
- security
- health and medical facilities
- the Olympic village
- hotels and accommodation
- transport
- the Olympic Games program
- proposed competition sites
- the cultural program to be run at the same time as the Games
- the IOC session to be held before the Games
- plans for the ceremonies
- plans to cater for the media
- telecommunications facilities
- data-processing services and links
- how we were going to finance the games
- plans for marketing the Games
- what we would do to promote Olympism
- legal aspects
- Australia's experience in handling high level sporting events.

Until that point, our office had been putting out press releases, organising travel itineraries and preparing brochures and videos and working on the plans for the Games. But suddenly we added new workload onto people's normal tasks. We had to put on more staff. It was seven-day-a-week work for some. The exercise involved working up fairly detailed plans on how Sydney would stage the Games — plans which would last the test of the next seven years. When they were finished they comprised three volumes of more than 500 pages. We had known from the start of the bid we would have to prepare the bid books, but after we got back from Lausanne in May with the specifics of what was wanted, everyone put their head down and worked very intensively. Everything seemed to build up momentum from then on.

While the books were not due in Lausanne until February

1993, they would have to be printed before Christmas, before the traditional January holiday shutdown. We decided we would draft it *all* before we went to the summer Games in Barcelona in July — only two months after the IOC briefing in Lausanne. When we came back, we would fine tune and finish it by the end of September. This was to give us plenty of time for translation — the books had to be written in both English and French — and printed before Christmas. It was a tight deadline and everyone began to focus intensely on their areas of speciality.

Around the same time there were some departures from the staff of the Sydney bid office and some important arrivals.

In April journalist and public relations consultant, Hamish Fraser, joined us to help with media relations. Hamish came from South Africa, although he had lived in Sydney for a long time, and specialised in handling the international media for us. I had known him before and he became a close adviser to me on many media issues during the bid. When I hired him, I told him I needed some work done but there were no promises; employment would be on a week-to-week basis. Bruce Baird kept a close eye on our staffing levels and we could never have anyone on staff who was not absolutely needed. But Hamish ended up staying there until the end.

We had linked into the programs run by the Australian Tourist Commission, the NSW Tourism Commission and the Department of Foreign Affairs and Trade to bring foreign journalists to Australia. Together they bring out about 1200 a year. We said we wanted to see any that came from countries which had IOC members. By the end of the bid, there had been over 400 international press visits into our office and Hamish had looked after every one of them. He took them out to Olympic Park at Homebush and all around Sydney. We got some great stories published. For example, a newspaper from Finland did a whole supplement on Sydney 2000 which was fantastic because Finland had two IOC members.

He also worked exclusively with the Olympic media — David Miller of *The Times*, Iain Macleod of the *Daily Telegraph*, and John Rodda of the *Guardian* all of whom were in London, and Karl Heinz Huber, the editor of *Sport Intern*. Hamish was on the phone at all sorts of ungodly hours feeding them information and helping them with stories.

Around the same time there were two departures — Peter Woolcott, our executive manager in charge of international relations and Susan Hunt, our head of communications. Peter had helped us establish the program to link into the diplomatic network and this was largely on track.

Susan Hunt had joined us the previous year from the federal government's Tourism Task Force. She was a very able woman with a good deal of promotional experience on tourism. She had worked hard to draw up our whole communications strategy. It was a good strategy and we never deviated from it. She had been very important in the early stages in insisting that concern for the environment would be an important issue in this campaign. She came on a trip to the South East Asian Games in Manila in November 1991 as part of our lobby team. However, as a result of a number of unfortunate differences with people outside the office — in which she was unfairly treated — she began to lose her confidence. She found herself being undermined by these people and it became difficult for her to implement the very sound communications strategy she had drawn up. I suppose there may have been occasions where I could have given her more support or done more to help restore her confidence, but I was travelling a lot which meant she didn't always have someone to turn to when these problems arose.

Unfortunately it was not working out and I decided it was best if she left. It is one of my singular regrets in the whole bid. There was no doubt it was a tremendous personal blow to her. But in a campaign such as ours, we only had two to three years to achieve our goal. If I felt that someone was not going to get us there, I had to make some tough decisions about whether they stayed on. Looking back, I suppose it was another lesson in being an employer. Sometimes you do have to spend the time bolstering the confidence of a senior employee to get them through the tough times — otherwise things can get to the point of no return and you lose someone who, in other circumstances, would have a lot to contribute. My being out of the office so much certainly didn't help Susan get on top of her problems with these other people. But ours was also a unusual working environment with two tracks of operation — one in the Sydney office and one on the road, lobbying. It was always going to have its own peculiar stresses on staff which would not be present in a more conventional office where the boss was often at his or her desk.

Bruce Baird sent us over Ian Dose from the NSW Roads and Traffic Authority to take over from Susan as head of the communications department. Dose was a very experienced government media man and had worked in Bruce's office before going to the RTA. He was excellent at handling the press and organising press conferences, either in Sydney or anywhere around the world. He would always do lots of preparation to maximise the impact of a story and made sure he followed up afterwards. He and his girlfriend, Dalila, carried box after box of satchels and press kits to the press conference at Barcelona. At the Mediterranean Games in Montpelier France in 1993 they made sure Sydney 2000 posters were up in all the shop windows. They both worked tirelessly for the bid. And if Dalila came overseas with us, Ian always paid all her expenses.

But we also needed someone else to handle our publications and the production of the bid books. We went back to Morgan and Banks, the employment agency who had helped us the previous year, and asked them to go through their books. They recommended a few people, one of whom was Laurel Taylor, the senior communications manager for the AMP. She was very talented, but after our first meeting both she and I came to the decision that she was really too good for the job. Our communications *strategy* had already been worked out. What we needed was someone who could implement it. I also needed someone who knew a lot about design, layout, branding, print and film production, merchandising and that sort of thing. She recommended a woman in her office, Silvana Griffin, who she said was very experienced in all these things. It was a wonderful gesture: Laurel gave us her best person.

Silvana worked with Ian Dose in the communications office. Dose handled the media relations side of things, with Hamish helping with the foreign press; Silvana handled all the printing and layout and design of all the publications as well as the production of the Sydney 2000 merchandise and all the gifts and souvenirs for the members.

Silvana was a tower of strength in the preparation of the bid books. As part of its move to cut down on the cost of bidding, the IOC had set down strict guidelines on the presentation of the bid books. They all had to be presented on A4 paper; stapled, not bound; have a flexible covering, not expensive hard covers. There was a clear instruction to limit the cost of production and to use existing documents where possible.

But of course we wanted to make sure we presented the IOC with a very impressive set of books. Silvana's job was a difficult one. She had to make the books look good, but not lavish. She had to produce the best bid books we could — but she couldn't step over the line and be seen to be too extravagant. It required a very detailed knowledge of both the IOC guidelines and production processes. Silvana became the master of all this which was one of the reasons our bid books ended up looking as high quality and professional as they did.

The Olympic Charter makes specific reference to the athletes' village which it sees as having the object of 'bringing together of all competitors, team officials and other team personnel in one place'. The idea of athletes from around the world coming together in one village and making friendships was a critical part of Baron de Coubertin's vision of how the Games would help promote world peace and understanding.

From the start, we had always aimed to make the Sydney games, 'The Athletes' Games'. In 1956 Melbourne had staged 'The Friendly Games' and broke new ground by suggesting a closing ceremony in which all athletes marched together, not as national squads. We always knew Sydney's climate and the conditions would be good for the athletes, but we wanted to make sure the athletes' village was outstanding.

Within our office we had a technical group working on the village proposal, including Keith Murton. A long serving member of the AOC and Australia's Olympic teams, Keith had lived in nine Olympic villages. We used him and other experts to work out things like how many people should there be in a bedroom, how many bedrooms per apartment and what had worked well in previous villages. They created a brief for a competition among architects to design the village. It would have to house 15 000 athletes and officials.

We had run a few architects' competitions for design work by then and they had proved successful. I'll never forget awarding the prize for the design of the velodrome. It was a cheque for $20,000. A young girl and guy from a small architectural practice won it and they were so pleased. It meant everything to them.

There was always a lot of interest in this design competition work, but when we asked for submissions for the design of the village, we got an unbelievable response. There were so many entries that we had to get a vacant floor in a government office building in Oxford Street to display them for the judges. The judging panel of eminent architects and planners was led by one of Australia's leading architects, Daryl Jackson from Melbourne.

The entries were displayed without any reference to who had done them — the same way we did with the competition for the logo. The judges looked at the entries for a day or so but they couldn't decide. All agreed there were five proposals that had a lot of commendable aspects. So I looked up the rules, using my skills as a lawyer, to see if we could defer awarding the prize of $50,000. We wanted them all to work together to incorporate the best of all five. We decided it was possible and the five groups were ultimately commissioned to do the village together.

One of the successful entries just happened to be submitted by two young architects connected with Greenpeace, Andrea Wilson and Rod Simpson. When we found this out, we couldn't believe our good fortune. We always knew the environment would be a strong issue in the bid. When we went to the IOC in Lausanne for the briefing on the bid books, we noticed that the environment was listed as a full chapter in its own right for the first time. The IOC was clearly trying to send a signal that it wanted candidate cities to regard the environment as an important consideration.

And now we had Greenpeace involved in the design of the athletes' village and the organisation had got there absolutely on their own merits. We encouraged Greenpeace to take a very active part in this group of five architects and the village was developed with a lot of advice from them on the environmental aspects of its design and construction. Then Greenpeace asked if they could give us advice on the environmental aspects of all our plans — including the design and construction of all our venues. We liked the idea and agreed. The process eventually led to the development of a set of environmental guidelines within our office for the whole bid. These were later set down in state government legislation for the Games. Under the guidelines, every tender for every venue had to include an environmental impact statement. The guidelines covered things such as the treatment of waste water, energy conservation and recycling of all the tickets, cups and paper.

The green movement was very effective and started to become very influential in many aspects of the bid, so much so that I had to slow them down at one stage. Greenpeace were starting to say that the bid's environmental guidelines should apply to *all* new government buildings. The state government became concerned that they might become an uncontrollable force affecting all new government construction work. There were some complaints and I had to draw a limit on their influence.

But we developed a partnership with Greenpeace and it was genuine on both sides. It was so important we decided to ask Karla Bell from Greenpeace to speak to the IOC's Evaluation Commission when it visited Sydney in March 1993. During the course of the bid, Paul Gilding, an Australian, became the head of the whole Greenpeace organisation in Amsterdam. We invited Gilding and Karla Bell to Monte Carlo in September 1993 to be part of our press conference on the environmental aspects of our bid.

The people from Greenpeace never compromised their integrity. They said they would support every bid city that did the same thing as we did. They made it clear they were not favoring the Sydney bid *per se*, they were in favor of what Sydney was doing. But the other bid cities didn't seem to pick it up. They tried to say they were environmentally conscious, but nobody had the degree of support that we had.

The Olympic Village design was so successful, there were inquiries from all over the world — most of them nothing to do with the Olympics. Developers from everywhere asked for the designs. The village came to be regarded as state of the art living for the next century; how people will build and live, taking into account environmental concerns.

We also attracted interest from other environmental groups, including a group called Ark. Part of Ark's strategy was to encourage support for the environment by having prominent people speak out on environmental issues — particularly from the entertainment industry. They got film stars to do videos for us. Tom Cruise and Nicole Kidman did one we released at Monte Carlo. They described Sydney's proposals as 'an environmental role model for the world' and 'an extraordinary example of how progress and development can work hand in hand with the environment'. They congratulated the IOC and the Olympic movement 'for making the environment an important part of the 2000 Games'.

Sydney's bid became known as the 'green' bid — helped by the fact that two people connected with Greenpeace came top five in an architects' competition. When the Enquiry Commission made its report the following year, it described the environmental aspects of our bid as 'outstanding'.

The whole thing was very good for the environmental movement. We set a standard that every Olympic bid city will have to meet if they are serious about winning.

We also broke new ground with our schools project. Virginia Chadwick, then NSW Minister for Education, Bruce Baird and I had a meeting to see what we could do to encourage interest in the Olympics in schools. My own strong memories of the Melbourne Olympics as a young boy left me in no doubt about the importance of getting the schoolchildren of Australia interested in the Sydney bid. But there was another good reason for this. One of the responsibilities of the IOC to promote the concept and ideals of Olympism. The Charter makes a specific reference to the importance of 'educating youth through sport'. We were being asked in the questionnaires for the bid books what we would be doing about this.

We knew the children of today would be the ones who would be watching and, hopefully, participating, in the 2000 Olympics as young adults. Getting children interested was also a good way of encouraging wider community support. But what should we do?

I thought we could develop some sort of school curriculum for NSW children on the Olympics. Virginia said if we paid the salary of an education officer, she would do the rest. So I bit the bullet and we paid the Department of Education to employ a woman, Susie Tuckerman, for a year to develop a curriculum.

Teachers were briefed, they taught it; children learned about the Olympics and they loved it.

But we went one better than that. Virginia said, 'Why don't we pair a school with each of these IOC members. Then that school can study that member's country and communicate with him or her when the member visits Sydney. They'll go out to the school and meet the children'. We did it with 90 odd schools all over the state, private and public.

Children were incredibly excited about the Games. They did all sorts of projects on it. Parents told me how the whole school would gather in eager anticipation when their IOC member came to visit. When Fernando Bello, the member in Portugal, came to visit the Lewisham Public School (which had a strong Portuguese community) 3000 parents and kids turned up to meet him. When Mohamed Mzali from Tunisia went out to Chullora, where there was a strong Arab community, there were over 3000 people from the Arab community to meet him and everyone of them said, 'You make sure you vote for Sydney'.

We sent speakers to schools. School kids came into our office, sat down on the floor and did their projects. We sent out thousands of Sydney 2000 kits to the schools. We had school kids on work experience. Every school adopted an Olympic project theme and we supported it all as part of our community relations program.

When they saw how it worked, the IOC members were so impressed they wanted all the details so they could highlight it at the Centenary Congress in 1994.

The schools also signed a kind of petition, asking the IOC to give Sydney the Games. We got thousands of signatures from school kids and bound them together in volumes. When IOC members came into our office, we would show it all to them, page after page of children's signatures saying, 'Please send us the Games.'

We had to keep the community interested and informed about what we were doing, but it was also important in terms of our relations with the Olympic movement. We were sending out the word that we were spreading the message of Olympism to our children. It also proved to be a successful technique to provide some personal contact with the members so they would think of

Sydney with fondness and realise that our bid had a lot of widespread community support.

The whole project was an example of our approach from the beginning. If we thought a project was necessary, we would work out the details, set down a plan of action and follow it through. We weren't the kind of organisation that would have a good idea but wouldn't bother to see it was properly carried out. I've always believed that if you want to get something done, you work out a good plan for it and then you follow it through. If you get both of those steps right, then you'll be hard to beat. It sounds simple, but in business, despite lip service given to it, a lot of good ideas do fail because everyone is 'too busy' to follow them through.

We regarded keeping the public informed about the bid as an important part of our job. We developed a bureau of people who would go out and talk about the bid. We never knocked back an invitation to speak. It started out just being the people in the office. I did a lot of speeches. But when we got snowed under, we added more speakers. Damien Keogh of the Sydney Kings basketball team was one of these and he turned out to be just fantastic. So was Ricky Walford, the aboriginal rugby league player who was a winger for the St George team. We put all the staff through speech and presentation training. We took them away for two days to a camp at North Head and had people from Rogen Australia teach them how to make a speech, how to use an overhead projector and how to present themselves so they would be good representatives of the bid.

I also wanted to have a scheme where we could use Australian business people as ambassadors for the bid overseas. I wanted to make sure that whenever they went overseas they were well informed about the bid and could promote it wherever they had a chance. Whenever they spoke — be it at a dentists' conference or whatever — they should also talk about the bid. The Beijing bid were doing this well, and so should we. We needed to have someone really good looking after the scheme and who knew the business community. So I asked Michael Yabsley, the Liberal Party MP for Vaucluse to handle the Overseas Business Strategy Unit for us. Michael had been the Minister for State Development and Minister for Tourism in the Greiner Government and was well connected in the Sydney business community. He made sure the business community all got kits and videos and all the information they needed on the bid. He did a good job — so much so he started to get a bit of publicity which didn't go down well with some other politicians.

He employed someone to help him with the scheme. He paid for some of it and we paid the rest. By and large, the scheme worked well. But on one occasion a travelling businessman got a bit overexcited about his mission and called up the South African Olympic Committee while he was on a visit there. The word came back to us and Phil Coles got very upset. He said the scheme was a disaster and said we should scrap it. But I said to him, 'Just calm down. It's all OK. We want these people out there working for us. If we lose, the business community will turn on us and say we didn't ask them to help. How would you look then?' So everyone calmed down and we went on with the scheme.

There was a very conscious view from the start that the bid should involve all Australians. We were particularly keen to have the involvement and support of the Aboriginal community.

When the original bid committee was formed Charlie Perkins, a former senior federal public servant and a prominent member of the Aboriginal community, was appointed. Bruce Baird also actively sought the support of the Aboriginal movement. The Aboriginal Land Council of New South Wales endorsed the bid and David Clark from the Council was also appointed as a member of the committee. We had a continuous program of liaising with the Aboriginal community. They insisted that we only use genuine Aboriginal merchandise in our promotional work — no cheap boomerangs made in Asia or any of that sort of thing. Bruce Baird gave a major presentation to the Aboriginal Land Council and the whole council came into our office for a briefing.

We made studies of Aboriginal issues and produced briefing sheets for anyone in the Olympic family who wanted to know about them and their culture. Personally, I believe that white Australians still have a lot to learn about Aboriginals and their culture. They are a very special part of humanity with a different philosophy to Western civilisation, one which has a lot to teach us. At the bid, we knew we would also have to be prepared to answer questions about race relations in Australia, particularly from black African members.

There were some interesting moments. When our Cultural Commission was formed, there was a complaint from Charlie Perkins that we didn't have an Aboriginal on it. When I checked I was told we did. I told Charlie who it was. He rang back later and complained: he said the person, Kim Walker, was not Aboriginal. Kim had been a star dancer for the Sydney Dance Company for a decade. He was black and had showed a strong interest in Aboriginal history and culture. But Perkins was correct. He wasn't an Aboriginal. Born of a West African father and a white mother, he had been adopted at birth by a white couple who had taught him a love of dancing. It was only when he joined the Aboriginal and Islander Dance Theatre at age 16 that he actually began mixing with Aboriginal people. So we added another person to the Cultural Commission — Justine Saunders, an Aboriginal actress.

There were some misunderstandings along the way. A few people on the overall bid committee thought they would be much more involved in the lobbying than was actually needed. I think Charlie Perkins thought that there would be a lot of international lobbying for him to do. Perkins, who had played soccer for Australia, had gone to the Youth Soccer Championships in Portugal in June 1991 for the bid and then flew to London to meet me and other members of our team who had also been travelling in Europe. Unfortunately he and I had a stand-up row at the Dorchester Hotel in London over how much he was going to travel, and he stormed out.

As it happened, he needn't have worried. Dick Humphry in the Premier's Department and I had in mind a specific program for him. We asked him to go to the African qualifying championships of World Cup Soccer in Mauritius and to continue promoting our bid in the international soccer community. I also hoped that, with the World Youth Football Championships in Australia in March 1993, he would travel around the Australian cities with the officials from FIFA and be seen to be part of the Sydney bid. He did so, graciously, even after our London barney.

I also wanted him to come to the opening of the IOC Museum

in Lausanne in June 1993, where we would be emphasising our cultural program for the 2000 Olympics, and then to Monte Carlo in September. He agreed.

Charlie's daughter worked at the NSW Art Gallery as an assistant curator specialising in Aboriginal art. In the course of her job she had a role in selecting some of the Australian art that was sent to Lausanne on loan for the IOC Museum.

We had our differences, but Charlie Perkins was willing and enthusiastic in the bid and was an effective liaison with the Aboriginal community for us.

The Aboriginal community has many different groups and factions, depending on tribal connections and where people stand on different issues. Some wanted to use the bid to bring their cause to the attention of the Olympic movement.

There was small demonstration of Aborigines outside the Darling Harbor Convention Centre where we had the GAISF conference. John Coates and the president of GAISF, Dr Un Yong Kim, had a meeting with the demonstrators. They wanted to write a letter to the IOC members. Coates agreed to make sure it got delivered — which he did.

And late in 1992 the NSW Aboriginal Legal Service announced it would campaign against the bid as a protest against the treatment of Aborigines. It sent all the IOC members a letter. We sent off a counter letter saying we did have the support of the Aboriginal community and we would be happy to discuss it with them.

The leader of the black movement in the IOC was the president of the Association of Olympic Committees of Africa, Jean-Claude Ganga of the Congo. He was the Minister for Tourism, Sport and Leisure in the People's Republic of Congo and a very eloquent and intelligent man. He asked if he could see the Aboriginal groups which supported the bid and those which opposed it when he was in Sydney.

So we set up the appointments. We also invited Aboriginal sprinter Cathy Freeman and hurdler Kyle Vander Kuyp to come on a harbor cruise with him. We didn't make anything of it, but he obviously noticed that they were successful Aboriginal athletes (Cathy had gone to the Barcelona Olympics). And, like all the black African members, Ganga was entertained at home by the Whitlams.

On the last day of his visit Ganga said there was no point in him meeting the groups who supported the bid. He would just meet those who were opposed to it. We set up a meeting with Paul Coe of the Aboriginal Legal Service. Coe passionately wanted to discuss the issue of Aboriginal deaths in police or prison service custody and other things which he regarded as human rights issues affecting the Aboriginal community.

Ganga, who is very formidable, said he only wanted to know about sport. The Olympic Charter talks specifically about the importance of 'sport practised without discrimination of any kind'. Ganga let Paul have his say. Gough Whitlam was also there and he gave a brilliant overview of Australia's contribution to the international covenants on human rights and what work had been done in the past to advance Aboriginal causes. He also mentioned that Australia abhorred racial discrimination and that we were the only country bidding which had signed *all* the relevant international conventions.

Ganga then said to Coe, 'I want you to tell me about discrimination in sport. I have seen Cathy Freeman and Kyle Vander Kuyp. Do you agree that, if they are talented enough, all Aboriginal athletes are welcome in the Olympic team?'

'Yes.'

'And they play rugby and cricket at an international level and there's no problem?'

'Yes.'

'I'm sorry. That's all I'm interested in. I'm a member of the International Olympic Committee and there's clearly no discrimination against blacks in the Olympic movement of this country.'

That was the end of the meeting according to Ganga.

When John Coates and I took Ganga to the airport, he said, 'I'm perfectly satisfied. I'm glad I've had that meeting with Mr Coe and I now understand the situation. You can be assured that my African colleagues will also understand.'

It was an important meeting for the bid too. It showed the importance of facing criticism head on. If you have a problem it's often best to be up front about it, talk to your critics and hear them out. In the end, you may find that the areas on which you differ are a lot smaller than you think.

11

Barcelona: Feeling the Heat

'What's the secret of my success? I always have a suntan, and I always look relaxed.'

Purportedly, Aristotle Socrates Onassis

I suppose it didn't help that my bags were lost on the way to Barcelona for the Olympics. Barcelona was very hot. It was hard to get around. We were working long days. My bags had gone all the way back to Sydney and I had to start buying new clothes. I didn't get the old ones back for a week.

I had often thought how wonderful it would be to go to an Olympic Games. As a child I wished I could have gone to the Melbourne Games. But going as the chief executive of a bidding city was just sheer hard work; exhausting, not exhilarating.

The Barcelona Olympics was my low point in the bid. But we learned a lot. And it was just a year away from decision week in Monte Carlo.

Barcelona is a city of some 4 million people, the second largest city in Spain after its rival, Madrid. It is the capital of Catalonia and is fiercely proud of having its own language — Catalan — and culture, distinct from the rest of Spain. Barcelona was also the home town of Juan Antonio Samaranch, who was born there in 1920. Some say it was always one of his great missions in life to have an Olympic Games staged in the city. Barcelona had bid for the right to host the Olympics in 1936 — only to be defeated by Berlin. Montjuic Stadium, on the hill of Montjuic overlooking the Mediterranean Sea, was actually built by the city in the hope of getting those games. The city was deeply disappointed when it didn't. It considered bidding for the 1972 Games — but was nudged out by Madrid, which became the Spanish candidate — and had been keen to stage an Olympics ever since. It won the right to host the 1992 Games at an IOC meeting in Lausanne in 1986, easily beating rivals Paris and Brisbane.

The Montjuic area — which also has a castle, an amusement park, an illuminated fountain and a model Spanish village — was the site of most of the major events of the 1992 Olympics. The central feature was the Olympic Ring — a complex of sports facilities including the stadium, the Palau Sant Jordi, swimming pools and a sports university. Montjuic is connected to the city by a funicular railroad and is also served by bus services, but, for the Games, the city built four giant escalators to take people up to the Olympic Ring area.

Barcelona has a rich history. The old town was once a walled city and the Gothic Quarter, which you could only see on foot because of its narrow alleys, had a wonderful medieval atmosphere and fascinating architecture. It was also known as the city to which Christopher Columbus returned after discovering the New World. It also had a strong artistic tradition with a Picasso Museum and the Miro Foundation, a gallery devoted to another son of Barcleona, Joan Miro, and a Museum of Catalan Art.

The city was situated on the sea between two rivers but the Games were staged in the height of the Spanish summer and for the athletes and other visitors like us, there was little respite from the hot sun.

By Barcelona, the campaign for the 2000 Games was on in earnest. Almost every IOC member was in Barcelona for at least a week, some for three. For our team there was much lobbying to do, a presentation to make, a press conference to give and a hospitality suite to staff. We had to take a big team: there was Annita Keating; the Lord Mayor of Sydney, Alderman Frank Sartor; Bruce Baird; and the NSW Minister for Finance, George Souris. Ros Kelly, the Federal Minister for Sport, was there for the Games and to support Adelaide's bid for the 1998 Commonwealth Games, which was to be decided at a meeting of the Commonwealth Games Association in Barcelona at the same time. Our lobby team also included Kevan Gosper, Phil Coles, Graham Lovett, Geoff Wild, Gabor Komyathy, Mahmoud Elfarnawani, Sallyanne Atkinson and Elizabeth Fox. John Coates was there in his capacity as head of the AOC. Dawn Fraser, Herb Elliott, Judy Patching, Geoff Henke and Peter Montgomery came as VIP representatives of the AOC. Ian Dose came to help with media inquiries and the press conference, Margaret McLennan and Alan Hoskins managed the hospitality suite and Sue Bushby came along to prepare all the gifts for the members.

In all 56 people from Australia went to Barcelona in association with the bid in some form or other — although the bid company only paid for 26 of them.

The group from the Sydney bid company also included a technical team, headed by Bob Elphinston, which came to check out the facilities at Barcelona. This included David Churches, the head of our planning and design operations; Robert Johnstone, our manager of planning; Paul Clark (no relation to the Paul Clark on the bid committee) who was in charge of logistics and sport; and Superintendent John Garvey from the police service to advise on security matters. Keith Murton came along to check out the Olympic village.

We already had the bid books drafted by then, but we saw the timing of the summer Games — in late July and early August — providing the cream on the cake. It was our chance to check out the latest in Olympic facilities and what was acceptable to the IOC before we finalised our books. The technical team worked virtually night and day. They saw nothing of the events themselves, but they came back with a lot of detail. We also added to our technical knowledge by establishing an Athletes Advisory Committee with a representative of each sport to report back to us on what worked and what didn't. And we asked the whole Australian team for their feedback too.

Surprisingly, no other bid city took advantage of the opportunity. Only Atlanta, which was set to hold the Games in four years' time, tried to make the sort of technical evaluations we did.

There was a lot of temporary seating. The swimming complex had seats that could be dismantled after the Games. We noted that the IOC didn't mind some temporary seating; that meant we did not need to build big expensive permanent facilities that were not going to be used afterwards.

We took a good look at how they managed the traffic. They had special Olympic lanes and the traffic police were well co-ordinated. We noted that the traffic worked much better during the Games than the week before. This was partly because Barcelona had arranged its school holidays for the two weeks of the Games. (And that's what will happen in New South Wales in 2000.)

On the face of it, the trip worked smoothly. But the logistics of being away with such a large group with a lot to do for such a long time had its strains.

One problem I found travelling with big numbers of people was that there were always those who wanted to react to every event by having a meeting. There's a kind of discipline in the minds of business and professional people about having meetings. They may be a good idea at head office and in many cases they can be invaluable in letting everyone know what's going on. But they don't necessarily work on the road. I was never happy sitting for hours in a room with our group in a meeting when I knew all the IOC members would be down in the lobby with people from the other bid cities. If you are overseas on a mission, your first responsibility is to do what's necessary to complete that mission and meet with the people you can't see at home.

In Barcelona everybody wanted a daily meeting which made it a very long day. We also needed to be at breakfast to be around the members. We would start with a strategy meeting every morning at 8.00 for an hour, then go to breakfast. Then I'd have a staff meeting and we'd be off to the Games. The second session of the Games would start about 4pm to 5pm and go to about 9pm to 10 pm. Then we'd go out to dinner and be served about midnight. Bed at 2 am and up again at 7.30 in the morning. No days off on Saturdays and Sundays. And we were looking at 16 days straight of this. It was terribly hot. It was hard to move between venues because our vehicles weren't accredited like the IOC members. Our staff were soon worked to a frazzle.

There had been some tensions developing between various members of our lobby team and these were exacerbated in Barcelona, which didn't help. Graham Lovett complained we had too many politicians in the presentation and questioned whether Bruce Baird should be involved. I wanted Baird involved. There was a dispute over what it was that Lovett actually said, which created more problems but in the end Lovett agreed to include Baird.

Our travel problems were eased with the help of two drivers we hired: two brothers who were some of the sharpest operators in town. Mercedes gave us a car to get around and we had another. Undaunted by the restrictions of what they saw as petty officialdom, our drivers made their own accreditation stickers so we could go anywhere. They would point to these and drive us up to the front gates of venues no-one else could get near. When officials stopped us, the brothers always talked their way through, saying what important people we were in Australia. At one stage Bruce Baird got worried that people would think he was masquerading as the prime minister. It was funny but it was also a lesson about lax security and how people can be fooled very easily.

But our broader logistical problems were not solved so easily. Even with our sizeable team, we simply did not have enough back up. The big thing we learned in Barcelona was that tremendously long hours will get to you in the end. We learned you've got to take enough people. You've got to have 'reserves' so that people can have time off. The fact that it sounds glamorous or fun to go to an Olympic Games or whatever should not in any way color your thinking on the need to use proper management principles when taking a large group away for a significant exercise.

The key is to get the planning right before you go. You need to be organised to the point where people know what they have to do before they get there, so you don't take up valuable time having meetings when you are away. Apart from being short staffed, we *were* very well organised for Barcelona. We had prepared a large briefing book for everyone and we all knew exactly what we had to do. But I found everyone looked to me to solve the inevitable logistical problems, when I wanted to be out and about mixing with the members. I knew it was something I would have to solve when it came to planning for future trips. It was a lesson in management for me. To be an effective leader of the sales team at a public event where you are under scrutiny, you have to be relaxed and free to mix with the customers. If your time is taken up and your energy drained by having to handle a whole series of minor operational details, it can defeat the whole purpose of the exercise.

I was so tired and preoccupied, I couldn't even enjoy the spectacular opening ceremony. Fortunately, every now and then, I actually got to the stadium and there would be a bit of talent there which would lift me out of the doldrums. Quincy Watts running the 400 metres was special. I saw Linford Christie win the 100 metres. Carl Lewis didn't qualify for the US team in the 100 metres, but he absolutely blitzed everyone on the last leg of the relay. But some of the field events — particularly the throwing — made me angry. The fact that track and field was now drug free meant that the athletes couldn't come near some of the records that had been set. In other words, the people who had set the records had cheated. And, of course, Australians had been trying to compete against these pumped up athletes for all this time. It was heart-breaking to think about what had been happening. I saw Kieren Perkins' gold medal for the 1500 metres in the pool. By then I was worn out. But it was very heartening to see the tremendous support for Australian athletes by the Australian spectators. At the swimming, the Australians were by far the loudest and most excited group. Even in events where the kids didn't even get a medal, our supporters were backing their athletes much more enthusiastically than anyone else.

Even though I was hot and tired, I still felt the excitement of the atmosphere in a city during the Games. I saw some of the architecture in the city and the museums and the concert halls which reminded me of Jose Carreras and Placido Domingo who were in the opening ceremony. Barcelona just buzzed. It was party time from go to whoa. The place never shut. The lights and the fountains were on all night. Everybody was wearing Olympic clothes. Walking around late at night, when the Mediterranean sea breeze took the heat off the day, was the greatest buzz you ever felt. I just knew it would be fantastic to be in Sydney when the Games were on.

But then you'd think of the latest argument that someone had on the team that day or what dispute would come up at the next day's morning meeting, and the joy of being at the Games would quickly fade again. Deeta and I would get back to our hotel room and she would say, 'I don't know how you stand it all.'

Much was later made of the press conference in Barcelona where we were quizzed about the ozone layer over Sydney. It was one of those things that was really only a minnow at the time but blew up into a whale.

In my view, the press conference was an easy one. It has since been written up as a mistake by me and a bad press conference. I don't agree. For a start, it was a big press conference, with about 120 journalists from around the world.

A German journalist asked a question about the ozone layer and I answered it. The guy pressed me again and I said, 'Look. I've already answered that. I just said to you we have no problem with the ozone layer in Sydney. It is a mischievous piece of information moving about.'

The German journalist tried to say we were accusing the scientists he was referring to of being liars.

'I think you're being mischievous. There's no scientific evidence that our ozone layer is any different from yours,' I replied.

To use the word 'mischievous' and to be a little firm in my tone might have been a little unwise in hindsight. But I certainly didn't raise my voice or lose my temper. I wasn't even irritated by it. I just thought he was being silly and mischievous.

Then he came back again, asking the question in German.

By this time Kevan Gosper, who was getting angry, stepped in:

'The preoccupation of the IOC is the health of its athletes. The preoccupation of a government of a nation is the health of its people. The sustained questioning in this area is, in my judgement, simply spurious and doesn't give your newspaper any credit. Nor does it give any assistance to the bid from your country.'

Although Gosper was on the Sydney bid, he was also a vice president of the IOC and I thought it was an unwise remark. But I didn't make it. And everybody at the end of the press conference was absolutely satisfied. Baird, Coates, Coles and Lovett were there too. They could be pretty critical at times but nobody thought any of us had made a mistake.

But when it got reported that I had lost my temper, some people started to worry. I had to start reminding people that they *were* all there and we *knew* what really happened.

The really heartening thing was the remarkable reaction to the allegations about problems with the ozone layer back in Australia. Scientists from the CSIRO and academics from universities on talkback radio and in the press said it was all a load of nonsense. The evidence was clear. The ozone layer in Sydney was no thinner than it was in Berlin. We had a wonderfully supportive response from Australian academia and the scientific world. Looking back, it was really a sign that there was a lot of underlying support in Australia for what we were doing.

That was like a lot of other media controversies which came up in the bid. You reacted to them at the time and wondered if you had done something that would hurt the Sydney bid, but in the end I don't think they counted for much.

Putting aside the personal wear and tear on ourselves, the Sydney bid team did well in Barcelona. We outperformed all the other bidders.

The Barcelona Games came at a critical time in our lobbying process. We always expected that the biggest concentration of IOC members would visit in the Australian summer — in the last months of 1992 and the first months of 1993. So we had to use the Games to nail down as many IOC visits to Sydney as possible.

After the success of the program in Birmingham the previous year, the Australian Embassy in Lisbon helped us with a visa service for IOC members. By the end of the Games the visa officer had issued 88 visas to IOC members and accompanying people who intended to visit Australia. It was an impressive total. We were expecting to get visits from more than 70 IOC members and after Barcelona most of them had visas.

A number of us — including Ros Kelly, Bruce Baird, Phil Coles, Kevan Gosper, Frank Sartor and myself — had a formal meeting with President Samaranch organised by Kevan Gosper. Frank Sartor handed over a letter — in Catalan, from all the lord mayors in Australia, saying that they were all behind the Sydney bid. The president was gracious as usual. He pointed out how important it was for the success of an Olympic Games to have your local team do well. He pointed out that when Spain had hosted the World Cup in soccer, its team got knocked out in the early rounds and few people went to the games. But in Barcelona, the Spanish team had done well right from the beginning which kept public enthusiasm very high. He said Australia was one of the most sports-loving nations in the world and if Sydney staged the Games, our athletes could be expected to do well.

We worked hard on the lobbying. Gabor Komyathy worked on the eastern European members. Elizabeth Fox and I on the

South Americans. Deeta, Mahmoud Elfarnawani and I made a concentrated effort on the Arabs and North Africans.

Sue Bushby had come to Barcelona about six days before the Games to set up the gift program. She took an un-airconditioned apartment opposite our hotel and worked day and night, sewing Sydney 2000 bands on more than 500 Akubra hats, packing Sydney 2000 beach bags with towels and wraps, and wrapping up small gifts for each member. Sue had masterminded it all — preparing the gifts in Sydney, getting them over to Spain and then putting everything together in Barcelona.

With the Barcelona sun so fierce and hot, the Akubras went down particularly well. Hundreds came to our office to get one. There were also Sydney bid pens and lapel pins and koalas dressed in Sydney 2000 tee-shirts. We estimated 500 people visited our little hospitality room — a hotel bedroom with the bed taken out. Istanbul and Brasilia had far fewer visits to their suites and closed them after several days. A number of accompanying people also helped with the staffing of the hospitality rooms. It was not uncommon to find Judy Baird, Sallyanne Atkinson, Beverley Lovett, Barbara Wild, Pauline Coates or Deeta helping out in the room alongside our staff members.

In Barcelona we made an important move for our bid. We reached agreement with Ric Birch, an Australian who organised all the opening and closing ceremonies in the Barcelona Games and was involved with the ceremonies at the Los Angeles Games, to advise our bid. Birch had been based in Barcelona for about two years before the Games to work on their ceremonies. But early on in the bid he wrote to us and said we may need him. He was very keen to be involved. So we kept up the correspondence.

Geoff Wild and I met him for the first time in Barcelona. We agreed to meet for lunch and it turned out to be the best meal I had during my whole time in Barcelona. We went down in the basement of the restaurant. There was meat hanging down from the walls and bottles of wine all over the place. The waiter came up and asked us what we wanted — there was no menu — then said, 'I think you'd like the fish. And this is what we have for you.' He took charge of everything and we had the most wonderful food.

Ric told us about what he could do in terms of the opening and closing for the ceremonies and his experience in working with President Samaranch and the Barcelona organising committee. The president had taken an active interest in the ceremonies. Barcelona was his hometown and he was particularly sensitive that the issue of Catalan and Spaniard be carefully handled. He didn't want any security problems or any political problems. With this in mind, he had insisted that Catalan be used as one of the languages for all the official announcements.

We signed a letter of appointment with Birch, saying that he would work exclusively for our bid. Birch agreed to provide suggestions on the bid books and advice about our presentations. He reviewed what we had already written for the bid books on our ceremonies and our cultural program. He also had a small input into the design of the main stadium, suggesting there be tunnels in and out which could be used for the ceremonies.

Birch agreed to work on an honorary basis, re-imbursed only for out-of-pocket expenses. He came to Sydney again for the visit of the IOC's Evaluation Commission in 1993. It was another example of how talented Australians were so willing to help the bid.

The power of the sponsor at Barcelona was overwhelming. Sponsors had tickets to just about everything. Obviously if a sponsor had said, 'If you want 200 million pesos out of me, I want tickets to everything,' he got them. Tickets were soldout, but the events were not packed out.

So every seat to every event in Barcelona was sold and nobody was worrying about the money. But there was hardy anyone in the stadiums. Some days the stands were almost empty. It was bad television not to have cheering spectators and roaring crowds. The Barcelona organising committee was not worried, it had the money. But President Samaranch told them they couldn't have empty seats on world television. He cranked up the organisers to get school children, anybody, to get the stands filled.

This was the great incongruity of Barcelona. The sponsors had tickets to everything, and at the end of the day they would throw a lot of them in the bin, because nobody had used them. At the same time, people were crawling around outside the venues, hoping for a ticket to anything!

Of course there was nothing in the Olympic Charter which said you had to have a full house at the Games. But television rights were one of the most important sources of revenue for the Games these days. If the big television networks decided the spectacle of the Games was no longer interesting, no longer exciting, the economics of the Olympic movement would be under some strain. I could understand the President's concern. But there was also something distinctly unfair and unOlympian to have people who desperately wanted to watch the events — and after all that's what the Games were about — and big quantities of tickets thrown away by wealthy sponsors. I was glad Sydney had not locked itself into any deals with major donors about the Games themselves. If we got the Games, I knew it was something we would have to think through very carefully. When we edited our draft proposals for the bid books, we developed some different ideas about ticket selling to overcome the problem.

As we saw with our cars with their 'official' stickers, security at the Games could be surprisingly lax at times. It was another message about using volunteers: when it comes to security, use big tough volunteers or don't use volunteers at all.

There were a lot of young people on the gates. If you were a big person like me with a bit of determination you could hustle your way in. I got Geoff Wild into the VIP session of the Olympic stadium for many sessions and he never had a ticket to anything. I'd just say, 'Excuse me. This man is with me. Out of the way please.' And because I am tall I got away with it. Security got worse as the Games went on; enthusiasm waned and the volunteers were hot and tired. You just can't have that at an Olympic Games. There are always heads of state at these venues and you've got to have proper security at them. The memory of the dead Israeli athletes at Munich in 1972 reminds us that athletes too can be political targets.

There were more lessons. Again there were problems with language, and many drivers did not know their way around the city. Volunteers are a great idea but are not always effective.

Before the Games was the usual meeting of the 11-person IOC executive board and a session of all the members. Much of their time in Barcelona was taken up with how to handle the difficulties which had arisen over the civil war in what had been Yugoslavia.

From the point of view of the Sydney bid, there were a number of changes to the board we thought would be helpful to our cause. Dr Un Yong Kim from South Korea was elected a vice-president, Richard Pound from Canada was re-elected and Ashwini Kumar from India, who was becoming a close personal friend of Deeta and mine, was also elected. Anita DeFrantz from the US was elected to fill the spot created by the resignation of her colleague, Robert Helmick. Anita was known to be very concerned about human rights, which even then was shaping up as an issue for the Beijing bid.

At the IOC session which followed there were two new members elected — Sheikh Fahad Al-Sabah from Kuwait and Sergio Santander from Chile. This brought the total number of IOC members at the time to 96. The young sheikh was well-known to Kevan Gosper and me and other members of our lobby team. He was keen to visit Sydney and was well aware of the support that Australia had given Kuwait in the Gulf War.

Suggestions that had come up in earlier meetings that voting procedures for Olympic host cities be changed to include five representatives of the International Federations (IFs) and five from the National Olympic Committees (NOCs) were deferred to be considered in 1993. So it looked like there would be no change to the voting procedures for September 1993: the vote would be decided as it had always been — by the 90 or so members of the IOC.

Eight cities were now bidding for the 2000 Games — Beijing, Manchester, Berlin, Milan, Istanbul, Brasilia, Tashkent and Sydney — so it was also decided that the presentation in Monte Carlo just before the vote would be cut back from 60 to 30 minutes with 15 minutes of questions. This was a good move. It would give us time to get across our message, but cut the cost.

All the bidding cities made a short presentation to the media. The only problem with ours was the video we had was a bit too long. Next time we knew to have a shorter, punchier video. When it came to the public face we presented to the Olympic family, I think the video was the only mistake we made during the whole trip. Of all the bidding cities, only Beijing, ourselves and to some extent Manchester had a successful time in Barcelona.

I felt that Istanbul and Tashkent were not going to be serious contenders and would fall away in the early rounds of voting.

The Berlin bid had suffered tremendously from the revelation of the files kept on the IOC members. These were apparently very personal and, for some, not particularly flattering. This revelation, combined with a lack of public and government support, was made life too difficult for the German bid. I sensed a widespread anti-Berlin view within the IOC members, largely because of the files. Little wonder when you considered their files revealed they had classified only seven members of the IOC as being honest — and the seven did not even include their own two IOC members! It was interesting that the German NOC had not said a word about the files, despite the controversy. We expected that — at the very least — it would have disassociated itself from them.

Milan, which had always taken a relaxed attitude to the new lobbying rules, distinguished itself by having its yacht expelled from the harbor at the direction of a member of the IOC executive. Its lobby team did not seem to be very organised and its technical bid was nowhere near the level of our's. Their team had some absolutely wonderful people and we had a few good hours with them drinking red wine. But they were not a threat.

Brasilia seemed to lose its way in Barcelona. The bid looked like it lacked financial backing and the ability to move among IOC members. Its team had been on the road as long as we had, but they were clearly not making the same impact.

The Manchester team were well organised. They obviously hoped that their lobbying effort would be highlighted by the arrival of Prime Minister John Major at the close of the Games. Only nine IOC members attended his cocktail party, and he was late for the start, which did not go down well with them. The Manchester team certainly worked hard. Indeed some would say they overdid it and became intrusive. Towards the end of the session, I was thanked by one European IOC member — the same one that Bob Scott had sat himself next to at breakfast at Albertville — for the 'non-intrusive' way the Sydney team went

The bid's audacious goal and Olympic idealism constantly brought out the extra yard in those the team came in touch with. Photographer Howe improved on the usual dull corporate team shot and placed us around the flag that spelled out our goal, over the logo. The team as it was in January 1992 (a full list is given in Appendix 1): *from left, clockwise:* John Shirley, Rosalyn Burns, Eddie Moore, Robert Johnstone, Kevin Simmonds, Lynne Jones, Alan Hoskins (*behind*), Sue Bushby, Melissa Petherbridge, Gavin Blatchford, me, Justina Tulloch, Sue Channels, Susan McElhone, Angela Meucci, Chris Barnum and Peter Woolcott (*behind*), Lisa McMahon, Magaret McLennan, Bob Prater, Jannelle Witschi, Sue Hunt, David Churches, Oscar Andreazza.

The senior talent bank. Space here prohibits description of the individual talents and contributions of these men, but I was able to draw on a fund of knowledge gained in two previous Olympic bids, long and deep involvement in the Olympic movement, business sense, contacts, sports history, sporting knowledge, and administrative, marketing and political talent and enthusiasm. *Clockwise, from top left:* Kevan Gosper, John Coates, Phil Coles, Bob Elphinston, Bruce Baird MP.

The Manchester bid. The gold flames denoting the Olympic torch always seemed predictable, safe and uninspired. We always felt Sydney's symbol was great.

The Manchester bid used British national icons like these Coldstream guards and ceremonial trumpets to stunning effect. Our Geoff Wild couldn't resist the photo opportunity it offered.

The Berlin bid. A German sports star signs a tee-shirt for a supporter at Berlin's hospitality booth in Stutgaart.

One day before the IOC executive met in Berlin, hundreds of Berliners demonstrated against the Games. Banners like 'IOC piss off', 'Olympics once was enough' and those in German opposing tax burdens it was feared a Games might involve could hardly be seen as evidence of public support for the German bid.

The Beijing bid. *Right:* A bricklayer's laborer showcasing China's bid for the visits of IOC members. Beijing was the bid that most worried us. Their team was almost invisible, but it was effective. Beijing's claim took on a life of its own. Some thought it was a certainty, unstoppable, and this irritated us, for there were powerful reasons why China should not be awarded the Games.
Below: China's human rights record was among these reasons and overseas Chinese, pro-democracy students inside and outside China, Tibetans and human rights activists marshalled against the Beijing bid world-wide. The Alliance for a Democratic China remind us of Tiananmen Square at a large rally in Belmore Park, Sydney.

Home entertaining. *Right: from left:* Russian-speaking Roman Korduba, Republic of Mongolia IOC member Shagdarjav Magvan, Sonya Lyneham, Mrs Marvan, Geoff and Barbara Wild and me. *Below: from left:* Barbara Wild, me, Belinda Hutchinson, IOC member from Uganda Major General Francis Nyangweso, his wife Naomi, Mimi Forwood and Geoff Wild.

Above: The bid office contained superb models of the venues, the big central model being Sydney Olympic Park at Homebush. These models gave the big picture in a way no amount of mapping, photography or computer modelling could rival. The concrete product we were selling centred on venue, village and city, and the task was to demonstrate the high technical standard of these, the credibility of what was planned or being built and every advantage they offered. Good products cannot be left to sell themselves.

Below: No visitor to Homebush, whether a city community group or potential corporate sponsor or an athelte or an IOC delegate with a vote to cast, was left in any doubt about what exactly the Park was for. Schoolchildren and The State Emergency service paint the logo on a concrete slab the size of eight football fields. They used up all the paint Wattle donated!

Lobbying went on pretty well constantly. *Above:* Barcelona press conference, where we announced that our Games, should we be successful, would be called 'The Athletes' Games'. *Above right:* President of the Chinese Olympic Committee, Zhengliang He (*right*) arguing hard for Beijing to Gunnar Erissson, leader of the Evaluation Committee of the IOC in Beijing. *Below :* Phil Coles (*standing*) seen speaking with Juan Samaranch, President of the IOC, on the first day of the IOC meeting in Barcelona. *Right:* Maria Vazquez Rana, one of Mexico's two IOC delegates and I on the podium in Darling Harbor.

The Bid Books, our key publication, available for reference for IOC delegates anytime, long after the brochures and fact sheets were discarded or filed. *Above:* Qantas CEO John Ward and I show them to Captain Ian Lucas before takeoff at Mascot. The photograph's publication showed Sydneysiders that things were happening, part of the vital task and duty of maintaining support and momentum at home. *Below:* Geoffrey Henke, Vice-president of the AOC, and I hand over the three volumes to President Samaranch in Lausanne, Switzerland.

CIRONNEEU/AP

Olympic hospitality. *Left:* Stiltwalkers in fantasy jumpsuits and helium-filled hats, part of the opening of Albertville's 1992 Winter Olympics. A magnificent, different and creative occasion that focussed our minds on opening ceremonies and acquiring talent for Sydney in 2000. Besides being a civic and national showcase, and a very important television event, the ceremony is a *welcome* to athletes, officials, the Olympic family and visitors. *Below:* Deeta and I, with IOC member from Algeria, Mohamed Zerguini (*centre*) and Mahmoud Elfanawani (*right*), the Toronto-based Egyptian-born volleyball player and coach we hired as an Arab specialist lobbyist, standing on the jetty before the Australia Day Regatta in 1993, waiting for the vessel *Ena*. We were stalling. The *Ena* was destined not to sail that day, but we made sure IOC members did.

The bid team wanted children involved. A girl just starting school in 1992 could conceivably make the Australian gymnastic team in 2000, and, it was part of our accent on youth. The kids responded enthusiastically and magnificently, and enjoyed their involvement. We also wanted the involvement of Sydney's ethnic groups, for practical reasons, and to demonstrate Australia's multicultural policies, as well as making vistors feel at home and fight perceptions of Australia as an Anglo-Saxon nation. Those communities exceeded our hopes. *Above:* dragons and festive masks enliven a Chinatown celebration. *Left:* Sydney's African communities lent support—and color. *Below:* Learne Lay from Strathfield Girls' High puts in some time painting for us.

The support of business was vital to the bid. Without the money, services, loaned equipment, discounts, labor, advice, expertise and support of the private sector there would have been little chance of mounting an effective campaign, and the drain on the public purse would have been politically difficult and financially burdensome in a recession. A full list of sponsors appears in Appendix 3. Here are just two uses sponsors made of their association—the big brewer, CUB, and a small business, the Woolloomooloo Bay Hotel. I called in at the hotel on my way back from the airport after Monte Carlo. Our keyring giveaway.

The IOC president could hardly miss this. Billboard on the road from the airport to the city. The space was donated by Paul Makucha.

President Samaranch views a model of the Olympic stadium at our offices, flanked by Bruce Baird and myself, ready to answer questions.

Go for it Sydney!

SYDNEY 2000 ©TM

DAYS TO GO

11

A Friendly City Can Host a Friendly Games.

Sydney prepares for the decision. We used activity and support back home right through the last days, feeding newspaper cuttings faxed from our office, video and audio tapes couriered in and anything else we could use to our lobbyists, even in Monte Carlo. *Above:* Countdown poster on the Hyatt Hotel, Kings Cross, unveiled by Premier Fahey. *Left:* Philips designed, built and installed a cunning reworking of that flexible logo on the ridges of the Sydney Opera House roof shells, and lit it up at night as the decision neared.

Monte Carlo, September 1993. *Left:* Musician outside the casino, in the heart of Monte Carlo, intriguing all and filling the very air with the sound of Australia. *Right:* Australians in Monaco hotels responded to our request to put out more flags all right, but the IOC and civic authorities ruled it wasn't on. *Below:* Our koala mascot Eddie Moore hands out a flag to a Monegaque policeman. We had a kangaroo mascot as well. Our cliches are others' exotica. *Bottom:* These look-alike besuited gents are the dance troupe Etcetera, who performed on the streets as a rule. They are shown here reading the *Herald Tribune* of 22 September 1994, with the wrap-around advertising space we organised.

Tanya Blencowe takes the microphone at our Monte Carlo press conference. *From left:* Graham Lovett, Kieren Perkins, Tanya, Paul Gilding, Elizabeth Fox and Perry Crosswhite.

Premier John Fahey pulls me to my feet in that now-famous leap of his when Sydney wins the 2000 Olympic Games at the 101st session of the IOC in Monaco, 23 September 1993.

And the Australians are rapturous. My wife Deeta, in Akubra, hugs Barbara Wild. Gough Whitlam is moved to a satisfied grin.

The job's not done until the ink on the paperwork is dry. Kevan Gosper smiles (*left, standing*) while Prime Minister Paul Keating and Premier John Fahey raise fists in victory, as IOC President Juan Antonio Samaranch (*middle, seated*), the IOC's Marc Hodler and Lord Mayor Frank Sator (*right, seated*) sign. IOC Director-General Francois Charrad (*standing, middle row*) observes.

Two cities thinking of one another, 23 September 1994. Monte Carlo. *Left:* Paul and Annita Keating savor the moment with an ecstatic Kevan Gosper. *Below:* Australians whoop it up, Lowes Hotel.

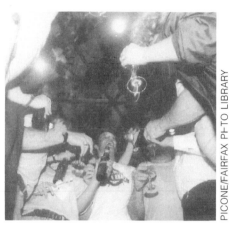

Sydney. *Above:* Centrepoint Tower, Sydney, our Olympic 'torch'. *Right:* Arguably our greatest Olympic athlete is still with the celebration as night gives way to day: Dawn Fraser.

Ticker-tape parade, George Street, Sydney, October 1993, courtesy of Telecom Australia. Sydney was saying thank you to us, but we knew we had a great deal to thank Sydneysiders for, too. *Above:* Deeta and I having a wonderful day. *Left:* Olympic champions Cathy Watt and Kieren Perkins join the celebration of the winning of the Athlete's Games.

about their lobbying. It was good to see our advice and our instincts on this approach confirmed.

It was also apparent at Barcelona that publication of *The Lords of the Rings* had hurt Manchester. Deeply critical of the Olympic family, it talked of 'the Lords of Lausanne' and was very personally offensive to President Samaranch. The two journalists who wrote the book had interviewed Bob Scott and members of the British Olympic Association and the association was specifically thanked in the introduction to the book. The book helped to generate something of an anti-Anglo-Saxon feeling at the Barcelona Games. It singled out four members of the IOC for particular criticism — President Samaranch from Spain, Primo Nebiolo from Italy, Joao Havelange from Brazil and Mario Vazquez Rana from Mexico — all from Latin countries. As I've said earlier, I thought the book took a few incidents, gave them undue prominence and attention and used them to tar the whole Olympic movement. Its authors showed no understanding at all of its history or the motivations of the vast majority of IOC members. Some suggested that the publication of the book had actually ended Manchester's prospects.

But I believed that Manchester were never to be underestimated. They were good lobbyists. Bob Scott may have come on a bit too strong for my liking at times, but he was an outgoing charismatic man who had led the city's previous bid and already knew a lot of the members. He was a theatrical entrepreneur in Manchester. His father, Sir David Scott, was a distinguished diplomat who entertained and travelled to help the Manchester bid. I always considered they were by far the strongest European bid when it came to courting the members.

But they were always battling the perception that they were representing a somewhat dowdy city and they seemed to have a very ordinary technical plan for staging the Games. By the end of the Games their lobbying team looked overworked and a little despondent. Clearly the heat was getting to them too. We felt tired — but we didn't let it show.

Beijing: always the city to watch, they were also the hardest to watch. They certainly had strong financial backing from their government. They had a staff of some 300 on their bid team while we only ever had about 50 at the most. When it came to lobbying, theirs' was certainly a different approach. While there

were people from Beijing present on most occasions, their lobbying process was not visible. You never heard open talk about
people supporting Beijing. It was hard to pin down more than
four or five IOC members who were categorically in favor of
Beijing. But you could feel it and read it in the press. It was
obvious that the Beijing bid had a momentum of its own. We
started to think about what more could be done to counter it.

There were rumors President Samaranch was backing Beijing.
But Kevan Gosper, closer to the Olympic family than me, was
adamant: the president had never indicated a preference for any
city. And another source said he had a private preference for
Sydney. From what I saw and heard, he played it straight down
the line.

I left Barcelona before Ric Birch's closing ceremony. We were
all exhausted. I had seen everyone I had wanted to see ten times
and I couldn't see the point in staying longer. When we got back,
Margaret and Alan Hoskins got sick. Margaret had spent 20 days
straight in the Princesa Sofia hotel with Alan running the
hospitality suite. She got a bad flu and had to take three weeks
off to recover when she got back to Sydney. We just couldn't
believe how badly we all felt. We were so drained. It was a very
critical moment for my management priorities.

'That's it,' I said. 'We are never going to go away short of
people again.' I knew this may involve some debate with the
premier and the minister over our travel submissions. But the
next time we went away, I was going to make sure we had enough
people to do the job properly. Fortunately, Bruce Baird supported
me because he was often on the road and could see there was a
problem if you asked people to do too much.

I was always a person with a very formidable constitution. I
could stay up into the early hours of the morning and bounce up
at 7am, never have a hangover, never need a quick sleep. But I
realised at Barcelona that even if you do have a strong constitution, you're not that good. It does get to people. If you are
exhausted, you get short-tempered and irritated quickly. And if
you're marketing to a client or a customer, you just can't have
that happen to you. It's not good enough having the best
product. The sales team also has to appear happy, relaxed and

confident. And lobbyists are in a selling game in a competitive market too.

Whenever we got back from a big international trip I always made a point of calling in all the staff in for a briefing where the travellers would tell everything. It was important that *all* the team were up to speed on where we were so that they could be well-informed ambassadors for the bid when they went out to their local school or community group or were talking to IOC staffers or corporate supporters or whoever.

At the staff meeting after Barcelona I said: 'We have just passed the easy part of the bid. Things are going to get tougher from here on in. We all have to get fitter. I'm not going to institute any physical exercise regimes or any bundy clocks. But let's all start to walk or go running or whatever we need to do.' I had never jogged for fitness before. But from then on I jogged every day. And I still do. I made myself much fitter and everybody else in the office did too — so we could stand more stress. We knew the pressure from then on was going to be twice as great.

I remember from Australian legal conventions papers like 'Stress and the Lawyer'. I used to think that it was absolute nonsense and it was for wimps. But I became very strong on the idea. You can't work people to a standstill and expect them to perform properly. It won't work. Particularly if you are handling an intensive assignment which involves very little time off. Being fitter means less stress, more effective work and the ability to perform over the long haul.

The return from Barcelona was an important milestone. We had been on the road for well over a year, but it was not until after Barcelona that the attention of the IOC and the rest of the Olympic movement started to focus on the race to stage the 2000 Olympics. Before Barcelona candidate cities were a minor item: everybody was focussed on how the Barcelona Games were going to turn out. Once that was out of the way, 2000 bidders became the major item of business and we came under much more scrutiny.

After Barcelona, the next major international event for us was in Acapulco — the annual meeting of the Association of National

Olympic Committees in November. Mario Vazquez Rana, from Mexico, was the president of ANOC and he made it a splendid event. It was held at the Acapulco Princess which is a complex of three hotel buildings along the beach, connected by long open-air corridors. There were lots of breezeways. Everything was open to the air except for the hotel rooms themselves. It was the same place we had stayed when we went to Acapulco in May 1992 for the annual PASO meeting. This time they had lots of grand buffet dinners with a different theme every night. One night Fidel Mendoza, the IOC member in Colombia, a surgeon who was normally rather shy, got up and sang some beautiful Spanish songs. He really had a wonderful voice. At the end of the night 'Share the Spirit' was played very loudly on the sound system and the music could be heard all over the hotel complex.

Everyone was given a little piece of crystal glassware and a set of satchels and pens — all at Rana's expense. Rana also gave John Fahey, who was on his first lobbying trip for us as premier, a big case of white rum. Fahey was very sensitive about taking anything that could be seen as an improper gift, so he handed it over to the bid team. Rana topped off the meeting by flying all the IOC members to Mexico City one evening for a meeting with the president of Mexico.

But for us, there was very serious business at hand. Although the NOCs wouldn't have a direct vote, their leaders had a large moral sway and personal influence in the Olympic movement. We knew we had to make an impact. If there was one issue which was a potential problem for the Sydney bid, it was the constant references to the long distances people would have to travel to get here. Bob Scott used to talk about it often when he was having a go at us.

Of course it was very unfair. The best point anyone ever made to me about the criticism that Sydney was a long way away was made by Jacques Rogge from Belgium:

'Australia has gone to all of the other countries of the world to compete. You are the only country besides Greece that has gone to every Games. People shouldn't have the temerity to say Australia was too far. It's the same as if you went to someone's place for dinner, but when you invited them to your home, they said it was too far to come.'

The reality is that distance equals cost for most of the Olympic committees. The athletes were keen to come to Australia. Australia had hosted many world championships and the athletes had performed at their peak. But we knew the issue of distance would have to be dealt with if we were to be considered on an equal basis with the other cities.

So we decided to make an offer to the NOCs that we would pay the airfares of the athletes and officials to come to Sydney. It had always been in our strategy that we would do this. It was mentioned in the original Baird report which had come out two years before and included in its budget estimates.

Again, we had learned from Melbourne's experience. Melbourne had devised a partial grant to pay the fares of some athletes. There was a logic in that. If you paid the fares of all athletes, the countries who could afford to send their own athletes just got a bonus. Melbourne decided only to give a grant to teams of less than a certain number, because the big countries were the ones who could afford to have teams of 400 and 500.

It was certainly cheaper that way. But the problem is it discriminates between teams. If you are trying to win votes, you are appealing to *all* IOC members. And the size of a country's team does not necessarily reflect the financial pressure on a particular national committee. In some cases, even when countries send small teams, the government pays, not the NOC, so the cost doesn't matter to them. But in a lot of other countries, the NOC has to struggle to raise the money. In the end we decided it was just not smart to offer to give money to some countries and not to others. This was Coates' view as head of Australia's NOC, and it was fully supported by the strategy committee. Of course it was expensive: all up, the budget to bring some 15 000 athletes, officials and other team personnel to Sydney was $35 million ($US24 million).

That was a lot of money by anyone's standards and it was important for us to think carefully about maximising the impact of our offer within the Olympic community. We decided the best place to announce this would be the ANOC meeting which was the annual meeting of all the world's NOCs. As these groups are the ones responsible for raising the money to send the teams to the Olympics, and many are former athletes themselves, they were the ones who would most appreciate the benefit of what we were offering.

We kept it secret and developed a plan to make the announcement and then hand out a letter signed by us to every NOC with the exact amount of money that they would get, based on the size of the teams that went to Barcelona. We had formed a committee with Qantas to work out how much it would cost. We had a special color newspaper, *The Sydney Spirit*, printed for the occasion, and the story of the offer was front page, in Spanish, French and English.

I spoke to the meeting and gave my usual high-sounding speech, then John Coates announced details of the offer. As president of the Australian Olympic Committee, he was talking to his colleagues. As soon as he had spoken, a team of our people went around the room handing out the letters. When the meeting broke up, our team were back on the doors, handing out copies of the newspaper, including the Premier and Bruce Baird. It blew everyone away. No other bid had done anything like it. It was just game, set and match.

I felt our attention to detail in the planning and execution of a strategy was standing us in pretty good stead as novice salesmen.

Manchester went around saying that we were trying to buy the Games and how dreadful it all was, but it went down very well with the NOCs, which was what we wanted.

There was one minor glitch. Our offer was for return airfares — that is fares to and from Sydney. But in the translation into Spanish, the word 'return' airfare created problems. People thought it only meant the fare back home again. So we quickly wrote a letter to everyone correcting the error. We couldn't allow that kind of mistake. It was understandable. Australians do say 'return' trip when they mean both directions but Americans and others use the term 'round' trip. These minor things happened. It was important to do what was needed to be done, make the corrections and move on. There was no point having any recriminations about it. And it didn't spoil the powerful impact of our offer.

Before Acapulco, our bid had become known as the 'green' one, the one with the best environmental considerations. After, it also become known as the bid which would pay for the fares of all the athletes and officials. Suddenly, every Olympic committee in the world knew that if the Games were in Sydney, it wouldn't cost them a cent or the time and energy spent knocking on doors and fund-raising. If a country's government paid for the airfares, Australia would still give them the money as a training grant for their athletes. And in the end, we didn't even insist they come Qantas. They could come on any airline, including Qantas. It was a stunning success.

Manchester later came out with what they called a Millennium Foundation which involved promises of money for scholarships and training. China also offered to pay for the athletes but it didn't give the NOCs any detail on what each one would get. We were the only one that had a detailed free travel plan.

There were the usual short presentations by bid cities to the meeting. Beijing outpointed us on the video. They showed a video made by a talented American called Bud Greenspan. It had superb historic footage of the Olympics and wonderfully panoramic views of China. It was just a knockout. But as it turned out it was only a one-off. I wondered if they realised how good it was themselves. They should have used Greenspan to make a video for their presentation in Monte Carlo. But, fortunately for us, they didn't.

The other event of direct interest to us at the meeting was the ballot for the order of the presentations at Monte Carlo. We were to be second — after Berlin and before Manchester. I said that was fine with us: it was still early in the day and the members would still be fresh and attentive to our presentation. But I wouldn't have really worried where we had been placed in the order of presentations. I'm a bit of a fatalist. I believe you just take those things as they come.

The Acapulco meeting was John Fahey's first experience of the Olympic lobbying environment. Fahey had taken over as NSW premier in June after Nick Greiner resigned. Fahey had not been a big overseas traveller and it was one of the few times he had been outside Australia. In the Olympic environment I found that people often jumped at shadows and rumors. There was always talk about who was winning and who was losing, and which member would vote which way. But you had to learn to filter all the information. You had to assess it and make your own judgement and then get on with it. Fahey went into this environment cold and was told by one observer close to the IOC that Sydney really didn't have a chance. At one stage in Acapulco, he came into our room and said he was worried we couldn't win. I think he came back from Acapulco a little flat.

But he was a great addition to our team. He was a very passionate sports person and he did a good job in our presentation. He made himself available for every social function and was actively involved in the whole proceedings. He seemed to strike up a particularly close relationship with Pat Hickey, the president of the Irish Olympic Committee.

I never had any great emotional ups and downs like some other members of our team — at least about who would win. I always felt Sydney had a good chance. But there were other things that did cause me a good deal of personal pain.

12
Tensions

Gentlemen, can you possibly believe that similar [unsporting]
incidents are not spread across the chronicles of the Olympic,
Pythian, Nemean games— all the great sporting events of ancient
history? One would have to be naive indeed to pretend that this
is the case.

Baron Pierre de Coubertin in an address
at the London Olympics, 1908.

The Olympic Games are supposed to be all about promoting
peace and harmony between people, and by and large they
do. But, as the good baron noted himself, the business of the
Olympics has never been without its peculiar politics and tensions. Nor was the business of running the Sydney bid.

When I met Patricia Rochford, of Rochford Williams, the firm
that was handling the search for the chief executive, she warned
me that there was a lot of politics in sport— particularly in the
Olympic movement; there were tensions between a number of
important people in the movement in Australia; tensions between
Sydney and Melbourne supporters over their separate pushes to
be the Olympic city; political tensions between government and
Opposition; and personal tensions within the government. I was
well briefed and went into the job with my eyes open. But
sometimes being told things and experiencing them first hand
can be two different things.

Essentially, I came in as the outsider into a lot of long time
relationships— most of them good, but some not so good.

When Billy Payne and Charlie Battle in Atlanta decided to
make their bid for the 1996 Games, Billy personally chose a
group of people who were good friends and who had already
worked together fund-raising. They had personal bonds— some
were members of the same church, some were members of the
Atlanta law fraternity who knew each other well. It wasn't until
after they had won that city officials and all sorts of outside
people began to get involved. Sydney's case was different. The

NSW government and the Australian Olympic Committee had come together to launch a bid. And they hired newcomers to the Olympic scene to help them carry it out, like myself and others.

It was one thing for me to insist on having the staff I wanted. And I know I generated enough flak with some of the changes I made there. But there was a broad range of people linked in various ways to the bid that I just had to work with, whatever happened. As CEO, it was part of my job to keep them all— if not happy— at least focussed on the main goal of winning the Games.

After I took over the job, I soon realised that there were some differences between supporters of John Coates and Phil Coles, who came from Sydney, and Kevan Gosper, who came from Melbourne. Jostling for position between Sydney and Melbourne for the right to bid for the Games had some part in this. There were different views about what Melbourne should and shouldn't have done in its campaign. As I found out, people involved in the Melbourne bid could be very sensitive to anyone from Sydney making comments about their campaign. But it went further. There was even a suspicion by a few people in Melbourne that Phil Coles hadn't voted for Melbourne in Tokyo in 1990! (I know he did.)

But there seemed to be a view among some that you were either a Coles and Coates person, or a Gosper person.

I had a lot of time for Kevan Gosper. One of only four vice-presidents in the IOC, Gosper was was well known and highly respected in the Olympic movement. He had often been mentioned as a possible successor to Juan Antonio Samaranch when he retired. In January 1994 Gosper was honored by France for his work in the Olympic movement when he was invested with the Legion of Honor.

Kevan was a great source of advice for me on many aspects of how to handle the Olympic family and particularly helpful in the final stages. He did a lot of lobbying and travel for the bid, even though he was in his final year for Shell in London. He flew out to Australia on a number of important occasions during the bid, and Deeta and I became very friendly with him and his wife, Judy. I would often confide in Kevan about how I thought we were going and what problems we were having.

But there were those that said because I was close to Gosper,

I was not on the side of Coles and Coates. This wasn't true. I also respected and valued the work and advice of Phil and John. Coles had gone out of his way to get me up to speed on the Olympic movement and to introduce me to the members. I had known and respected John Coates as a lawyer before I joined the bid. He was a man of tremendous capacity and ability, and a tireless worker. Whenever there was paperwork to be done he always turned it around very quickly. He was very experienced in dealing with the Olympic movement and had very sound views on how the bid should be handled. The paper he prepared on lobbying for the Games provided the basis for our whole campaign. He had been *chef de mission* for the Australian team in Barcelona and Seoul, and would later be appointed to the same task for the Atlanta Games. Phil and John were both very committed to the bid. And we were all part of the one team.

But problems would arise at unexpected moments.

At one point during the winter Olympics in Albertville, when we were in the thick of some of the problems with Visa and American Express. Kevan Gosper, Dick Pound (from Canada, the IOC's finance expert), and I met in a bar to talk about it. Phil Coles was somewhere else in the bar and John Coates wasn't there. After we had finished, Coles came up and accused me of shafting Coates over the Visa-Amex matter. I told him I wasn't, I was just discussing the problem with Gosper and Pound and trying to work out what to do about it. But he had got it into his head that we were cooking something up in a dark corner. The incident, unfortunately, hurt the on-going relationship.

Tensions between myself and Graham Lovett were unfortunate too. Lovett was on the board and was very experienced in sports marketing, particularly rugby league and tennis. When I first started the job he was very kind to me and took me to a lot of football games and introduced me to all his sporting colleagues.

We got on very well initially but had a blow-up in relation to a number of personal matters. On the flight of the lobby team to Copenhagen for the Association of European NOCs in April 1992, we quarrelled over several things that were out of my control, including the intervention of a senior bureaucrat from the Premier's Department, but Graham took it to heart. There was a lot of vitriol and things deteriorated from then on.

At the conference in Copenhagen, Lovett complained that we

didn't have our brochures in French as well as English. By the end of the conference, I noticed that none of the other cities did either, which I pointed out. I tried to sort it out and told Lovett if he wanted an apology, he had it. But I knew I hadn't got anywhere. We had some other differences in Barcelona over who should be involved in the presentations, which didn't help.

After the Copenhagen trip, there was another difference of opinion which saw my relationship with Graham deteriorate further. I didn't believe he was a great public speaker and I thought this was particularly important for us as we addressed IOC members around the world. He disagreed. Bob Elphinston was a great people person and an excellent public presenter, so I included him in our lobby team when I could and Graham's international lobbying role was not as extensive as he would have liked. He was not happy about it and blamed me for it.

As the bid progressed, the tensions between us meant that I didn't include Lovett in the entertaining of IOC members I did at my home— and I did a lot. As chief executive, I was very careful to extend to him all the rights, entitlements and courtesies of a director. I also made a point of praising him in public. But I certainly wasn't going to invite someone I wasn't comfortable with into my home. For various reasons, the same thing started to happen with the individual entertainment by some other lobby team members. It was all very difficult for Sue Bushby who was handling all the entertainment schedules for the visiting IOC members. She found herself in the middle of all these strains with different lobby team members having instructions about who was and wasn't to be included on their guest lists.

But Graham did a magnificent job in convincing the 25 international Olympic sporting federations that Sydney had the best bid. He and Bob Elphinston worked together on this and they were great. By the time we finalised our bid books, they had got all 25 IFs to give our bid their seal of approval. It was an important step in our campaign of selling Sydney as having the best technical bid for the 2000 Games.

On reflection, I'm not proud of the way I handled the problem. I should have addressed the situation, sat down with him before relations got too strained and worked out some other ways for him to contribute. It may not have changed the result but at least it would have been a more constructive approach to the problem.

Of course, in any large organisation, personal differences between senior executives are inevitable. To an extent, tensions between the CEO and a senior executive may not rule out effective co-operation between managers— as I saw with Graham and Bob. But personal problems with another board member were something I could have done without.

As chief executive of Sydney Olympics 2000 Bid Limited, I had to keep on side all board members, politicians and other members of our lobby team; I had to cope with the demands and restrictions of being a public enterprise while trying to focus on the main game of winning the Olympics. In private enterprise, people often sort things out directly, with the chief executive having the power to decide on his or her own team. But our operation was a very different animal. I found when it comes to a public service operation, people who have the power to do so, often do not confront personality differences head on. There seemed to be a tendency to agree about problems privately but a reluctance to take the kind of direct action that may have straightened things out.

The structure of our organsiation contributed to tensions. The premier was both the president and the chairman, but he was inevitably very busy with other duties. If we had had a chairman who could have been around a lot more, as has been since established with the organising committee of the Sydney Games, it might have been easier to sort out some problems from the beginning.

There were other tensions that went beyond individual personalities.

When the bid campaign was well and truly underway, another group of people emerged, almost as a second informal strategy group. Although we had a board, a large overall bid committee, a strategy committee and other specialist groups, about halfway through the bid I had to start incorporating this other group into the matrix.

Sometime in 1992 a perception had taken root in some people's minds that the Sydney 2000 bid was not doing enough; that things were not happening fast enough. We were very involved at the time preparing the bid books, getting ready for

Barcelona, and with our international lobbying campaign— as well as developing things such as the schools program and pushing ahead with the design of venues such as the athletes' village. None of it was particularly visible and I began to get feedback through John Valder that some people around town didn't think things were going very well. When were we going to get the signs up around town and the whole place rolling?

These matters had been discussed and a strategy agreed. We decided we didn't want to burn the city out by getting over-excited too early. We wanted to put the signs up around Sydney in late 1992 when all the IOC members were starting their visits. We knew what we were doing. But it's hard to stop people from criticising you when they are speaking from ignorance.

Others began asking if we really knew what we were doing about getting enough votes. There was a very real and under-standable desire to avoid the Melbourne situation where the bidding committee had been very confident of a good result but, in reality could only line up 12 first round votes.

In June 1992 the premiership also changed. Nick Greiner resigned and John Fahey took over. Fahey took over as president and chairman of the bid and Nick remained on the board, which was expanded to 16. I had known John Fahey for many years from our time in the law. When Bruce Baird was making his phone calls, checking me out for the job, John Fahey was one of the people he spoke to and Fahey was very supportive of me. But, as the incoming premier, Fahey had to quickly get himself wised up about the business of bidding for an Olympic Games.

In September 1992, after Barcelona, we had a meeting to finalise our budget submission for the bid books on a Sunday evening at the Intercontinental Hotel. At the end of our delib-erations, John Valder said he thought some things were not going right. He'd obviously been in John Fahey's ear. So we decided to form another committee, a kind of macro-strategy committee which would look at issues such as what we were going to do about the strength of the Beijing bid, what more we should be doing in terms of community support and what we should be doing to promote the bid in our region. It included Nick Greiner, Greg Daniel, John Valder, myself and some other board mem-bers. But I sensed another group out there was trying to become involved.

I was soon to find out about it.

They turned out to be a group of people led by Ross Turnbull, a Sydney businessman, who had strong influence with Premier Fahey. Turnbull had been a good rugby union player in his day, playing many games for the Wallabies, and later managing some Wallaby tours to Britain. He had been chairman of the NSW Rugby Union for eight years before retiring in 1989. Trained as a lawyer in Newcastle, his business interests had included various property developments and investments. The group also included John Morschel, the managing director of Lend Lease, Kim Santow, Geoff Levy and David Gonski from Freehill Hollingdale and Page, and Bob Mansfield, the chief executive of Optus. I was asked to go to a meeting with this group and the premier in his meeting rooms.

They believed they could do a lot to help the bid. 'We've got business connections and international connections. We want to help and we want to do something,' they said. We talked about various things. I gave them a report on how we were doing on a number of fronts which eased things a bit. But they still said they wanted to do something, and John Fahey said, 'Well Rod, I think we ought to involve them, don't you?'

I agreed. Fahey had effectively directed me to have further talks with them, but it wasn't against my will. I did know some of its members— particularly the lawyers Kim Santow, who later became a Supreme Court judge, and David Gonski— and had a high respect for them and their connections.

I started to give them some jobs to do. I looked at areas where I thought our formal strategy group was not making headway. We needed some help in seeking the support of the major television networks around the world. The networks were one of the major sources of funding for the Olympics and we wanted to make sure that they weren't lobbying behind the scenes for Beijing to get the Games. There seemed to be a belief in some quarters that because China had 1.1 billion people, the networks would want a Beijing Games. For similar reasons, we also wanted some further help with our plans to seek the support of all the major Olympic sponsors.

There was also a group of about eight IOC members that I didn't think we were penetrating properly— members of royal families and important banking people. If these people could help us on areas where our strategy committee was weak, I didn't think there was anything to lose by trying to work with them.

So, as things evolved, I began to run what became two strategy committees. I appointed Mark Jackson in our office to look after the Turnbull group. At first, my official strategy committee did not know about the other group. When they found out they were angry. And then it started. Coles, Coates and Lovett were deeply suspicious: 'Who are these guys? We're running this bid. Tell them to get lost.' They worried that things might drift into the hands of people who didn't know what they were doing and mess things up. But I always approached the group with an open mind; I took the view that they may have had something to offer— which they did. Maybe it was because I was an 'outsider' to the official family to start with myself that I was more open to suggestions from intelligent and well-connected people. They might not have been expert on the bidding process but I knew they could open other doors— in some cases, doors we had never even thought of.

I've always felt that while there are official structures and proper ways of doing things, a leader should also be prepared to indulge in a bit of lateral thinking and be open to some independent advice. Just because we started out with an official strategy committee did not mean that we couldn't accept advice from anyone else.

So there was the initial group of people who were formally a part of the process, and a second informal group and I was in the middle. It was difficult for me although I had the Premier's imprimatur to deal with them. The Turnbull group never caused me any great problems, but my official strategy committee resented their existence.

I never put the two groups together. But I did tell the Turnbull group that there had been some objections and criticisms about them from the official strategy committee. So Ross Turnbull rang Phil Coles. Turnbull said he wanted to help. He was told that things were already under control. But Turnbull said to Coles:

'You were involved last time and you went into a room thinking you had all the votes and you only started out with twelve. What's to stop that happening again? You can't possibly allow Sydney to end up with the same result as Melbourne did.'

When Turnbull told me about the conversation, it drove the

point home to me even further. We just couldn't afford to go down the same track as Melbourne had in 1990 and end up with only 16 votes. With their experience to build on, we had to do better simply to be able to say we did as well. So I got even more determined as a result of the emergence of this new 'committee'. The existence of a second force was a strain on me, but I was determined that we should leave no stone unturned in our campaign to get the Games.

The Turnbull group started out a bit naively at first. They had a lot of ideas which we had already thought of and discarded.

They had grand plans to throw a big party in London at the Dorchester Hotel around the time of Wimbledon in the northern summer of 1993. We knew there were going to be about 20 or 30 IOC members going to Wimbledon, so it was a sporting event we had to be at. President Samaranch was a tennis fan and we thought he may well be there too. Ross Turnbull said he knew Lew Hoad and could arrange something. But the strategy committee was concerned that anything we did at Wimbledon should be *low* key, because it was Manchester's patch; they believed that if Sydney had a big reception at the same time it would just offend Manchester and put the IOC members in a difficult position.

The Turnbull group involved Jim Wolfensohn. A very successful Australian merchant banker based in New York, Wolfensohn had high-level connections in the US and around the world. Kim Santow and David Gonski were friends of his. Wolfensohn was an Olympian, having fenced for Australia in 1956. They asked him if he could help, and we gave him the list of members we were having trouble reaching. He opened doors for us among some of the big US companies and provided some useful connections in high level international circles.

But the real coup of the Turnbull group was to get us in contact with President Samaranch's lawyer, Samuel Pisar.

Pisar, who lives in Paris, was the general counsel to the IOC. When I looked at the IOC handbook, he was there. But the name didn't mean anything to me when I first saw it. Pisar was 12 years old when he was put in a Nazi death camp in Poland. His mother and younger sister died in the gas chambers. His father was a resistance fighter and was executed by the Gestapo. He was in Auschwitz and Dachau, and was liberated by the Americans at the end of the war. Two of his uncles, who were living in Melbourne, traced the 17 year old after the war and brought him out to Australia. The boy, who had not held a book in his hands for six years, studied law at Melbourne University where he got a first-class honors degree. In 1954 he won a scholarship to Harvard where he did his doctorate and later studied at the Sorbonne in Paris. Pisar became a very prominent international attorney with offices in New York and Paris. He was an adviser to US president John F Kennedy and French president Giscard d'Estaing.

It was the combination of his legal skills and his ability to speak Russian which brought him into contact with the Olympic movement. In the late 1970s, after the IOC chose Moscow to host the 1980 Games, they needed a lawyer who could speak Russian to help them with the sponsorship contracts and television negotiations. Juan Antonio Samaranch was also the Spanish Ambassador to Moscow at the time. From then on, Pisar become closely involved with the Olympic movement and Samaranch himself.

Pisar came out to Australia in April 1993 to give the Holocaust Address at the University of NSW, commemorating the 50th anniversary of the uprising of the Jewish ghetto in Warsaw. David Gonski arranged for me to attend. He gave a very moving speech. The defence of the ghetto in Warsaw is something that the Jewish people regard as one of the key events in the Holocaust because it was such an heroic battle. Afterwards, I was introduced to him. He was about five foot nine, balding, very elegantly dressed, a quiet, precise man. Pisar was a man of a few words. He talked slowly and deliberately. He seemed intrigued that I had come. I was not Jewish, of course, but I explained that I was interested in Judaism and had read a lot about what had happened to the Jewish people. I took along a friend of our family, Rosalind Reines, who was Jewish, and she was touched by the evening and was very pleased to meet Pisar.

I met Sam again a few days later in Premier Fahey's office, where we talked in some detail about our bid. He was a cautious man and very, very conservative, but he had an ear on everything. He said he thought Beijing was going to be very hard to beat.

Fahey got quite depressed about his verdict on Sydney's chances. I didn't, because I knew how we were going. Pisar may have been sceptical about our chances but he still retained an affection for his foster country. He never openly favored any city, but I came to regard him as a friend of our bid. He was always concerned that we understood what a huge task it would be to take on the might of the forces behind the Beijing bid. Maybe he appreciated the full extent of those more than we did— which was just as well.

Sam had a marvellous wife, Judith, a very striking woman. Judith really liked Deeta and they became friends. Deeta acts for Remy Martin in Australia and one of the Remy Martin family was on the board of the American Cultural Centre in Paris which Judith ran. This provided another connection with the Pisars. Pisar and David Gonski also talked a lot by phone.

Whenever I met him, Pisar would always tell me that the contest was going to be tough. And I would say, 'Sam, it's going to be all right.'

I never really knew what influence our friendship with Pisar had on the final decision. But I believed he helped us where he could. He certainly wasn't on our payroll and he never did anything improper, but he did give us cautious encouragement and advice. He was always very concerned for us and worried about me personally, because he felt the task was too great for us.

It was a wonderful association for me. If I had to count the ten most interesting people I met during the bid, Samuel Pisar would have to be one of them. And it was the Turnbull group which got us access to him. Our official strategy group hadn't even thought of him.

The Turnbull group also set up a meeting for me with Dan Colson. Colson was a Canadian lawyer who advised Canadian media baron, Conrad Black, and was a member of the board of the John Fairfax Group. Fairfax is one of the two big newspaper groups in Australia with publications including the *Sydney Morning Herald*, the *Age* in Melbourne, the *Australian Financial Review* and the *Sun-Herald*. Although he was based in London, Colson was still very well connected in Canadian business circles. He was a partner in a law firm with Dick Pound, one of the two IOC members in Canada and a member of the IOC executive.

In an indirect sense, the existence of a second 'strategy' group put a bit of ginger into our board. They made us re-examine ourselves and put us under a little more pressure to make sure we were doing all we could. Any board can become insulated at times. We had set out a strategy early on and the board met each month to see if that strategy was on track— which it generally was— but it didn't hurt us having another outside voice feeding in some different information, and asking us, 'Have you thought of this? Have you thought of that?' This was Australia's third bid to host an Olympic Games. If we failed this time, it would probably be the last for many years. There were no excuses for not doing everything we could; we had to check out every possible avenue of support. I never felt the Turnbull group was anything but well meaning— the task for me was to try to harness its strengths without causing too many problems with other people involved in the bid.

I saw Kerry Packer personally early on. Packer was a devoted Sydneysider and I think he really believes Sydney is the best city in the world. He said he would do anything he could to help the Games, and we did call on him several times. He and Ros hosted an important dinner party for Mario Vazquez Rana and lent us his two Sikorsky helicopters for the visit of the Evaluation Commission. And his television station, Channel 9, was very supportive all the way.

I also thought Rupert Murdoch, an influential ex-Australian with the highest level contacts around the world, might be able to help. Murdoch had helped fund the lavish garden party for the Brisbane bid at an IOC meeting in Berlin in 1985 which had rated a mention in *The Lords of The Rings*. A huge amount of Australian seafood, including Queensland mudcrabs and oysters, was flown in for the occasion. It was a big party, reputed to have been the biggest ever thrown by a city bidding to host an Olympic Games.

But in the Sydney bid, Murdoch took a much lower profile. I went to see Ken Cowley, who runs News Limited's operations in Australia. Ken said Rupert wanted Australia to have the Games but he was an international businessman and it was not in his interests to be seen to be supporting or opposing any city.

Murdoch had not made his big investment in Star television in Hong Kong then, but he was clearly interested in the region through his ownership of the *South China Morning Post*. Murdoch also had big interests in Britain with his newspapers and his interest in Sky satellite television. Ken said Rupert had lot of things happening around the world; he might help us privately but there would be no great song and dance about it.

Cowley asked what he could do to help. So I gave him a lot of briefing papers and the same difficult list of IOC members we had trouble reaching that we had given Jim Wolfensohn. He couldn't have been more charming.

I never did get to see Murdoch personally about the bid but I believe he helped us where he could. And Cowley went out of his way to be personally helpful.

There were the usual petty tensions as well. There were many functions in the life of the bid. A few of our wives (ours was a predominately male group) got left out of some events. It was nothing personal, just the perennial problem of having limited numbers— but they were unhappy about it and it spilled over into relations between some of the board members. Whenever I did guest lists, I always had to be very wary about who was included and who wasn't. Privately, I always thought that people should be bigger than to fight over whether they were invited to a dinner party or a cocktail party or not. Sometimes you wondered if people hadn't forgotten that our goal was to win the Games, not to be a source of social events. But it was all part of being the CEO.

Then towards the end of 1992, after Barcelona and the Acapulco meeting, there were more serious problems. There were a few stories appearing in the press with some critical references to me. Late in November, there was a story in the *Sydney Morning Herald* written by journalist Roy Masters which talked about the structure of the organisation which would run the Olympic Games if Sydney won. It talked about a meeting between John Fahey and John Coates the previous day. It mentioned that Nick Greiner would not be asked to be president of the Games organisation because they both felt that person should be apolitical. But the article also contained a comment about myself. It said:

> The new president, who may double as the chief executive, will have to straddle the Australian Olympic Committee, the organisation which will be awarded the Games, and the NSW Government which will be the principle source of funds. It is a task the current chief executive of the bid, Rod McGeoch, has found difficult.

It then quoted John Fahey as saying he would 'canvass nationally and internationally for the full-time executive' who would run the Games.

Before I read the article I had been told in a meeting about other matters, that Roy Masters had the benefit of a private briefing by Fahey and Coates the previous day. I knew it wasn't the first time such views about me had been rumored. Before the article I had been advised by several people that media speculation about me was damaging my reputation and the bid. But it was the first time the sentiments had been aired so frankly in public. I was upset. I decided it was time to take a stand. I didn't think I should do nothing and be criticised, even by inference, for things that weren't true. I was also worried that public speculation about who might head up the organising committee could damage the bid. The Olympic family likes continuity in the people they deal with in a city which is going to host a Games. Whatever was thought privately would happen if Sydney won, it was not a good idea to raise questions in the mind of the IOC at this point in the bid. I had little doubt that the senior people in the IOC would see the article as it has an excellent international monitoring service of any media coverage of anything to do with the Olympics.

So I wrote a letter of protest to John Fahey:

> You are aware of my views about the agendas and motives of some of the persons associated with this bid. You are also aware of my views regarding the reason some persons are pressing ahead with the details of the structure [of the committee to run the Games]. There has been no need at all in my view for the position of chief executive of the OCOG [the organising committee] to have been even discussed in the public domain. That it has, is most unfortunate for the bid and now, as it turns out, myself.

I noted that none of the views expressed in the article had ever been formally transmitted to me. Nor had they been raised at any board meeting. Then I went on:

> I am quite incensed at the manner in which people associated with this bid have allowed their own agenda and sensitivities to have allowed this situation to occur. I am even more incensed with being the subject of the kind of comment that was in the paper today. If it is your view that I am justified in my feelings, then at the very least, I would expect you to publicly correct the impression of Mr Masters as soon as possible.

But then I went an important step further:

> If it assists you in making such a decision, I would be prepared to give you whatever commitment you like in relation to the position of chief executive of the OCOG. In other words, I am prepared to provide an undertaking now that I am not a candidate for the position, if that is what it will take to remove this matter from the agenda and to have people assist me in dismissing the imputations that have arisen from the last few weeks.

When some of my staff read it, they asked if I was sure I wanted to include the final statement in the letter. I told them I did. I gave the letter to John Fahey at a function that day. I spoke to him later at the rugby at Waratah Park. He was very sympathetic and supportive. Bruce Baird also telephoned me. As usual, he was also very supportive.

We were coming into the most critical time of the bid, 1993, and it was just something I had to live through. But I did feel that it was important I take a stand. I knew what was going on behind the scenes. There were some people with their own reasons for wanting the issue of the possible chief executive of the organising committee to be debated at that stage. But I wasn't going to have press speculation undermine me or the bid. If those press comments had kept up, there would have been no need to debate the future chief executive of the OCOG because there wouldn't be one. I believe there are times when a chief executive has to roll with the punches and take critical public comment and live with unfavorable unsourced press stories. But when it starts undermining confidence in your own position and your organisation as a whole, it's time to take action. After I did, the leaks stopped and we all got on with business.

But it took a personal toll. I began to sleep badly. I developed a skin rash on my hand— the doctors said it was stress eczema—

which never quite went away. It had never happened before. It gradually went away after Monte Carlo.

But there was a greater goal and, in the end, we all had to rise above our differences. And we did. Everybody put their shoulder to the wheel and got the job done.

The only way you can deal with the inevitable personal tensions in such an exercise is keep reminding people of that greater goal, the main objective. You have to try to put the tensions down as a *de minimus* thing; to tell people not to worry and to get on with the job. But it often took a tremendous discipline to keep my temper and try and diffuse the tensions by talking about the greater goals.

In any business or in any major organisation, there will be people who don't get on or spouses that don't get on, but if you are the chief executive, you've got to make it work. It's like being the captain or the coach of a football team. There will always be differences between the players and debates about who should have been in the team and who shouldn't. But when you run onto the field and you've got to play the game, you've got to get on with each other.

You'd better.

Otherwise, you're going to get beaten.

And I had no intention of letting that happen.

13
Bell Lap

I just kept my eyes on the tape and went flat out.
Betty Cuthbert on her gold medal,
Melbourne Olympics, 1956

As 1992 neared its close, we came to the final critical lap of the bid. No-one rang a bell, but we all knew that we would be running flat out until the finish line in September 1993. Whatever the behind the scenes tensions, there was a huge amount of work to be done. There was the preparation of the bid books which had to be taken to Lausanne in February, visits by around 70 IOC members to Sydney, the inspection visit of the IOC Evaluation Commission in March, followed immediately by a trip to Atlanta for the annual meeting of the Association of Summer Olympic International Federations (ASOIF), then the visit by President Samaranch in May, an intense schedule of international travel for a final round of lobbying, the preparation for Monte Carlo and then the big week at Monte Carlo itself.

The most pressing task was getting the bid books done. Preparing the bid books — our plans for the venues and for staging the Olympics in 2000 — was one of the major tasks in our office from the beginning. As soon as we finished the budget for the bid itself, our business plan and our strategy plan, many people in our office did nothing else but work on this big project.

A lot of Bob Elphinston's time was spent supervising the selection of the designs for all the venues for the Games and all other aspects of the venues plan. We had already completed 18 venues for the preliminaries and the competition. The construction of the canoeing and rowing course at Penrith Lakes had started back in 1988 and was due to be ready in 1994. Work at Olympic Park had started in 1992 — including work on the

Sydney International Aquatic Centre and the Sydney International Athletic Centre. But we had to initiate and supervise the design of the 80 000 seat Olympic Stadium for ceremonies, athletics and the football finals, a 15 000 seat indoor sports and entertainment venue for artistic gymnastics, volleyball and handball finals, the Olympic baseball centre, the indoor velodrome for cycling and the athletes' village.

David Churches, head of our planning and design group, had been working on the Games planning with the government since the late 1980s, and handled a lot of this in conjunction with Bob. The detail was all being done in our office while we were pushing ahead with our lobbying campaign. Paul Clark also did a huge amount of work on the bid books. He handled all the writing of the chapters on ticketing and accreditation, security, health and transport.

After we came back from Barcelona, we incorporated some of the things we learned into our proposals. The biggest change we made was a shift from permanent to temporary seating in some of the venues. In Barcelona, Dick Pound from Canada had reminded us that we could use temporary seating. So we were able to review venues such as the proposed tennis centre to see where we could use temporary seating. All this helped save money. The athletes had also pointed out the need to have large stair wells in the housing for the athletes' village: someone had a heart attack in the Barelona Games and it had been difficult to get medical equipment up the stairs to their room.

The preparation of the budget for the Games was another major task. It was important for us to show the IOC we had a viable financial plan for the Games — that Sydney could genuinely afford it and the 2000 Games weren't going to be frustrated by any cash shortage after the IOC had made its decision. Far better for the IOC to make its assessment of a candidate city's budget at this stage, than to find a city that has run out of money a year or two before the Games were to begin. Although much had been done to prepare for a Sydney Games, it was also a good discipline on us to have to make up-to-date assessments on potential costs and revenues.

The budget was prepared by our Finance Commission, chaired by David Smithers. Our financial director, Bob Prater, did a lot of the work. Representatives from the commission went to

Atlanta and Barcelona to see how they had put together their budgets. There were several telephone conversations with Dick Pound. Pound was one of the experts in negotiating television rights for the IOC. Finance Commission members also went to Lausanne to check their numbers with the marketing people in the IOC, particularly Michael Payne.

David Smithers started off with an overall budget for everything connected with the Games — the cost of every new venue that would be used and the cost of all the modifications to the existing facilities to make them usable for the Olympics. If Sydney won the Games, there were about $400 million in new facilities that would have to be built in addition to the facilities already under construction. Then he said, 'Let's take out of the budget the cost of the permanent facilities that Sydney's going to have for the next 100 years and only leave the cost of converting existing facilities and the new facilities at Homebush Bay. That's what the Olympic Games budget ought to wear.'

We all agreed. If you have a facility like Darling Harbor, you don't expect to pay for it in one year. You have to look at it in the context of its useful life. Any company looking at investing in a fixed asset always assesses the cost over its useful life. Berlin was planning to use the stadium which was used for the 1936 Olympics in its proposals for the 2000 Games.

So we drew up a smaller budget for the organising committee of the Games and it was that which was included in the bid books. It included all the costs for rental of government-owned facilities, upgrading and fitting out facilities such as the athletes' village especially for the Games. We estimated this would cost about $127 million. This included a rental fee on the facilities built by the Olympic Construction Authority especially for the Games of 10 per cent of their gross construction cost.

On the revenue side, the biggest single source of income was to come from the television rights. The IOC controlled the negotiation of all the television rights with all the major broadcasters around the world. It was to keep 40 per cent of the total, passing on some of its share to the IFs and the NOCs. The host city would get 60 per cent.

Throughout the budget process, we took a conservative approach to the television revenues as we did with everything else. We estimated that the television rights to the 2000 Games would bring in $US 813 million worldwide in 1992 dollars, comprising $US368 million for the US rights and $US445 million for all other rights. The Sydney organising committee would receive $US488 million of this. (All the figures prepared for the IOC budgets had to be in US dollars.) Our total figure was only 30 per cent higher than the $US618 million received in television rights for the Barcelona Olympics. We figured that this was a cautious estimate given the fact that the revenue from the Barcelona Olympics was 55 per cent higher than from the Seoul Games.

The television revenues from the Olympics Games had risen substantially from Games to Games in recent times: $US1.6 million for Tokyo in 1964, $US9.7 million for Mexico in 1968, $US17.8 million for Munich in 1972, $US34.9 million for Montreal in 1976, $US88 million for Moscow in 1980, $US286 million for Los Angeles in 1984, $US399 million for Seoul and $US618 million for Barcelona. So budgeting for a 30 per cent increase on Barcelona, two Games and eight years before ours, was very conservative.

In our favor was the fact that the timing of events in Sydney would be suitable for prime time viewing in the US, and our Eastern Standard time zone was also favorable for viewers in Japan, Korea and other Asian regions. We also calculated that the price to be paid for an Olympics after 1992 should also rise as the summer and winter Olympics would no longer be staged in the same year, putting fewer budgetary constraints on the networks as they bid for each Games.

John Fahey took a very active interest in the preparation of the budget, vigilant about every item. He really drove the Finance Commission to get it right. There were many drafts. Fahey would reject things and say we weren't going to do this and that was too extravagant. We didn't know exactly what was driving him at the time, but from subsequent press reports it would appear that he may have been under pressure from the NSW Treasury. He never indicated that to us but he certainly asked lots of questions and challenged lots of figures and sent us back to the drawing board to put up more modest proposals throughout the whole process. We had a representative from the NSW Treasury, Ian Neale, on the Finance Commission who was part of all our deliberations and everything which emerged from its meetings was unanimous.

At one stage in late 1992, Fahey said if the numbers weren't going to work, Sydney would withdraw the bid. That would have been very difficult at that stage and would have had significant political repercussions — it was a mark of how serious he was about getting the numbers right.

But the whole process meant Sydney's budget for the Games income was the most conservative of all the bidding cities. Our estimate that Sydney would receive $US488 million from television rights was well less than the $US572 million which Berlin had put in its budget for television rights and Manchester's estimated $US600 million and just under Beijing's $US500 million estimate. We estimated that the Sydney Games would receive $US297 million from international and local sponsorship — far less than estimated by all the other cities. Berlin was looking at $US455 million, Manchester at $US478 million and Beijing was looking at substantial $US630 million!

In calculating our costs, we also included a contingency allowance of $US61 million to cater for any unexpected expense, the only city apart from Istanbul to do so.

Every line item in the budget had to be certified by the sub-committee that was responsible for it. When it was all done, David Smithers and I went up to Macquarie Street to brief Cabinet on it. I wondered what would happen in such a powerful environment. But when the Cabinet members came into the room they were friendly to me and all wanted to know how the bid was going. When it was all approved and finalised, our methodology for the figures was audited by accountants Price Waterhouse, the auditors for the IOC.

We estimated that the Sydney Organising Committee of the Olympic Games (or SOCOG) would make a profit of $US15 million from staging the Games. (*See table opposite for summary accounts.*)

Of course, this was the budget for *staging* the Games. It did not include all the cost of building the venues and it did not include the $A700 million for the construction of the athletes' and the media villages which were to be financed by the private sector.

All this was spelled out in some detail in our presentation to

Receipts	$US million (1992 dollars)
Fees from television rights	488
Australia's share of the income from the IOC's international sponsorship program, TOP	90
Local sponsorship	207
Coin marketing royalties	18
Licensing fees	33
Tickets	139
Total	975

Payments	
Events, ceremonies and programs	301
Construction reimbursements (for temporarily upgrading existing facilities, special fitout of athletes' village and officials' village, rental of government venues)	127
Media facilities and cost of being host broadcaster	187
Catering	8
Transport	46
Security	30
Medical	8
Olympic organisation	14
Administration personnel	48
Advertising and promotion	28
Other costs and contingencies	163
Total	960

Surplus	**$US15 mil**

the Evaluation Commission of the IOC by David Smithers when it visited Sydney. We had his presentation recorded and there was no secret about any of the figures. So I never understood how the budget suddenly became an issue after the Monte Carlo vote, with people alleging that we had somehow misled the IOC or the people of Australia.

Getting the bid books ready was to provide another lesson for me as chief executive. We had been working on them in earnest virtually from the beginning of the year and we thought we had it well in hand. But in about September, after we got back from Barcelona, when things should have been well underway, Bob and I got a bit of a shock — we found that things hadn't been moving along quite as well as we had expected. In retrospect, our mistake was not to take a more hands-on approach to the task in the first place.

Some draft documents for the books were sent to the Australian Olympic Committee without either Bob or I putting our official stamp on them. We just had not read them thoroughly enough. They were only draft documents — but they were not at the standard that either Bob or I would have wanted. And that sent red lights flashing. There were some harsh words from the AOC. Everyone was starting to send us in amendments to the documents.

Suddenly, the pressure was really on. We virtually had to start again. The timetables were slipping. Bob, John Coates and I realised we all had to step up our involvement. We decided we would have to sign off on every single word that was to be in the bid books.

We went through every chapter in detail. I was still travelling, so we were faxing things back and forth around the world. We were correcting things, reading them and correcting them again. But until we were all satisfied with it, it was not going to the printers. As chief executive, I was responsible for the quality of the work that would be published by the bid and I simply couldn't have bid books which set anything but the highest standards. In any organisation, paperwork and publications are something that the chief executive probably *shouldn't* ordinarily get too involved in. But, for us, the bid books were a very important exception. They were our major written statement to our customers, our most important sales document.

There was a lot of detail to check. We had to supply answers to all 23 'themes' and give details on every venue. John Coates also insisted that the details of every travel grant for every sport be included in the chapter on all 25 sports — as well as the general introduction. So, for example, if someone interested in rowing only read the rowing section, they would know how much we were offering to pay to bring their rowing shells to Sydney.

I agreed with the IOC's moves to cut down on the cost of the production of the bid books. In the past, candidate cities had gone to all sorts of extremes, binding them in expensive leather and putting them in cedar boxes, accompanied by electronic maps, compact disc and videos. We had to comply with the new rules — but there was no way we were going to be beaten on either the look or the content of our books.

ISIS/FHA Design, the design house based in Pyrmont headed by Simon Pemberton, had won the creative rights to design the books and they worked very closely with Silvana Griffin on them. And Silvana herself was also a wizard on the creative look of the books.

Even in the last stage, when we were at the printers with the proofs, we were fine tuning them. Silvana was actually taking corrected proofs from me, one by one, page by page, as I was working on them and handing them to the printer and saying, 'OK, print. OK, print.'

In the end, the bid books comprised three glossy volumes containing a total of 550 pages. The green-covered Volume 1 had general information about Sydney and Australia, customs and immigration, the weather, security, health and medical facilities and the environment. The red-covered Volume 2 was the big one with all the details and plans of the Games venues, the ceremonies, the Harbor of Life cultural program and the IOC session. The blue-colored Volume 3 had all the technical information about financing, media and telecommunications facilities, computer facilities and the legal aspects of the Games. The three volumes contained about half a million words and 1500 photographs. Melbourne had spent $1 million dollars on their bid books; we spent less, around $600,000. Atlanta had set a new standard for the bid books — but ours were better.

There was one small blow up afterwards — in the chapter on telecommunications. Telecom had played a large role in writing it and was also a big sponsor of both the AOC and our bid. In the last few days, between Christmas and New Year, Karen Lang, who had been working with Silvana, was selecting photos. She wanted some photos on communications. Telecom had submitted some but she didn't like them. She scurried around and found a wonderful photo of a satellite dish. But what we didn't realise was that it had 'Optus' — the name of Telecom's new rival — written right across the middle of it. It was one of those mistakes which happens in the heat of the moment. It didn't make one bit of difference to the IOC, but Telecom got very upset, complained to the premier and made a lot of noise. It was unfortunate, but in a huge production exercise like that, one or two minor slip ups were almost inevitable. We could live with them as long as they didn't affect the bid itself.

I saw the bid books prepared by the other candidate cities and the Sydney bid books were by far the best. We heard suggestions that Berlin complained that we used too many photos and broke the rules. But we didn't. There were a whole set of rules about this that only printers understand. Silvana understood them. It was a masterful piece of work.

At the end of it, I had never seen anyone as overworked as Silvana. I went to John Shirley, our office administrator, and said, 'This woman is going away for a couple of weeks. And I don't want any nonsense about leave forms. She's not losing it out of her holidays.' So off she went and had a well-earned break.

Australia Day, January 26 1993, saw Bruce Baird and I and 15 IOC members standing in the foyer of the new ANA Hotel in The Rocks. Because there were 15 of them, the ANA Hotel agreed to take them for nothing. The hotel had just opened and it was a prestigious thing to be doing. It was the biggest single gathering of IOC members in Sydney since the GAISF conference in September 1991. With the members and their accompanying persons and their visit officers, it became quite a large group.

It was a wonderful, sunny day and we were going to take them all on a harbor cruise on the famous old wooden steamboat the *Ena* to see the Australia Day Regatta. It was about 10 in the morning and we were all in our boating outfits.

Then my mobile phone went. It was *Ena*'s captain saying that the boat couldn't come, it had broken down. I said, 'Where are you?'

'We're about 10 minutes from our own the jetty and we're drifting back towards it.'

The *Ena* certainly wasn't going on any harbor cruise. And there I was, looking at a potential 15 votes and their accompanying persons.

I turned to Bruce Baird, the Minister for Transport, the

Minister for the Maritime Services Board, and gave him the mobile phone.

'Bruce, I don't know how you're going to do it, but I need a boat and I need it right now.' He got out this little green booklet that cabinet ministers carry with phone numbers in it. The Maritime Services Board harbor command vessel, a 55 foot cruiser, was out on the harbor with the entire board of the MSB enjoying the regatta. Baird got on the phone, 'I don't care what you do, get them off the boat. We want the boat right now.'

And so the entire board and their spouses were put off the boat at a public jetty. The boat came around and picked up the 15 IOC members and the rest of our party. By this time they knew that the original boat had broken down and they couldn't believe we had provided another one only a few minutes later. That was the kind of backup we had from the state government. And, as they say in the business books, there are no problems, only solutions and opportunities.

We had deliberately encouraged members to time their visits to Sydney to co-incide with the Australia Day celebrations. We realised that Australia Day could be a big occasion for us. It was always a big event for Sydney with lots of festivities. The weather was usually good and it was an excellent time to show off the city. John Valder was the chairman of the Australia Day Council. He had been making the point at board meetings saying, 'We can really make this a strong day for the bid as well.' So we massaged itineraries and worked hard to get as many members as possible in Sydney for the day.

In the end, 15 IOC members came. They included the powerful Dr Primo Nebiolo, long-time president of the International Amateur Athletic Federation; Willi Kaltschmitt from Guatemala who was a good supporter of the Sydney bid; Mohamed Zerguini from Algeria; Tony Bridge from Jamaica; Philippe Chatrier from France; General Gadir from the Sudan; Fidel Mendoza from Colombia; and my friend Mohamed Mzali, the member for Tunisia. Some brought their wives and some brought children. Kevan and Judy Gosper flew out from London to help.

The whole day was very impressive. It started out with the Australia Day ceremony at Tumbalong Park, Darling Harbor. All the IOC members were officially acknowledged, one after another. The announcer forgot Philippe Chatrier's name and I had to quickly get a note to him to make sure his name was read out.

We knew it was very important in trying to win an Olympic Games to be able to show that the citizens of the city supported the bid. And around Australia Day especially, it was very easy to do that. The city was sparkling with Sydney Olympics 2000 signs and street posters. We had a helicopter trailing a Sydney bid flag all over the sky.

The children from the 'twinning schools' were also involved. It was school holidays, of course. So instead of having the members go to the schools, we invited the schools which were twinned with the 15 IOC members to come to Government House to meet the members for afternoon tea. All the mums and dads and the kids came and spread out all over Government House lawn. The members were overwhelmed.

We were to have a fly over of F-111 fighter planes but it was cancelled because of some differences between the state and the federal governments. I didn't know the details. It was a shame, but it didn't really matter.

In the evening there was a State Reception at Darling Harbor. There was the most unbelievable fireworks display over the water I had ever seen. Centrepoint Tower was lit up so it looked like an Olympic torch. When that happened, John Fahey turned to me and said, 'If that doesn't impress them, nothing will.' It certainly did.

On another day, we took them to a spectacular sports show in the five halls at Darling Harbor. It was a wonderful thing for the members to see. Inside the halls, there was a full swimming pool, a basketball court and a volleyball court. There was mountain climbing and car rally races and a 60-metre indoor sprinting track and displays of sporting equipment. It was really done well. Kevan Gosper went through it and he was surprised at how good it was. We were able to tell the members that Darling Harbor was where we would be holding basketball, boxing, judo, table tennis and weightlifting if Sydney got the Games.

Some of the members decided to try out the rally cars which people could drive around one of the halls. I went in a four-wheel drive with Mohamed Zerguini from Algeria. It was such a tough course that I hit my head on the side of the door, driving round a corner. Zerguini said, in French, 'Same roads as Algeria.' And we both laughed.

About half way into our journey back from Darling Harbor by bus, I said, 'Well, ladies and gentlemen, have you seen any red lights yet?'

They hadn't.

'That's because we turn them all green when we want to. Watch.' With the co-operation of the police and the Oxford Street traffic control centre, we were able to turn every light green as we approached an intersection. There was never any traffic hold up anywhere. They thought it was hilarious, and laughed. We did it for all the IOC member visits. It was probably the only time in my life I could be guaranteed a clear run in the Sydney traffic. And, in their heart of hearts, everybody hates red lights.

We gave all the members a presentation about the bid. We got the specialists from the various committees to do their own briefings. It proved to be a very good rehearsal for the Evaluation Commission which was due to come to Sydney in five weeks' time.

The day after Australia Day, we took them out to Homebush to inspect the work at Sydney Olympic Park. Primo Nebiolo officially opened the Sydney International Athletic Centre there. Dr Nebiolo was gracious in his comments. Sydney, he told the *Sydney Morning Herald*, had a great chance to win the 2000 Games.

'What can I say? You have it all. One of the most beautiful cities in the world, a great spirit of the people and great projects.'

He made an important point. One of the keys to a successful Olympic Games was public support. And he could see that Sydney had it.

'I have found a great enthusiasm in the people that is very important. I see the people are very keen about these Games and I have found all the authorities are supportive. . . Sydney can organise a fantastic edition of the Games. You can have the best facilities, but the wishes of the people and the willingness is not so easy — but you have this.'

That day we learned the news that Tashkent had formally withdrawn from the race. This left seven cities.

The IOC visits involved a heavy round of entertainment by members of our lobby team. The IOC had banned lavish entertainment of members which I thought was a good idea. But it meant a lot of emphasis on more low-key entertainment, such as private dinners.

There were usually three nights of entertainment for a visiting IOC member — Bruce Baird's night, John Coates' night and mine. Baird lived at Wahroonga which was a fair way out of the city, so he did his entertaining at Bilson's Restaurant on Circular Quay, opposite the Opera House. Coates had six children so he usually did a harbor cruise. If there was a fourth night, it would usually be at The Opera House. Donald and Janet McDonald would look after them and take them to supper at the Bennelong Restaurant.

Deeta and I ended up doing most of the home entertaining. While my house isn't the grandest, I had always felt there was something special about having people in your own home. My father used to do it all the time. And my house was close to the city. So I never thought for a minute I was going to entertain anywhere but at my place.

At one stage, around Australia Day, Deeta and I counted that we had entertained every night for 30 nights in a row, many of them in our own home. In total, we entertained more than 60 IOC members in our home over the course of the bid.

Lindemans and Tullochs donated all the wines for the functions. If anyone was entertaining, Sue Bushby, our hospitality officer, would estimate how much was needed and make sure it was delivered to the appropriate venue.

There were some memorable nights. One night there was the Japanese member, Shun-Ichiro Okano, the Irish member, Kevin O'Flanagan, and four African members and their wives. Deeta was away and it was a big dinner party. We had Japanese music and Irish music.

I got Warren, the cartoonist from the *Daily Telegraph-Mirror* to come along. He was just sitting in the room, sketching people and giving the drawings to them. It was a bit of an experiment. He drew me smoking a big cigar, blowing out smoke in the shape of the Olympic rings. It was very funny. But the Africans had no idea that these things were supposed to be a bit of a joke. Warren did a cartoon of Rene Essomba from Cameroon. Rene had been a surgeon and was professor of medicine. He had a bald head and

Warren drew him with a solar panel in his head and a spear in one ear. When Rene looked at it, he said, 'Rod, is this really me?' And I thought, 'Oh, no. That's one vote gone.'

But we all had a great time. At about 10.30 pm the cars arrived to take them back to their hotel. But the music had started and things were going pretty well. Somebody got up to go and I said, 'You're not going now guys, let's get into it.' That was all the encouragement they needed. We drank two bottles of Cognac and smoked all the Monte Christo cigars I had in the house. I remember a visit officer — a girl called Christine — smoking a big number one Monte Christo. They all left at about three in the morning.

The trouble was that they all had to go on a harbor cruise the next day and everyone turned up a bit worse for wear. Coles and Gosper and everyone else was asking what the matter was. They all said, 'We were at Rod's place. It was the greatest party in the history of the Olympic movement.' Unfortunately, one of the women in the party got sea sick about five metres out from the jetty. And I thought, 'We've really done it now. That's another vote gone for sure.' But it really was a very funny night. It was the best party and they've never forgotten it.

Others also entertained people at their homes. Elizabeth Fox and her husband looked after a lot of the members from South America. Gough and Margaret Whitlam would always entertain the black African visitors, normally at the home of their son, Nick, and his wife, Judy. The Greiners entertained visitors from eastern Europe — and old Mr Greiner, Nick's father, was usually there as well. Renata Kaldor, the head of the NSW Government's Women's Advisory Council, was on the bid committee. She and her husband Andrew, who comes from Hungary, and were part of the Kaldor fabric making family, also helped out with entertaining eastern European members.

Kerry and Ros Packer hosted a dinner for Mario Vazquez Rana, the media magnate from Mexico. Ros Packer did all the organising. Rana seemed impressed that the Mouton Rothschild was flowing freely.

There was talk that we should be using grand homes overlooking Sydney harbor to entertain members. Many people volunteered to have members in their home. Sue Bushby inspected a lot of homes and talked to a lot of people, but in the end we didn't use a lot of harborside houses. We tried to match the interests of the IOC member with their potential hosts. Where a member was not comfortable in English, we looked for multilingual skills.

We also decided to approach Australian ethnic groups for some entertainment, a very successful strategy. The Indian community did a dinner for Ashwini Kumar at the Minar restaurant near Central Station, a great night. Kumar could not believe the way the Indians — Sikhs and Punjabis; Moslem, Hindu and Christian — all sat together, their traditional differences less obvious in the more relaxed, egalitarian Australian society.

The Arab League entertained Mohamed Mzali, Mohamed Zerguini and Bashir Mohamed Attarabulsi from Libya. Deeta came to the dinner for Mzali and Zerguini. We weren't allowed to drink alcohol. The women all had to sit separately.

The Chinese community looked after Ching-Kuo Wu from Taiwan (or 'Chinese Taipei' as it was officially called within the IOC) and Zhenliang He from the People's Republic. Henry Tsang, the deputy Lord Mayor of Sydney, hosted the dinner for Mr He. Of course we didn't expect to get his vote, but under IOC rules any member could visit any candidate city bidding for a Games. Mr He came to Sydney, just as Phil Coles and Kevan Gosper made their visits to Beijing as Australia's IOC members. With several rounds of voting expected, you couldn't take anything for granted. Who knows, Beijing might have dropped out in any early round and Mr He could have been in a position to give us his vote.

Sonya Lyneham from The Planning Workshop, and her husband Michael Bray, looked after Shagdarjav Magvan from Mongolia because she speaks Russian, and David Smithers entertained Nat Indrapana from Thailand at his home.

There was one person who helped us out looking after an IOC member who's name I will never know. Roque Munoz Pena from the Dominican Republic was set to arrive in Sydney one morning at 8am. But he changed his flight without telling us and arrived at 6am. Normally, we would go up into the cabin of the aircraft to greet them. I was overseas for this visit but his visit officer was set to meet the 8am plane. Somehow Roque got his luggage off the carousel and out into that melee of Sydney airport. The only problem was that he couldn't speak much English. All he was saying was, 'Rod. Olympics. Rod. Olympics.' A hire car driver at the airport twigged to what was going on, went over to Roque and asked could he help him. Roque kept saying, 'Rod. Olympics'. He said, 'You come with me.' The driver took Roque out to his car and got on the car phone and was eventually connected to my house where Deeta was sound asleep.

'I've got a man at the airport who seems to be looking for Rod,' he said.

'Oh, no. He's not coming until 8am,' said Deeta.

'Well, I've got news for you.'

That driver took Roque Munoz Pena into the Park Lane Hotel, got him into his room, fixed everything up and then went back to the airport. I still don't know who he was, but Roque never stopped telling everyone what friendly people there were in Sydney.

All the members were escorted throughout their stay by their own visit officer. The visit officers would pick the member up from the airport (Coles, Coates and I were usually there as well), make sure of their transport, help them with any additional tours they might want and generally escort them around Sydney. This meant some long days and a lot of weekend work for these people, most of them volunteers. Sergio Santander from Chile arrived at Sydney airport at 6 o'clock in the morning and didn't get back to his hotel until 5 am the next day because he went out dancing. The poor visit officer and the driver had to stay up all night!

When the members who had been to the GAISF conference in 1991 came back for their second visit to Sydney, we matched them up with the visit officers who had looked after them before. By that time they had exchanged a few Christmas cards and letters and some very good friendships were formed.

In some situations we found problems getting a suitable visit officer from the state government's volunteer program to match the needs of a particular member. So we started using the services of a small company which actually specialises in taking people around Sydney, called Sydney In Style. It was a wonderful little operation run by two women, Penny Wise and Kate Weir. They had access to a lot of people with many different languages and turned out to be a very helpful adjunct to our hospitality program. They came up with a young man of about 30 called Sean Burke who spoke Russian, Italian, French and Spanish. He became the hospitality officer for the visits of Vitaly Smirnov and his wife from Russia and Magvan from Mongolia. Later on, he came to Monte Carlo with us as a translator. Sydney In Style also found us Jane Delandro who spoke Spanish. She came to dinner at our house twice, because she was got on very well with the Spanish-speaking IOC members.

At first I was very sensitive about using a professional hospitality company. We had lots of offers from people to take people around Sydney. It sounds great but using too many untested volunteers could have its own problems. We needed to have people who really knew Sydney, had some experience in dealing with international visitors and a good grasp of foreign languages. With more than 100 international visits to host, it would have been a huge task to check out suitability and co-ordinate the large numbers of volunteers needed.

I cautioned Sue Bushby about using Sydney In Style too often. I thought they were great but I was concerned someone would object to us actually paying a hospitality company. But I was away a lot and Sue was a very determined woman. She continued to use them and I could understand why. They were an excellent company. They never missed a beat. Whenever they were needed, they were always there. And they seemed to be able to get access to people with a wider range of languages than we could with the government volunteer program.

It was a lesson. There are times when it really pays to use professionals. We had to have people for our hospitality service who were committed and willing to work all sorts of hours. If we'd insisted that they were all volunteers, we could not have guaranteed that they were all of the standard we needed. With so much at stake, we just could not afford to have anything go wrong.

Working with the NSW Protocol office and David O'Connor, we prepared a booklet for every visit by an IOC member, setting out their itinerary with all sorts of useful information about Sydney. It was the responsibility of each visit officer to produce it. They would come into Protocol's office about four or five days before the member was due to arrive and prepare it so they knew exactly what was going to happen. When they met the member at the airport, with Phil Coles, John Coates or me, they would give it to them straight away.

In planning the visits, we took great pains to find out what the individual members wanted and tried to show them something of special interest. One visitor liked zoos, so we took him to Taronga Park. Another liked judo so we arranged a visit to a judo school.

We took Magvan from Mongolia out to the zoo in Dubbo in the central-west of New South Wales which has a horse-breeding program where there were some Mongolian horses there that were actually extinct in Mongolia. So we got in touch with the Federal Government and plans were made to send some of these Mongolian horses back to their country of origin.

Someone discovered three of the IOC members were pilots. And that led to another brainstorm. We thought it would be a good idea to let them experience a flight simulator for a 747 jet. All three went out separately to the simulators at the Qantas base at Mascot Airport. Simulators are essentially an exercise in virtual reality, giving one the feeling of flying the plane without leaving the ground. What we didn't realise was that Qantas had had its own brainstorming session on how to impress the members. It had actually filmed all of Sydney's Olympic venues from the air. So when they 'flew' the Jumbo, they could see where all the events would be held. They went out over Darling Harbor, Homebush, and out to Penrith Lakes, where the rowing was to be held. They could see it all without moving from the simulator.

When Flor Isava from Venezuela came out with her grand daughter Alexandra she had just been in Beijing. She had a dreadful eye problem which had flared up again. When they got here we sent to her an eye specialist, who fixed it up in two seconds flat. We continued to send her medicines for it after she left — and she paid for them every time. She and Sue Bushby became particular friends and they corresponded after she went home. We knew that Flor was a very well read woman so we invited author Bryce Courtenay to a dinner for her during her visit to Sydney. Bryce autographed a copy of his book, *The Power of One* for her and it made an enormous impact. She was particularly intrigued about his descriptions of boxing and felt she understood boxing much better after she read it. When I went to visit her in Venezuela, later in the year, she asked me to bring a copy of the video of the movie and a copy of Bryce's subsequent book, *Tandia*.

Of course we were trying to win their friendship and their vote. But we also wanted to show them the high standard of technical competence Australia had in a wide range of areas; that Sydney had a resourceful, well supported and efficiently run bid which could cater for all the interests and personal needs of people from all over the world. In other words, what we would have to do on a much grander scale if we were hosting the Olympics.

But there was no doubt that they did get the red carpet treatment around Sydney. Take a night at the opera. Any one of us mere mortals who are late for the opera know you can never get in until the end of the first act. But at one stage we had three or four IOC members who were late for the opera through no fault of their own. So Donald McDonald, who proved to be a tremendous asset to our campaign, just said, 'The opera doesn't start till they get here.' And it didn't. One IOC member's wife was caught in the powder room at interval. The Opera House manager came up to McDonald and said, 'Look. This show has got to start.' But McDonald said, 'Until Mrs K is in her seat, this show doesn't resume.' And it didn't.

In my early days in the bid, I heard all sorts of rumors about IOC member visits and what might be expected of us as hosts. There was one story about the bid for the 1996 Games, about an IOC member visiting Toronto. The member had complained that his wife had lost a very expensive piece of jewelry in their hotel. The Toronto bid people immediately called in the Mounties and, after some questioning, the complaint was dropped. No-one really knew what had happened, but the piece was never found.

Once, an IOC member who had just visited Sydney called me and said his wife had lost a valuable earring. I must confess I was a bit worried at first. I wondered whether we would be asked to pay for it. We searched high and low everywhere they had been and — sure enough — we found the earring on the floor of a car. It was duly returned to her.

There was only one other occasion when I was asked for

anything even vaguely unusual by an IOC member. I was having breakfast with some members in a hotel at the IAAF meeting in Stuttgart, in the last few weeks of the bid. Another member, who was standing at the door, called me over and gave me a piece of paper. When I went back to my hotel room I read it. It was a small list of items — two bottles of whisky, six cartons of Kent cigarettes and some medicine for a diabetic child. I suspected that the member could not get the medicine in his own country. But it was nothing. Cigarettes and whisky were the kind of things we often took to members when we visited them, much the same as guest would take on a special visit.

In the whole bid, despite the inferences of the dumped Berlin bid files, I was never asked to comprise myself, never asked for big gifts, money, drugs, favors, sexual partners, or influence. Nor did I hear of such requests made to others. Not once.

In all my time in the bid, people just didn't give any expensive presents, nor did anyone even vaguely suggest we do so. Sure, we would go out of our way to find that small special thing that a member would like such as a tape of a rugby game or a Bryce Courtenay novel, but it was nothing more than the kind of thing anyone would do would do for a good friend.

No sooner were the Australia Day visits over than I was on a plane to Lausanne with Geoff Henke from the AOC to formally deliver the bid books. I had an awful fear I would be late. I wasn't. But sometimes you get that dreadful feeling before important events that something might go wrong.

By this time, media interest in the bid was really starting to step up. We held a press conference on our departure to mark the occasion. At it, I described our books as, 'the most comprehensive analysis of why Sydney is the best city in the world to host the Olympic Games. Until now, the bid is only something that we've talked about. This book represents our application.' The television crews actually filmed me putting the books in a case and getting on the plane.

When I got to Lausanne, I gave a little speech and the books we had worked so hard and so long to produce, were handed over. After it was over, there was a lunch to mark the occasion, a very modest repast in the IOC staff canteen. I was to be seated on President Samaranch's right and Bob Scott from Manchester on his left. It was the first time that the president had really recognised me as the leader of the Sydney bid.

Throughout the campaign, there was always a bit of competition about who was sitting where. I remember as I stood at my seat, waiting for the president, Bob Scott said, 'How come you've got a seat like that there?'

'Bob, you're on the other side of me. It's not as though I'm getting ahead of you at all.'

Bob never seemed to miss an opportunity to take a shot at the Sydney bid. He would say we were 'the bid that peaked too soon', or that we were 'the glamor bid' with no substance, and Sydney was 'too far away'. I thought it was a bit silly. Phil Coles would often say, 'Just let him go because he's only hurting himself. People aren't impressed by that.' Despite all the times he would have a go at us, I only ticked Bob off once during the bid, when I went to Damascus for the Arab Games. I got there two days before the opening ceremony. I was there with Mahmoud Elfarnawani, our lobbyist for the Arab countries. There weren't too many IOC members, but Prince Faisal of Saudi Arabia and Sheikh Fahad from Kuwait were there.

I had extremely good meetings with them. I had become very close to the Egyptian community and people in its Olympic movement, and they were helping me get to know some influential people in the region.

Bob blew in, virtually on the morning of the opening ceremony. He couldn't believe I was there. I think he thought he was going to have it all to himself. He asked: who was there? What was happening? So I told him that Sheikh Fahad was there and gave the room number, and Prince Faisal was in the Sheraton and that he was leaving soon. Bob and I went down to say hello to him before he left.

When he got back to Manchester, Bob was quoted as saying that he was the only bid city that had been at the Games. So I wrote a letter to the Manchester newspaper and said, 'He must have a bad memory or something, because I was there two days before him. Sydney was certainly there.' And then I wrote to Bob and told him I didn't think he should have done that. He wrote back to say he had been misquoted.

But Bob was a really great impresario, a fine and colorful

character. But he had great pressure on him. It was Manchester's second bid and he wasn't getting the kind of support from his IOC members that we had. And he was always having to battle with the widely held view that it was a Sydney-Beijing battle. So he always had to say things to keep up his team's morale. We were always a good target.

Despite Bob's remarks, I enjoyed the lunch and had a good, long discussion with President Samaranch. It was obvious he was beginning to work out who was who.

The next big hurdle was the visit of the IOC's Evaluation Commission in early March. The commission was made up of 11 men and two support staff led by Gunnar Ericsson, the IOC member from Sweden. I had met Ericsson, a member of the IOC executive, several times before. Grey-haired, 73 year-old, a former Swedish politician, he was always immaculately dressed and extremely courteous. He was an experienced hand at the job, having been chairman of the Evaluation Commissions for the previous two Olympic bids.

The commission included five IOC members, three heads of international sporting federations (swimming, weightlifting and basketball) and three heads of NOCs. Its purpose was to check out all the facilities Sydney was proposing to use for the Games and look at technical aspects of our bid. In part, the Evaluation Commission's role was to check out the *truth* of what candidate cities had put in their bid books.

In many ways it was one of the most important official visits we were to have during the campaign. We always felt the technical side of our bid was superior to the other candidate cities, but we had to make sure the commission members were properly briefed and reached the same conclusion.

We started preparing months before. John Landy, the famous Australian miler, had been very involved in the Evaluation Commission visit to Melbourne in 1990. So, in November 1992, we brought Landy to Sydney and asked him to talk to all the people who would be involved in the visit — the health service, the police, the head of security, the transport people and the financial people. We asked him to tell us what it was like. How much detail did the committee want? How thorough were their inspections? He was a great help. He reassured us that they would not be checking every venue seat and every hospital bed. He agreed with our suggestion that it would be a good idea if the medical briefing were done at Westmead Hospital, which was to be the Olympic hospital, rather than in our office. And he gave us all sorts of other tips.

Bob Elphinston and I got very involved in the preparation for the visit. We knew there would be 11 people plus a couple of IOC staffers. When you added that to our people, it was going to be quite a team to move around Sydney and all the venues over the five days. So we asked Kerry Packer if we could have a loan of his two big Sikorsky helicopters. No problem.

Sydney was the first city to be inspected. That was good because the members would be fresh to absorb all the details of our plans. Kevan Gosper flew out again from London to help. We gave them a three-hour briefing on the Sydney plan in our office. I spoke to them about how we ran the bid, our relationships with the Olympic family, our Olympic programs and how everything came together. Bob had all the technical information on venues. Donald McDonald and Ric Birch spoke to them about the cultural program. Ewan Waterman, from the Federal Treasury, talked about the outlook for the Australian economy and David Smithers did our financial presentation.

We knew that the environment was becoming an important issue with the IOC and our relations with Greenpeace were developing well. So we got Karla Bell from Greenpeace to do the presentation on the environmental aspects of the bid. She praised the environmental sensitivities in the design of the athletes' village and the other facilities, and the environmental guidelines we had developed for our plan. It was pretty hard to beat that.

We knew the state of Australia's industrial relations would also be an issue. The commission was well aware of Australia's poor history of industrial disputes. This had all changed in recent years but a bad reputation often sticks long after it is no longer justified. There had been the threat of a general strike in NSW just before the GAISF conference in September 1991. Although it was headed off, there was enough publicity for the IOC to learn about it. And around the Australia Day visits, when we had the 15 members here, there was a baggage handlers' dispute which affected one member who had flown to Melbourne afterwards.

We were a little nervous about these incidents, so we asked Michael Easson of the NSW Labour Council, and a member of our Bid Committee, to give a presentation for us. He told them the union movement supported the bid and its position had been approved at the senior levels of its organisational structure. He told them that the union members working on the construction site at Homebush had contributed to the bid from their pay packets.

Then he made a very telling point:

'Gentlemen, just remember, the Australian union movement supported the Australian team going to the Moscow Olympics in 1980. The Federal Government wanted us to boycott the Games and the union movement said that we were for the athletes, we were for the Olympic Games. On no occasion has the Australian union movement ever supported a boycott.' Easson got some questions but they weren't aggressive. He did a wonderful job. After that industrial relations was not an issue.

We did the health presentation at Westmead Hospital while we were out west, touring the venues. We zoomed into Westmead by helicopter and our entire Health Care Committee, including Dr Daniel Stiel, the chairman, and Dr Bernie Amos, the director general of the NSW Department of Health, were there. They gave a memorable presentation with slides and a film about the quality of Sydney's water and our hospitals and the structure of our health system. They also talked about what plans we had for medical facilities at the athletes' village and the venues. The briefing on our plans for security at the Games was done at police headquarters by Assistant Police Commissioner John Garvey.

And of course whenever we drove around Sydney, we always turned the traffic lights green. We told them what we were doing and they laughed.

We took them on a bus trip out to Sydney Olympic Park. Francisco Elizalde, the IOC member in the Philippines, who was a member of the Commission, used a stopwatch to time the trip. Our bid documents had said it could be done in 24 minutes. We did it in 22 minutes! And this without fixing the traffic lights. Elizalde was impressed. It confirmed that we had not been inflating our promises in the bid books.

We showed them the Sydney Football Stadium, the Entertainment Centre and the exhibition halls and the Convention Centre at Darling Harbor. They did a helicopter trip over the venues, from Sydney Harbor to Penrith Lakes, Eastern Creek and out to the Royal National Park.

The trip involved one very memorable stop off.

John and Ashley Dawson-Daimer had a country property near Camden. It was on our way from the rowing venue at Penrith Lakes to the Royal National Park where the road cycling races would be held. They invited us to stop off there for lunch. Ashley Dawson-Daimer had magnificent rose gardens with hundreds of plants. Unbeknown to us, Henry Adefope, the IOC member from Nigeria who was with us, just loved roses. You couldn't have had a more wonderful coincidence. These two big choppers settled down on their lawn, we got out and he was in the middle of a magnificent rose garden. He started talking roses with Ashley and had a great time.

We had a very simple lunch of cool drinks and sandwiches in their lovely old home. Then Dawson-Daimer asked if anyone would like to see his racing cars. When we walked down to the machine shed, we found out he had 11 Lotuses! (One had been driven by the famous Jim Clark.) They all got in them and we took photos of all the IOC members in 'their' racing cars. It was something they all remembered. Whenever I saw them later, they mentioned those cars.

We'd got the message that there were to be no parties and that the visit was to be very low key. But we did have to eat: we had a dinner on the 31st floor of the State Office Block, a great view of Sydney, and Premier Fahey and Gunnar Ericsson made a few remarks.

They all stayed at The Regent Hotel. Ted Wright, the manager of The Regent, even put private fax machines in their rooms. Richard Carrion, one of the IOC members on the commission, had flown in from Puerto Rico. He was president and chief executive of the Banco Popular de Puerto Rico. Carrion came to see me the day after he arrived and said, 'I just want you to know how much I appreciated the fax in my room. I just had my bank's monthly figures faxed to straight to my room. I couldn't be happier.'

A few days into their trip, the commission members got a surprise visit. The Prime Minister popped in to see them. It was election time and Keating's office telephoned and asked if we would like him to come. Of course we did! Keating saw them at The Regent. The rooms have a great view of the harbor, it was a beautiful day outside and we could see Circular Quay. All our Sydney 2000 banners were flying in the breeze. Keating said, 'I suppose you've seen Sydney out there — the life and everything?'

They had.

'Well, Beijing is no fun city, but of course their crowd control is better than ours.'

It was taken in good spirits. The Prime Minister spoke about the strength of the economy and the importance of our ties with the Asia-Pacific region. He told them if there was a change of government, the Opposition leader, John Hewson, would stick to everything the federal government had said about the Olympics. He was very worldly and above party politics. He was there as Australia's leader to commit the country to the Games and he was terrific. They really appreciated him coming.

The five days went off pretty much without a hitch and the team moved on to Beijing. Not only did we have the advantage of being the first city they saw, when they were all still fresh, but all 11 members were present. After Beijing, I gather, some members dropped out which disappointed some cities. But it is a big call to ask that many busy people to travel around the world together on the same days.

But they had all been very tight lipped. We would hear of their verdict in July, not before.

We put the commission members on the 11 am flight to Beijing on 5 March, and got on the 5 o'clock flight that afternoon to Argentina. We had to give a bid-city presentation to the Pan-American Sports Organisation (PASO) meeting at Mar Del Plata, on the coast. We stayed in an old hotel there which I don't think had been touched up since it was built in the 1930s. It was an important meeting for us to attend. There were 19 IOC members in the Americas and most of them would be there.

It was also another opportunity for presentations. Because of the conventions of bidding, none of us could stand up and say that Sydney was the best place to have an Olympics. But someone had the bright idea of getting a child to say it. So in the video for our Mar del Plata presentation, we used a child's voice, saying, 'My Mum and Dad say we will have the best Games in 2000.' There were tears here and there in the audience and everyone said it was fantastic.

Whenever we travelled, we always brought home everything we could from our rival bids — tee-shirts, brochures, knick-knacks, whatever — so we could show it to our creative team. Time was ticking by and our team needed to know exactly what we were up against out in the field. We often took a guy from the Public Works Department called Bernie Ward, an expert on computers and electrical equipment. I called him Bernie the Gadget Man after Joe the Gadget Man on television years ago. Whenever bid cities had to make presentations, Bernie would film everybody else's presentations.

We were watching the other presentations at Mar de la Plata. Bernie had everything set up on remote control. Normally he would just set it, walk away, sit down and watch from another part of the room. But this particular room was crowded and I asked Bernie if everything was all right. Bob Scott, who was standing near me, said, 'What are you doing, Rod?'

'We always video everyone's performance, Bob.'

'That's your trouble, McGeoch. You always know what the rest of us are doing.'

He meant it cuttingly, but I thought it was the *least* we could do. With everyone starting to think about their presentations for Monte Carlo in September, why wouldn't we be studying our opponents closely? It was so easy to videotape it all so everyone on our team could see it when we got home. Manchester or anyone else could have done it too. It was all part of evaluating your opponents and trying to learn from them at the same time. We weren't trying to be smart. Just well organised and professional. I don't think anyone should have to apologise for that.

After the PASO meeting we flew north to Atlanta for the annual meeting of the Association of Summer Olympic International Federations (ASOIF) which was held in conjunction with a meeting of the IOC executive board. Acapulco November 1992 had been the meeting of the NOCs of each country. The Atlanta ASOIF meeting was for the association of international bodies of the 25 sports in the summer Olympics.

This was in the period after the bid books had been presented to the IOC in Lausanne but before they were distributed to the members. There was a rule that you couldn't make any new commitments for the Games after your bid books were presented to the IOC. But we had a window of opportunity to surprise the Olympic community by announcing something that *was* in the books, but unread as yet.

In our books, we had included an offer to pay for the freight of all the equipment needed for the athletes — all the horses, canoes, rowing shells, yachts and kayaks. It would cost us a total of $7 million (or $US5 million), but we hadn't publicly announced it.

And Atlanta was just the place to do it. Just as we had told the NOCs they would not have to pay for their athletes to come to a Sydney Games, we would be telling the heads of the individual sports that they would not have to pay to bring their equipment. We said to the Equestrian Federation we would pay for all the horses, the Rowing Federation that we would pay to bring out their shells and so on.

In addition to all this, we had also put in our budget a smaller allocation to meet some of the cost of federations who might want to hold their meetings in Sydney in the seven years between the decision and the Olympics. We announced that at the ASOIF conference as well.

I had to leave early to get back to Sydney, so John Coates and Bruce Baird made the presentation. When they announced our two generous offers, it sounded very impressive. None of the other bidders had anything like it and the news was a pleasant surprise for most.

The whole thing was timed to be delivered to the right audience. Again, as we did in Acapulco, we printed a special color edition of *The Sydney Spirit* newspaper and it gave it out to everyone as soon as we had spoken. It had a lot of impact and was extremely effective. And no-one else could match it later because they had not included it in their bid books.

After the meeting, John Coates had a brush with the Germans. They accused Sydney of trying to buy the Games. This was ironic because we had always thought that Germany, one of the most powerful economies in the world, could easily outspend our bid. But they were really upset because we were leading the initiatives of the bid cities all the way. Again, it was something that they could have done too. But we were the only bid who had thought through the concerns of the different organisations in the Olympic family and were prepared to pay the funds to make it easier for them to come to a Sydney Games.

The IOC meeting in Atlanta confirmed what had been expected ever since Birmingham — votes for candidate cities would be kept secret during each round, the aim being to stop sympathy voting in the early rounds for candidates which did not have high quality bids. It was a good thing for us. It would mean IOC members who were serious about supporting Sydney would have to give Sydney their vote from the start, not to some other city with a less impressive bid just to give them some encouragement for next time.

I had to brave a blizzard in Atlanta to get back to Sydney to meet IOC members in town for the World Youth Football Championships. I thought I'd never get out of the place. The visiting members included the powerful Joao Havelange, the IOC member from Brazil who was president of the International Federation of Football Associations (FIFA). The championships were a major event in the football world. With the IOC studying Australia's capacity to host the Games, our handling of such an event would be watched closely at this critical time. We expected worldwide publicity and it was a great opportunity to show off Sydney. Our office worked closely with the Australian Soccer Federation and sponsors Coca-Cola, to have an outstanding opening ceremony and provide VIP treatment to all the FIFA people and the IOC members. We even went to the extent of finding short films about Australia and Sydney in particular which could be shown on television if there was a break. Before and after each match, at half-time, during injury time viewers around the world saw what a great place Australia was. SBS had the world television rights and were very co-operative. A lot of people said the 1993 World Youth Football Championships were the best ever. And it showed off some of our best football facilities to sports officials around the world.

March saw another small but important development. Milan withdrew. This effectively freed up the votes of the three Italian delegates — Giorgio de Stefani, a life member who was 89, Franco Carraro and Primo Nebiolo, head of the IAAF. They all would have had to support an Italian candidate in the early rounds. Now they could make an independent choice. We always thought that European members would support us against Beijing. This just made it that little bit easier.

The people from the Milan bid were great people but they clearly didn't have anything like the quality of our bid and the venues in place. I never thought they were going to win — despite talk that IOC members' spouses would not have minded shopping in Milan — but the reduction in the number of competing cities was good for us as it meant the votes were not going to be scattered around so much.

(Sadly, Giorgio de Stefani died before the vote in Monte Carlo. He was a wonderful man who had fond memories of Australia. He spent his honeymoon in Melbourne and I had counted him as a Sydney supporter.)

At the time, British betting house Ladbrokes had Sydney 4–7 odds on to win; Beijing 2–1; Berlin 7–1; Manchester 9–1; Istanbul 14–1 and Brasilia 33–1.

By the time of the Youth Football Championships most of the IOC members had made their visits to Sydney, although a few came later. Of the 90 or so IOC members 77 visited during the campaign — not counting the 21 or so that had already come for the GAISF conference in 1991 and others who had come out for other sporting events over the two years.

One of the last visits, in April, provided one of the most emotional moments for us in the life of the bid, that of 73-year-old Jan Staubo from Norway and his wife.

Staubo had been a Spitfire pilot in World War 2. He was shot down by the Germans and held in the notorious Stalag Luft 3 prisoner-of-war camp. The prison later became famous for some of its successful and not so successful escapes through a series of underground tunnels. Australian journalist Paul Brickhill wrote *Escape to Danger* and *The Great Escape* based on interviews with many of its prisoners. Had there had been any Australian POWs in the camp with him? We asked the RSL to advertise. There were 17! They included Sir Rupert Steele, a former chairman of the Victorian Racing Club. We brought them all to Sydney for Staubo's visit for a re-union.

They gathered in the boardroom of our office an hour before the meeting with Staubo. In Anzac Day ceremonies, servicemen meet according to their units, not what prison camp they were in. They hadn't seen each other for 45 years. Most of them wept. It was the most emotional reunion I had have ever seen. I was humbled by the stark intensity of it.

One was cartoonist Bill Fordyce, whose drawings in the camp were preserved and given to the Australian War Memorial Museum in Canberra. The museum lent us his book and Kodak reproduced it perfectly and bound it in leather to give to Staubo. The re-union and presentation was to take place in Victoria Barracks in Paddington. Staubo didn't know how it was going to work. He had a walking stick. He was still carrying two bullets in his body (he had to walk around the metal detector at the airport).

At the barracks, they all wept again. They lined up, single file to meet Staubo. They were an unlikely lot to help you win an Olympics Games bid, but they were real Anzacs. Bill Fordyce was about fifth in line.

'Remember me?' asked Fordyce.

'No.'

'Well, you ought to. Your bloody tunnel fell in on me twice!'

Staubo has never forgotten that day. He told me it was probably the most 'significant' day he had ever had in the Olympic movement. He wrote me a beautiful letter afterwards and made me promise to come and see him again in Norway.

I did. Gladly.

14

The China Syndrome

How, you may ask, can the Games be denied to Beijing and the world's most populous country? Sydney, Manchester and others will try to provide the answer to that.

David Miller, Olympic Revolution, *1992*

David Miller, Olympic correspondent for *The Times* of London and President Samaranch's official biographer, summed up the race for the 2000 Games in his 1992 book, *Olympic Revolution*: 'How, you may ask, can the Games be denied to Beijing and the world's most populous country? Sydney, Manchester and others will try to provide the answer to that.' The onus was on Beijing's rivals to prove why it should *not* get the Games, or at least why their bids outweighed Beijing's inherent lead, rather than on Beijing to show why it *should* get the Games, like everyone else. Miller's comments summed up much of the conventional wisdom which seemed to be developing in support of Beijing. China had more people than anyone else in the world, therefore its capital, Beijing, should get the Games — almost by sheer weight of numbers.

Forget about the fact that China had not been an active participant in the Olympic movement for a large part of the century. Forget about the fact that it was not exactly known as one of the great sports-loving nations of the world. Forget about what it would be like for the athletes to compete in the heat and dust of a Beijing summer. Forget about the problems any ordinary foreign tourist in Beijing faced with hotels and transport. Forget about the lack of English, French or Spanish or any other foreign language. And forget about Tienanmen Square and human rights in China. If the country with the most people in the world suddenly decided that it wanted to host an Olympic Games, then it should be allowed to go to the top of the queue.

Of course there was a logic to it if one could translate people into dollars. Many people could not see past the purchasing power of more than a billion potential customers, all supposedly buying Cokes, eating Mars bars and using Visa cards and Brother typewriters and Ricoh faxes or whatever. But the billion people-can't-be-wrong school never seemed to give the Olympic ideals a second's thought. The cynical view of the almightly power of the dollar in the modern Olympic movement had been fed by works such as *The Lords of The Rings*. I never believed it.

In the bid for the 1996 Games, there had been a clear view from the top of the IOC that, for historical reasons, it would be a great idea if Athens staged the Centenary Games. In that contest, it *was* up to Atlanta, Melbourne and the other cities to show why they could do it better. In the bid for the 2000 Games there was no quasi-official favorite; no-one had a break. But the Beijing bid did begin to develop a momentum of its own during the campaign, and we began to feel people were using different standards to judge the merits of its bid.

Of course we knew from the beginning Beijing was the city to beat. In 1990 the Baird Report named Beijing as the serious competitor. And so did a lot of other members of the Olympic movement. It was in Birmingham in June 1991 that Vitaly Smirnov, the IOC member from Russia, had made his pronouncement to me about this being the battle of the giants, Sydney versus Beijing.

The other two cities we watched with some seriousness were Berlin and Manchester.

Berlin had also been mentioned in the Baird report as a serious contender but as the campaign progressed, our initial fear of Berlin, in spite of its substantial financial backing, fell away. They clearly did not have widespread public support and lacked effective lobbying. Their best asset was their second bid leader, Axel Nawrocki. But he hardly ever travelled; we could never work out why. Their campaign was beset with all sorts of problems from protesters to the discovery of the files on IOC members. The IOC's move to tighten up on gifts and lavish parties also helped put Sydney on a more equal basis when it came to competing with a country with more economic power like Germany.

We felt Manchester could not be ignored. This was the second time the city was bidding — and the third time running for

Britain. After us, they were the most effective lobbyists — particularly with the European members. Bob Scott was a wonderful guy even if he seemed to come on a little too strong at times. The Manchester bid was always battling with the image of being a rather dowdy city with a campaign which never seemed exactly flush with funds.

What we had thought in 1991 began to become widespread in the various arms of the Olympic family by 1992 — Beijing bid was the one to watch.

The strange thing was that it was hard to put a finger on exactly why we and so many others felt this. Only one country, Ecuador, came out publicly early on in the campaign and said they were voting for Beijing. (In fact the comment came from the president of the Ecuadorian Olympic Committee who was not an IOC member). The Hong Kong Olympic Committee came out early in 1993 and supported the Chinese bid — but that country did not even have an IOC member. Throughout the campaign, it was hard to find many members who would come out and say they were going to vote for Beijing.

On the road, Beijing had very friendly people. Their IOC member, Zhenliang He, was fluent in French and English and charming. But when it came to lobbying, their team didn't seem to have that kind of assured internationalist style which was necessary to strike up relationships with IOC members — and their spouses — across the range, from the Latin Americans to the Africans to the Europeans. We kept hearing messages that the Beijing team was entertaining heavily at Chinese restaurants around town whenever there was an IOC meeting or a gathering of candidate cities. But we never saw any of it. This may have been partly due to the fact that the Beijing members were often allowed VIP access, by virtue of their positions as senior government officials, that our team couldn't get. But if they had been as active as the rumor suggested, I would have thought we would have bumped into them more often.

There were also rumors and press speculation that the big Olympic sponsors wanted to have the Games in Beijing because of the marketing potential of more than a billion consumers. But when we talked to big sponsors like Coca-Cola, we saw no evidence of this.

There was some suggestion that the Beijing bid had strong

support from the Latin American countries. The Brasilia team itself had publicly talked of swapping preferences with Beijing. There were also suggestions that third-world countries, particularly those in Africa, which had received foreign aid from China might be under pressure to vote for Beijing. Joao Havelange, the IOC member from Brazil who was head of FIFA, was meant to have wanted Beijing to get the 2000 Olympics to make it easier for him to achieve his goal of having the 2002 World Cup soccer finals in Tokyo; if China didn't win the right to host the 2000 Olympics, it could well have been a rival for Tokyo to stage the 2002 World Cup. There were suggestions that the African members had been promised an extra qualifying team in the World Cup if they voted for Beijing, suggestions too that Havelange wanted to support Beijing for the 2000 Games so that Beijing would support another Brazilian bid for the 2004 Games. Havelange was very influential in South America and, of course, football was important within the IOC, representing about 20 votes. There may have been something in all that.

Like any good marketer, we did a lot of homework on our major competitor.

In the early days of the bid Ken Baxter from the NSW Premier's Department and I flew down to Canberra and saw the China desk in the Department of Foreign Affairs and Trade. We wanted to learn about the country and understand the Australia-China relationship. A very plain signal was sent at that meeting: Australia had a very close relationship with China and that was more important than any Olympic Games bid. I thought this could prove to be interesting later on.

The bid office collected all sorts of newspaper clippings and other information about the Beijing bid. We did it with all the cities — but far more so with Beijing. Melissa Petherbridge, our librarian, put together a formidable collection of data.

As the campaign went on, the Olympic media, including David Miller, were increasingly speculating that Beijing was a strong candidate. There was clearly a fascination with China as an emerging economic superpower and the idea of the Middle Kingdom opening up to the rest of the world, but there was surprisingly little analysis given to how it would actually stage an Olympic Games.

In any normal business or sales campaign, part of the game is to keep stressing the advantages of your product and — to varying degrees — point out the shortcomings of your competitors. There was no doubt in my mind that our bid was better than Beijing's; that Sydney would provide a far better environment for athletes to perform at their best and a far more enjoyable place for spectators.

But bidding for an Olympic Games is a very discreet affair with all sorts of long-standing conventions. One of the strongest was that you did not publicly criticise your opponents. One had to subtly point out one's own strengths and leave it to others to conclude how well you shaped up compared to your rivals. Comparative advertising — in any of its forms — was just not on.

We often discussed the Beijing bid in our strategy committee meetings. Of course, there were the natural competitive juices running about one's most serious competitor — the fierce pride in one's own product and the great desire to tell the world how we were better. But what irked me the most was that Beijing's push seemed to be developing without any real assessment in the market of the facts. There wasn't any open and critical discussion about the true situation in China, its technical capacity to host an Olympic Games and the serious issue of how its record on human rights sat with the Olympic Charter. We felt we were playing the game with one hand tied behind our back; the playing field wasn't level; the rules of the game seemed to be easier for them. We didn't want to criticise China — we couldn't anyway — but there was a growing concern that the truth about China was never going to come out.

If Beijing were to host the Games in 2000, it would have to invest heavily in upgrading the infrastructure of the city. There were many reports that the Asian Games in Beijing in 1990 had been poorly run. Hosting the Olympics in Beijing would be even more difficult. The city had big problems: a shortage of international standard hospitals, roads and transport facilities; a severe shortage of five-star international-class hotels; few world class health and medical facilities; anyone that didn't speak Mandarin or Cantonese found it extremely difficult to get around; poor drinking water; dreadful pollution; airport a shambles . . . It was not as if it was *impossible* for Beijing to stage the Games in the year 2000, but what would have been the financial and human cost of the investment in infrastructure needed to get it there? Sydney was there now.

There are many factors involved in the decision about who should be awarded an Olympic Games, but when it comes to judging the technical competence of a city to hold the Games, I believe the decision should be made on which city is better placed to hold the Games based on the information available at the time — not on what might happen between then and the Games. Sydney could easily show the IOC a sophisticated infrastructure — roads, hotels, computerisation, telecommunications, medical and health facilities of world class standards. We didn't have to get there.

There were other questions too. Having been a lawyer for 20 years, I may have had a more acute sensitivity about human rights than some others. The Olympic Charter had lofty ideals about 'encouraging the establishment of a peaceful society concerned with the preservation of human dignity', 'respect for universal fundamental human principles' and encouraging a 'spirit of friendship, solidarity and fair-play'. I believed in them. They were why I felt so strongly about the Olympic Games and what a positive force Olympism was for the world. But the more I studied China, the more I felt that China's approach to human rights was an anathema to the Olympic ideal. After the killings in Tiananmen Square in 1989 thousands of people were imprisoned without a hint of a trial or right of hearing. There were many other reports of arbitrary imprisonment and exceutions. I formed a very strong intellectual view: it was wrong for China to get the Games.

But the argument gained currency during the bid that a Chinese Games would open up the world's biggest economy, allow better world trade prospects, create more jobs and put pressure on Beijing to improve its human rights position. Beijing's theme, A More Open China Awaits the Year 2000, hinted at reform. There was the parallel argument that having the Games in 1988 had been good for reform in South Korea. But the political situation in Korea was a far cry from that in China. And in any event, it seemed to me that Beijing should make its changes *before* it is awarded the Games. You don't give a city the Games in the *hope* that it will make big changes.

Giving Adolf Hitler the Games in 1936 didn't do much to

change the way he ran Germany. Berlin won the right to host the Games in 1932 under the old Weimar Republic, a democratic government. But Hitler came in and manipulated the Games for his own advantage. The athletes' village was built with signs saying, NO JEWS, NO DOGS. The Olympic movement fought him all the way, but, in the end, the Games were turned into a propaganda exercise for Hitler.

I thought the world's perspective on China getting the Games was all out of kilter. Everyone seemed to be swallowing the More Open China line — the greater economic prospects, the wouldn't-it-be wonderful dream — and ignoring the reality of the system and the plight of a lot of its people.

But, of course, I couldn't say anything.

The Chinese themselves were very sensitive about anything in the press that could be seen as a criticism. At one stage author Bryce Courtenay wrote a very pointed article in the *Australian* newspaper saying why Sydney should be preferred over Beijing. There were some other strong articles in the Australian press and letters to the editor criticising Beijing. Ross Turnbull, the Sydney businessman who led my 'other' strategy group, also wrote a letter that appeared in *The Times* of London, unfavourably comparing Beijing to Sydney. The Chinese complained about it to Kevan Gosper. They said it was not fair and asked if the Sydney bid team was behind it. We weren't. But Kevan was quick to pass on their concerns to us. In retrospect, I wonder if it wasn't very good tactics on their part to object so strongly to these articles, as a way of heading off any more serious criticism.

People kept asking me what we were going to do about Beijing's momentum. Peter Montgomery in a strategy committee meeting said what a masterful campaign they were running: how Beijing had got to be the favorite when by all the external criteria they had no right to be there; how everyone somehow accepted that they could stage the Games; and how everything would turn out fine.

There was a growing belief that we really might need to do something, despite the straightjacket of the convention. So I decided that we should do some more analysis of the Beijing bid, at least.

Around the middle of 1992 I engaged a woman called Gabrielle Melville to help me. The year before, Gabrielle had just missed out on Susan Hunt's job as head of communications for the bid office. Very able, very bright, she was an international communications strategist who had worked for a number of Australia's largest blue-chip companies. I gave her the task of getting on top of the whole Beijing issue. We gave her all the papers we had collected on China and the Beijing bid and I spent many hours with her talking through what I thought were its weak points. I asked her to do a complete review of everything, analyse what the Chinese were doing, work out what their strategies were and what counter measures we should consider.

Over the next few months she prepared a detailed paper covering a wide range of issues associated with the Beijing bid which I presented to the strategy committee.

The paper talked about political problems. Potential political instability. Questions about the future of Hong Kong after 1997. What might happen after the death of Deng Xiaoping? Would there be another Tiananmen-style response to political dissent? Details of the human rights problems. The leadership's poor record in handling any kind of dissent.

Gabrielle noted that China was high on the list of Amnesty International's most consistent offenders on a whole range of human rights issues. In 1991, according to Amnesty, there were 1600 death sentences passed and another 1000 official executions. The unofficial figures were estimated to be much higher. There was a concern that if China was awarded the Games, they could be used internally for propaganda, as an international endorsement of its regime.

There was also the question about the nature of China's commitment to the Olympic Games. The issue of the representation of Taiwan has always been a sensitive one for the Olympic movement which has tried — more than most other international institutions — to balance the interests of both sides. In his book, *Olympic Politics*, published in 1992, British academic, Christopher R Hill says the first Chinese IOC member was elected in 1922. China sent one athlete to the Los Angeles Games of 1932, 54 to the Berlin Games of 1936 and 26 to the London Games of 1948. But after the Communist takeover of the mainland in 1949, the issue of which 'China' was to attend the Games became a serious problem which the Olympic movement wrestled with for the next three decades. In 1951, according to Hill's research, most members of China's National Olympic Committee fled to Taiwan where they continued to be recognised. The Taiwan-based Chinese continued to take part in the Games as the 'Republic of China'.

The IOC has an official rule that it only recognises one NOC per country and that only countries with a NOC can participate in the Games. In the lead up to the Helsinki Games in 1952, the IOC effectively broke its own rule when it decided that both 'Chinas' could participate in the Games, although only the NOC in Taiwan would be officially recognised. Only one athlete from the Peoples' Republic of China turned up at Helsinki and none from Taiwan. In 1954 the IOC finally recognised the NOC of the People's Republic of China, while maintaining its recognition of Taiwan's. The PRC boycotted the Melbourne Games of 1956 in protest at the fact that Taiwan was allowed to remain in the Olympic movement. In 1958 the PRC withdrew from the Olympic movement and all the international sporting federations. Its IOC member, Shou Ti-tung, resigned with an angry letter dubbing IOC president Avery Brundage 'a faithful menial of US imperialists'.

By the early 1970s, things changed. In 1971 the United Nations recognised the PRC and expelled Taiwan. In December 1972 Australia become one of the first Western countries to officially recognise the regime in Beijing. As the western world began to shift towards recognising mainland China, the IOC officially resolved that the PRC should be encouraged back into the Olympic movement — but, unlike the UN, it made it clear that it would not be expelling Taiwan. The mainland Chinese began to rejoin the international federations and return to the Olympic movement but the 'two Chinas' issue was still a difficult one for the IOC, which worked hard to keep both countries onside.

In 1970 the IOC elected a Taiwanese member, Dr Henry Hsu. But in 1976 in Montreal the Taiwanese team left the city the day before the Games began because of complications over the Canadian Government's One China policy. In 1979 the IOC made another move to bring the PRC back into the official Olympic movement, recognising its NOC as *the* Chinese Olympic

Committee. It ruled that athletes from both countries should be allowed to compete in the Games, but under different names. This followed a recommendation in 1978 by Juan Antonio Samaranch, then a member of the IOC executive, that the IOC should do everything in it powers to allow the PRC to be recognised.

From then on, the PRC became an active member of the Olympic family. The country sent a team to the winter Olympics at Lake Placid in the US in 1980. Both China's boycotted Moscow in 1980 but, in 1981, Zhenliang He was elected as the PRC's IOC member. In the 1984 Olympics in Los Angeles the PRC resumed its participation in the summer Olympics with a team of more than 350 competitors.

Mr He became a member of the IOC executive board in 1985 and was made a vice president in 1989. In September 1989 the Chinese Olympic Committee announced that Beijing was a candidate for the Olympic Games of the year 2000. But Taiwan still remains part of the Olympic movement. The IOC still has a member in what it calls 'Chinese Taipei', Ching Kuo-Wu, and Taiwan continues to have its own officially recognised NOC.

Gabrielle Melville's paper noted that support for Olympic sports had only been a relatively recent interest of the communist regime. In the past individual competitive sports had been derided by the communist regime as being ideologically unsound, another example of 'bourgeois liberalism'. It was only in the last 15 years or so that attitudes began to change and the importance of doing well in international sport and the idea of China's staging an Olympic Games began to interest the powers in Beijing.

By the time it lodged its formal bid for the 2000 Olympics, the regime was building them up as the highest international accolade a country could be given. In 1978 Deng had outlined a 20-year plan to modernise the economy and transform China into one of the world's superpowers. Staging the Games in 2000 would be the crowning symbol of international acknowledgment of his success.

Melville's paper noted the infrastructure and organisational problems that had arisen in the Asian Games in September 1990. The organisers had underestimated the cost and time needed for the construction and had to scramble to get the facilities completed. They were a financial disaster, losing from $US60 to $US100 million and the Chinese had shown little understanding of how to handle sponsors. The standard of judging was low, transport and air conditioning was poor, and there had to be a big crackdown on crime and violence before the Games.

Beijing would also have to address its pollution and potential health problems. During the autumn, when the Games would be staged, strong northerly winds blow and cause heavy dust storms. There was a risk of sinus and bronchial problems as athletes were trying to perform at their physical peak.

The Beijing of the early 1990s was already struggling with infrastructure problems — crowded roads, an over-stretched airport, rats and open sewers and an inadequate medical system. What would it be like in 2000 when its population was expected to grow by another 9 million to 23 million?

The facilities which Beijing was putting forward as venues for the Olympics begged questions. While there were plenty of training venues, many of the facilities mentioned seemed too small for full scale competition. And there looked to be particular difficulties in staging yachting and equestrian events.

The paper concluded that China was capable of staging the Games in 2000, but that the cost of the investment needed to bring its infrastructure up to standard would put an enormous strain on its economy and could push more urgent issues such as political and economic reform lower down on the agenda. 'To award the XXVII Games to China would be premature: the country has more urgent national priorities if it is to have a long term, sustainable growth. It lacks economic and political stability, is internationally unacceptable in terms of human rights policies and lacks the loyalty and commitment to sport which is the hallmark of the Olympic family. . . Placing additional financial constraints and international faith in the current Chinese government, and by implication, endorsing the methods they must use to ensure the staging of the Games, will raise serious questions regarding the motives of the IOC in managing their task.'

Gabrielle suggested a number of ways the Sydney bid could try to counter the push from China. The most feasible, in protocol terms, was her recommendation of a public relations campaign with the objective being: 'to illustrate how the awarding of the

Games to Beijing would be a gross betrayal of the ideals of the Olympic charter'.

The paper surprised the strategy committee in its detail. Peter Montgomery wrote to congratulate me and its author (who was then anonymous) on such a cogent overview.

We used the paper to plan how we would go about executing such a strategy. Gabrielle argued strongly that we should only push for the truth to come out; we did not want to bash Beijing; we just wanted to make sure the correct information came out.

It was a sensitive issue of handling. We wanted a public relations campaign to air and debate some of these issues but not one sourced back to the Sydney bid. Ideally, it would operate out of another city, such as London or New York. We had to create a strategy which looked like it came from somewhere else and had nothing to do with us.

The Turnbull group introduced me to Sir Tim Bell, an Australian-born public relations expert living in London. Tim had been the chief executive of advertising agency Saatchi & Saatchi in London, had advised Margaret Thatcher on her three election victories and received a knighthood from her. He had since established his own firm, Lowe Bell Communications. Bell kept up his contact with Australia and often came to Sydney for Christmas holidays. He handled the public relations for Freehill Hollingdale and Page when the Australian law firm opened its London office. Kim Santow, who had been an important part of the Turnbull 'strategy' group, went over to become the firm's London partner.

I met Bell in London in late 1992 and talked about the possibility of him handling a China campaign for us. Gabrielle then went to London to talk about the Beijing strategy, get it organised and work with Tim Bell's firm on it. Bell was going to be my private weapon. He was going to set up a campaign that could not be sourced back to Australia. There were strict instructions that the public relations company we eventually appointed to help with our European lobbying were not to know about it.

Part of the campaign was to fund a human rights group based in London to speak out about China issues. It was to culminate in a book being written about China, *The So-called Suitable*

Candidate, which would be released about a month before Monte Carlo. It was to have been produced by the London-based organisation but we would mastermind it with Tim in London. It would have nothing to do with Australia. It was imperative that the campaign be a subtle one. If people felt there was a force out there trying to kick heads, it would be assumed that it was another bid city doing it and could have rebounded on us.

Tim came to Sydney a few times and we talked more about the strategy and the budget for it. Figures between $50,000 and $500,000 started to be mentioned.

At the same time, we were moving ahead on other fronts. We made a direct pitch to the other countries in our region to support us.

We asked Paul Keating to write to the leaders of the countries in the South Pacific, asking support. He agreed and letters were sent out in early 1993.

John Valder also had plans for us to seek support in South-East Asia. John had been the prime mover in generating interest and financial support in New Zealand, arguing that an Olympic Games in Sydney would have spinoffs for that country. Following his success there, he was keen to do something similar with the South-East Asian countries. We felt we shouldn't allow the Chinese to assume that all the countries in the region would back them. There were some obvious advantages for these countries in Sydney winning. People travelling to Sydney for the Games from Europe or even the US could well stop over in Bangkok, Hong Kong or Singapore for a few days on the way there or back. If China got the Games, there would be little real spin off for these countries. They had more to gain with a Sydney win.

We were also a little disturbed when the chairman of the Commonwealth Games Federation, 'Sonny' de Sales of Hong Kong, came out in February 1993, saying he supported Beijing's bid for the Games. De Sales' comments were published on the front page of the *South China Morning Post* where he also promised to argue the case for Beijing to the 13 IOC members who would pass through Hong Kong on the way to the East Asian Games in Shanghai in May. The article also suggested Hong Kong officials were hopeful the city would be awarded one or two sports — possibly soccer and equestrian events — if Beijing were to host the 2000 Games.

De Sales had been in our office on a visit to Sydney. He was very helpful and I liked him. We were surprised at his comments, given his role as head of the Commonwealth Games Federation. There were 16 IOC votes in the Commonwealth. In a sense, Manchester's and Sydney's bids could be seen as constituent members of that association. Kevan Gosper spoke to him about it and he quickly said he was speaking in his capacity as president of the Hong Kong Olympic Committee. But we still thought it was a little strange for a person in his position to be making such a public endorsement of the Beijing bid.

While John Valder was considering what we could do in the region, Peter Wills, the chairman of Sydney-based property company CRI Limited, telephoned to suggest we should be doing more in South-East Asia. CRI is a property developer which has specialised in major building and infrastructure projects and has done work in Asia. He was supported by Charles Curran, a Sydney lawyer and businessman. Curran was on the board of QBE Insurance which has a growing business in Asia. They were both particularly keen to help us in the region.

I had a series of meetings with them and asked Mark Jackson to work with them in developing some ideas. They wanted to create a Friends of Sydney group in the region. This would involve holding some lunches and dinners in Hong Kong, Singapore and Bangkok to try to get influential people to commit themselves to Sydney rather than Beijing, arguing that there was more in it for these countries if we won.

Wills and Curran decided that the seven-a-side rugby tournament in Hong Kong in March would be a good event to target. (An extraordinary number of English-speaking companies from around the world have board meetings in Hong Kong around the time of the Sevens' tournament! All the major accounting firms suddenly seemed to have a partners' meeting there.) It was a very fertile time to appeal to people with a significant commercial influence in the region. And because the Sevens is a major international sporting event, sports journalists from around the world would be there too.

I flew up there, armed with press kits and all sorts of Sydney 2000 gear. The Australian High Commissioner gave a cocktail

party for me and I made a short speech. Wills and Curran gave
an impressive dinner for the Sydney bid at the Grand Hyatt
which was attended by some pretty high powered people there.
Nick Greiner, who was in Hong Kong for a board meeting of
QBE Insurance, came along to the dinner and was very helpful.

The morning after the dinner — before the tournament
started — I gave a full press conference at the High
Commissioner's office. I gave out our press kits and other
information about the Sydney bid. It was very successful and
there was quite a lot of television coverage.

At no stage did I make any criticism of de Sales' position. That
was up to him. I acknowledged Beijing was our biggest competitor and argued that there would be more benefits for the other
countries of the region if we won. But I also argued that, at the
least, everyone in our region should agree that it was time the
Games came back to the Asia-Pacific region and that it should
not go back to Europe again in 2000.

As for the rugby itself, I found it disappointing. I'm a rugby
fanatic but I found the Sevens tournament half-baked. My work
there was done and I was lonely. I had an exhausting schedule of
international travel ahead of me for the rest of the year so I didn't
even stay for the finals. We weren't able to do much more in
South-East Asia. Time was running against us.

Maybe we did have some effect — even if it was only to
remind Beijing that it couldn't take it for granted that it had the
support of other Asian nations. Later on in the bid, there were
more substantial reports that China was talking to Hong Kong
and Taiwan about the possibility of having some events in their
countries. It was always going to be difficult to stage the yachting
near Beijing but there were good facilities in Hong Kong. When
we heard these reports we were very pleased as we thought it
would help our bid. There is a strong emphasis in the Olympic
Charter on the athletes' village as a place where competitors from
around the world can meet and, hopefully, form friendships. The
IOC members don't like having several athletes' villages either;
they see the Games as a time to get together with their colleagues. One of the big attractions of our plan was the centrality
of the events and the athletes' village. Under our plan, it would
be the first time that the athletes could actually walk to most
events from their village. I don't think this talk helped Beijing's

strategy at all — but they may well have thought it was a way to garner more support from Taiwan and the South-East Asian region.

The media speculated that the major sponsors were in favor of a Beijing Olympics because of the potential to appeal to a market of more than a billion people. It was written that Coca-Cola in particular wanted to have a Beijing Games. It was an argument I never really bought, but it gained currency, so we checked it out.

We saw Dean Wills, the chief executive of Coca-Cola Amatil in Australia, and asked him if he could make sure that Coca-Cola in the US played the game down the middle. He said, 'You've got to be joking. Of course, it's going down the middle.' A US vice-president of Coca-Cola gave a letter to Bruce Baird saying that the company would not be favoring any country for the Games. What most of those peddling the line that Coca-Cola would push for Beijing didn't seem to understand was that Coca-Cola already had 13 bottling plants in China and was already widely known throughout the country. Coke had been in China before the Communist takeover in 1949 when its bottling plants were nationalised. In 1978, only days before the US Government 'normalised' its relations with Beijing, the company reached an agreement to re-enter the Chinese market. In 1992 it sold 73 million cases of soft drink in the country. There was no special marketing advantage for Coke to have the games in Beijing. Coke didn't need an Olympic Games in China to let the Chinese people know about its product. There was also the potential of offending franchisees if it favored one country against another. Most Coca-Cola bottling plants around the world are franchised, not directly owned by the US parent. In Australia Coca-Cola Amatil is half owned by Coca-Cola in the US and has the local franchises, a very important link in the product's international marketing chain. CCA had pushed very aggressively into South-East Asia and eastern Europe, where it controls a significant number of Coke franchises. It would have been be a very game company that favored one franchisee over another. Coca-Cola Bottlers in Sydney, one of the biggest franchisees in Australia, was a major supporter of our bid, donating $250,000 to our campaign. Dean Wills would have been most upset if he believed that Sydney lost the Games as a result of some unfair pressure from Coke in the US. It just wasn't logical.

I also discussed the issue with senior officials from the company I met at the opening of the Olympic Museum in Lausanne in June. Coca-Cola was a major sponsor of the museum and we were all there for several days. Gary Hite, the head of marketing for Coca-Cola worldwide, asked to have a meeting with me there and he flatly rejected any suggestions that his company was backing any city in this contest. The company has its headquarters in Atlanta and there had been a lot of ill-informed press speculation that it had used its financial muscle to help that city get the 1996 Games. It didn't want to go through the same thing again in the run up to the decision on the 2000 Games. I made a point of explaining Coke's position at a press conference later. The company told me that they really appreciated the way I defended them and were grateful that I had been prepared to take a public stand when there had been so much inaccurate speculation about their position.

There was also an argument that the US television networks — a key source of funding for the IOC and the Games — also wanted the 2000 Games to be held in Beijing for similar reasons — of somehow appealing to a market of a billion people. Through the Turnbull group, and with the help of Jim Wolfensohn, we got access to top levels of the US networks. Graham Lovett also spoke to his contacts in international television. The television executives were surprised we were trying to lobby them; surprised that we thought they may have some influence over the IOC or the decision; surprised that we even asked them. They said, 'Why are you worrying? It's obvious we would want the Games to be in Australia for technical reasons.'

The Beijing campaign was discussed in some detail in our strategy committee meetings in late 1992 and early 1993 but not at board level. But in the first quarter of 1993, the board started to push me, complaining that we didn't seem to be doing anything about China, asking what I was going to do about it. Until then I had felt that the quiet campaign we had planned to come out of London was the sort of thing the board might not want to know about. But as they were pushing me about it, I told them we had a paper prepared on China and that we were working on a China strategy. They should leave it to us.

Half an hour later, Dick Humphry and Ron Brown from the Premier's office phoned, saying, 'What is this paper all about? Have you got a paper that's going to destroy the entire Australia-China relationship?'

'If you people don't want to know, don't ask.'

I calmed things down a bit. But in the course of some meetings, I told Kevan Gosper about it. He didn't know about it because he was not on the strategy committee and was based in London. He got concerned, became quite involved, spoke to Premier Fahey and argued that we shouldn't be doing it. Too risky — if it ever came out it would destroy the Sydney bid.

Eventually the board passed a resolution to stop me. John Coates amended it to make it very broad, very clear. I was not allowed to become involved in any public relations exercise on the China bid in any shape or form.

I got very firm at the meeting because I didn't agree with them. I argued that we had millions of dollars in corporate money riding on our performance. Our supporters all wanted us to win. All we were doing was trying to get the truth out about our opponent. If they knew, I would have thought that most of corporate Australia would have said, 'Go on. Give it everything you've got. We want to win.' I told the board it was tying one arm behind my back, 'Look out if we lose, because if there's one or two votes in it, we'll all have to bear the responsibility of not doing everything we could.'

They argued that some of the information on China was already coming out, so we didn't need to worry.

Not long after that board meeting, I went to a meeting in Nick Greiner's office in Macquarie Street with the Turnbull group which included Kim Santow, Ross Turnbull and Geoff Levy. The group had been a strong supporter of the idea of the Beijing project and they had been expecting me to come from the meeting with specific instructions to go ahead with a campaign. After all the talk, they were hoping that things would finally start happening. But instead I had to tell them that we were not allowed to do it. They were surprised. I explained to them that we had a pretty forceful debate about it at the meeting but I could go no further. It couldn't be done.

'What do you mean, it can't be done?'

'I can't do it. My hands are tied. The document will never come out of the safe.'

It was fortunate that Nick Greiner was there. Nick backed me up and said, 'Forget it. It's not going to happen.'

They were amazed but they accepted it. They didn't try to encourage me to do any private deals. They just said, 'If that's that, forget it. Let's get on with it and try to win votes some other way.'

Around the same time human rights organisations made statements on China's human rights record and the US Congress took up the issue. Groups such as the US-based Human Rights Watch and the International Campaign for Tibet were arguing that China should not be allowed to host the Games. In June a foreign affairs subcommittee of the US House of Representatives passed a resolution 'strongly opposing' Beijing getting the 2000 Games and urging the US IOC member, Anita DeFrantz, to vote against Beijing. The motion quoted a 1992 State Department report on human rights which claimed that the Chinese Government's 'human rights practices have remained repressive, falling far short of international norms', and referred to the persistence of 'torture and degrading treatment of detained and imprisoned persons' and the suppression of Tibetans and their culture. 'Holding the Olympics Games in countries. . . which engage in massive violations of human rights serves to shift the focus from the high ideals behind the Olympic tradition and is counterproductive for the Olympic movement.'

Then US Senator Bill Bradley, an Olympic gold medallist in basketball, wrote to President Samaranch expressing 'strong opposition to awarding the Games to Beijing while its government denies fundamental human rights to its citizens'.

The problem was, this action began to generate its own reactions within the Olympic movement. The Olympic Charter specifically declares that its members will not accept any interference from governments on their freedom of action or their voting decisions. The IOC had always been very active in defending its own independence from any government. As the issue began to gain momentum in Congress, an anti-US mood began to develop in some sections of the IOC. The IOC felt compelled to assert its independence from any attempts at political interference. Rumors started to circulate about a possible Chinese boycott of the Atlanta Games in retaliation for the actions of Congress.

In late June 1993, at a press conference at the opening of the IOC museum, Kevan Gosper, in his capacity as an IOC executive vice-president, spoke out against the attacks on Beijing and raised the issue of a possible boycott. 'This is interference,' he said. 'It takes us back 13 years to the Carter boycott [Moscow, 1980] when the movement was almost brought down. Let's say Beijing is not successful in winning the bid and feels it's because of this US campaign. How does Beijing feel then about Atlanta? The worst case is that you go back to the 1980 syndrome.'

President Samaranch was upset that anyone would even hint at a boycott in public. His first experience of organising an Olympic Games was dominated by the tensions over the Soviet boycott of the Los Angeles Games. Barcelona was the first time since 1960 that not one of the 172 member nations had withdrawn for political reasons. At the end of the session in Lausanne, he made the first of many statements, appealing to the US Congress to stay out of it. 'We are very sensitive to public opinion, but we must be free from political pressure. We respect all the other international institutions, but, please, I will ask these institutions to respect the independence and autonomy of the IOC. The issue of human rights is one of many factors each member will consider. For some, a poor human rights record will be a reason not to vote for a country. For others, it could work the other way. They may consider that the experience could help to open up a country and change many things the way it did in Seoul in 1988.'

But his comments did not stop the US Congress from pushing ahead. In July the House of Representatives voted overwhelmingly to oppose the Beijing bid and in August 60 Senators wrote a letter to all IOC members urging them to reject Beijing. Giving Beijing the 2000 Olympics, the letter said, 'would confer upon China's leaders a stamp of approval by the international community which they clearly do not deserve. The propaganda value for the current regime would be enormous, China's democracy activists would be demoralised and the image of the IOC would suffer as it worked closely with an authoritarian government to stage an event televised around the world.'

Further moves by Congress also re-inforced the determination within the IOC that it should not be pressured by any government in its deliberations, particularly not a superpower. Anita DeFrantz, who was always very concerned about human rights, was upset that her government was publicly telling her how to vote.

We began to worry that the anti-China push would have the contrary effect, actually generate sympathy for Beijing. We were particularly worried that it would polarise the Latin American vote in favor of Beijing. The Latin Americans have always been sensitive about anything that could be seen as the US throwing its weight around.

On the Saturday before the vote, SBS Television aired a documentary about China by reporter Jane Hutcheon. It quoted a Chinese official saying that it may consider a boycott of Atlanta if China did not get the 2000 Games. It became an issue early on at Monte Carlo until the Chinese delegation gave an undertaking that they would not boycott Atlanta.

So we didn't get any joy. The anti-US feeling also strengthened the argument of people in Sydney who didn't want to do an anti-China campaign.

With the benefit of hindsight, the anti-Beijing strategy probably proved to be unnecessary and the opponents of our proposed strategy could argue that they were vindicated by the hostile reaction to the moves of the US Congress. In the months leading up to the vote just enough emerged about the true situation in China. Not a lot — but just enough.

Had the board not stopped me, I would have had no doubts or qualms about going ahead with our strategy. I didn't know we were going to win at that stage. I thought we had a good chance — but until the final vote was cast, no-one could be sure. We were in the final stage of the campaign and we needed to throw everything into the fire. The strategy I had envisaged was only ever going to bring out the truth.

It was frustrating that we had put a lot of effort into something that never saw the light of day. But at no stage in our three-year campaign did the Sydney bid ever — directly or indirectly —

instigate or become involved in anti-Beijing activity. Nothing happened.

In a way, the exercise is an important lesson on the importance of the wise counsel of a board in an organisation. As chief executive, I was passionately committed to achieving our goal of winning the Games for Sydney. It dominated my whole existence for almost three years. It was my responsibility to look at every possible — legitimate — means of turning our goal into a reality. I was angry that our competitors seemed to be able to get away with things that no-one else was allowed to. And maybe my background as a lawyer made me a lot more emotional about human rights issues than was wise for a person in my position. But — with the wisdom of hindsight — the board, led by Gosper, Coates and Coles, were right to stop me. As board members, they were able to take a more considered view than some-one involved in the day-to-day heat of the battle as I was. They were very attuned to the potential repercussions of what I was proposing. They had many years of learning about the sensitivities of the Olympic movement. It was right for me as chief executive to look at everything that could be done to help our cause and it was right for them to take a more dispassionate view and say that this was not the sort of thing our organisation should be doing. Collectively, the right decision was made.

15
Ninety-one Votes

Every military operation must be directed toward a clearly defined, decisive and attainable objective.

US Army Field Manual

There comes at time in any operation, any campaign, when you must get your goal into very sharp focus again. A time to step back from day-to-day activities, take another look at where you are headed and work out your final plans for getting there.

For me, that time came in about March 1993. The bid books were safely with the IOC in Lausanne. The Evaluation Commission had gone. We had made our presentation to the summer sporting federations. We only had to focus on one thing — the most important thing of all: securing the votes of the 91 men and women of the IOC who were going to Monte Carlo in September.

As Sydney's autumn settled in, the great bulk of IOC members had made their visit. The challenge was always going to be keeping the Sydney bid fresh in their minds. They would visit other major cities in the northern summer and we feared the attractions of these cities might be uppermost in their minds when they voted in September. We just couldn't let them forget us.

Everything seemed to be going well. But the challenge was to push ahead with one final intensive lobbying campaign in the last six months from April to September. In some of our darkest days over the life of the bid, we would think, 'What if we only got the four Oceania votes and one or two others?' That would have been total humiliation for Australia's third consecutive bid. But by this time we were pretty confident that we had a core of at least 30 votes for the first round. If 91 IOC members were voting, that meant we then had to pick up another 16 votes in the subsequent rounds. Thirty was a long way in front of the 12 votes that Melbourne began with and a good base, but until those members put pen to ballot paper in Monte Carlo, nothing could be guaranteed. The most serious danger at this stage — as Kevan Gosper said publicly during the Australia Day visits — was complacency. We couldn't leave anything to chance.

We had our own ideas about how to go about courting IOC votes, but I also wanted to consult the experts.

Early on in the bid I had a chat with Wal Murray, the Deputy Premier and the leader of the National Party in the NSW government, a veteran politician and an experienced numbers man.

'You *are* going to ask for the vote, Rod?'

'What do you mean, Wal?'

'In politics everyone knows you must *ask* for the vote. If you don't ask, you don't know what people are going to do. If you do ask them and they say "no", you at least know where you stand and you might be able to do something about it. If they say "yes", you take that into consideration, add up all the promises of a "yes" vote — and discount them by about 30 per cent.'

I wasn't a numbers man, but it made sense to me. I told the strategy committee we should be able to build our relationships with people to the point where we could ask them if they were with us or not. Phil Coles had a problem with that: 'I don't think we should do that. These are my colleagues and we're not going to be doing that.'

'I'd like you to think about it, because I really think it's the key. We're not going to go down the same path as Melbourne did last time,' I said.

While working on our final lobbying strategy in early 1993, we contacted Senator Graham Richardson for advice. John Coates was a long time friend of Richo's. The Senator was the Federal Minister for Health and had been Minister for Transport and Communications, but we wanted to draw on his experience as a numbers man. I had already taken Wal Murray's advice on board, but I thought Richo's advice would also be valuable. You had to admire the way the Labor Party had worked its numbers. I didn't think there had been anybody better on political strategy in recent times, in Australia or overseas. We sent the Senator a lot of briefing papers and I called him up. He had helped with the Melbourne bid and knew more about the Olympic movement than I realised. We arranged a meeting in Sydney, not long after Labor been re-elected in a surprising victory. Given the weak state of the economy, it was another example of the skill of Labor's political strategists. The party had developed an excellent reputation for focussing its limited resources on areas which yielded the best results. It was a good lesson for everybody.

I asked him about Wal Murray's advice on vote-getting and the importance of actually asking people if they were going to vote for us or not. Richo agreed: 'Wal Murray was absolutely correct. You must ask.'

He went through all the techniques of working a room. If you were going to ask somebody if they were going to vote for you, he suggested you did it by surrounding them with two other people so that they made the commitment in front of them. He wanted to know a lot of details about the election process itself. Who were the returning officers? What was the room like? Did they write the vote down on paper? Did they came out for coffee between rounds? He asked about all the logistical workings of the voting room on the day. He suggested that we looked for supporters among the members who could lobby for us between each round of voting.

I also asked for his advice on the details of the lobbying process. Should we lobby them almost to the end, but leave them alone on the last day or should we work them right up to the ballot paper? You worked them right up to the ballot paper. None of what he said was a total surprise to me but it confirmed much of what we were thinking. Given the high standards we were setting with everything else in our campaign, I wanted to make sure we went about our final lobbying efforts with the same degree of professionalism.

Graham and I agreed that he would meet our lobby team to talk it through in more detail. I reported to some of my people that I had met with him and it leaked to the press. I have never spoken to Graham about it, but I'm told that he was not pleased that his role was publicised. So things sort of cooled and he didn't come to a lobby team meeting. But he taught me a lot and I was able to pass it on.

I also had a meeting with Ian Kortlang about the same sort of issues. Kortlang had been an adviser to the Greiner government and had established his own strategic consultancy, Kortlang Sydney. Having consulted experts from the Labor Party and the National Party, I wanted to talk to someone who had advised the Liberal Party. Kortlang stressed the importance of having a strategy for getting second preference votes. He asked if we thought we could win on the first round. Probably not. So he asked, 'What's your strategy for getting second preference votes? That's got to be your primary strategy. You've got to go to all the people who you know are going to vote for somebody else first and make sure they vote for Sydney second.'

I know that all sounds obvious. But is helpful when people who are speaking from experience say that's the way it is. It confirms you are going in the right direction and it makes you more focussed on the strategy.

It wasn't that we didn't have our own ideas on how to do it. We did and, of course, John Coates was an excellent numbers man. But my view was that if there was a valuable source of experience we could tap, we should tap it. There was as much professional expertise in the business of lobbying for a vote as in any other aspect of our campaign or selling in general, for that matter. And, when it came down to it, getting those votes was our *raison d'etre*.

So, as it came closer to the vote, we would ask people if we had their support. It wasn't difficult because it was generally the main topic of conversation with the members by this time anyway. If they told us they weren't going to vote for us, we would then ask them for their vote in the later rounds if the city they were supporting was eliminated.

At the same time, we also worked out a revised plan of action on our final lobbying effort for the last six months from April to 23 September.

I decided to create a strategic unit to supervise the administration of the final contacts with the members. Bid books complete, there were people we could move into this unit. We put together a team led by Mark Jackson and Louise Walsh, another talented young lawyer on secondment to the bid who had came to us from Allen Allen and Hemsley. They were backed up by Alan Hoskins, Margaret McLennan and Kevin Simmonds. The world was divided into two sections. Mark was in charge of organising and providing the backup for the lobbying in Africa and Asia while Louise was responsible for Europe and the Americas. Mark's responsibilities included organising a major trip to Africa by John Coates and Gough and Margaret Whitlam. Louise was to help Phil Coles and Doug Donoghue set up their office in Paris and provide the logistical backup and the liaison with our office.

The unit reported directly to me and to Bob Elphinston when I was away. 'I want to know that all 91 members will be covered all the time — which lobbyists are targeting them, when was the last time we contacted them, what's coming up, were they receiving all our newsletters and videos?' I told them.

They devised a general public relations program to contact all the members over this period. Each of them would get three issues of our special *Share the Spirit* magazine, five specialist brochures detailing the Sydney Olympic plan for each of the 25 Olympic sports, a summary of our bid books in a special presentation which would either be sent to them or delivered by their local Australian Ambassador and a video showing various activities of the bid around Sydney and its level of public support. The schools would write another three or four more letters to their IOC member and those members who had visited Sydney in 1992 would get a series of photographs showing how the construction work had advanced at Sydney Olympic Park and the rowing course at Penrith.

There were plans for each individual member. The strategy unit drew up a list of IOC members and wrote down what further action was needed to get their vote — which lobbyists would make contact with them, who else could be helpful in soliciting their support and ways to follow up on any areas of interest they had shown during their visits to Sydney. We already had a lot of this in progress, but the strategy unit developed the few last steps for each member. It was circulated to the members of our strategy committee and then we decided which of us would actually ask the particular member for their vote. Coates and I felt that nothing less would do it.

The lobby team itself also divided the world up, according to our specialities.

Coates was to travel into central and southern Africa. His close relationship with Sam Ramsamy would be very helpful there.

I was developing good contacts in northern Africa and Latin America, so I planned several trips there. I had just got back from the annual Pan-American Sports Organisation meeting in Mar del Plata in March and I was to go back again to Ecuador in May for the COPA America football championships with John Warren, coming back via Western Samoa, which was hosting the Oceania basketball championships. Then I was to go back to South America again later in the year. I would consider another swing through North Africa.

Coles and Donoghue lobbied the European members and sporting federations from their base in Paris. Coles was on the move all the time, attending canoeing and gymnastics championships and meeting up with other IOC members. He stayed with Fernando Bello in Portugal and Gunnar Ericsson in Sweden.

Nick Greiner went through eastern Europe with Gabor Komyathy. Bruce Baird did a trip through Scandinavia. Bob Elphinston went to sports meetings in Sweden, Finland, Norway, Czechoslovakia, Turkey and Malaysia, and the International Baseball Congress in Rome. A group of us were also going to the Mediterranean Games in Montpelier, France in June and the International Amateur Athletics Federation World Championships in Stuttgart in August. Kevan Gosper travelled to Panama, Brazil, Kuwait and Belgium for the bid in those important final months.

We also decided to boost our final lobbying effort by hiring a firm of public relations consultants to work on the 38 European members. Europe had by far the biggest single concentration of IOC members. After that, there were 19 members in the Americas, 16 in Africa, 14 in Asia and only four in our region, Oceania. We felt we were in good standing with the European members and they would also be very important in terms of second preference votes. If the Games were not going to go back to Europe in 2000 — and there was a good chance of that, given that they had been in Barcelona in 1992 — we wanted to make sure the European members supported Sydney and not Beijing as their first or second choice. We wanted to do an intense PR campaign in Europe. We were going to have our own people living there and others working there. As far as I was concerned, we would work Europe until we dropped — those 38 members were not going to forget us.

We created a brief and concentrated our final efforts on two PR companies in London — Hill and Knowlton, and Shandwick.

Hill and Knowlton had helped the Atlanta bid in the last campaign but Shandwick owned International Public Relations in Australia which did the PR for the Australian Olympic Committee. Hill and Knowlton sent out their boss, David Wynne-Morgan, to Sydney to meet us. David was a wonderful, gregarious man who knew everyone in England, sat in the front row at Lords and all that. We knew he was well-connected but we also knew the day-to-day campaign would be handled by someone further down the line.

Shandwick sent out the young guy who would be working on the campaign, David Fuller. Shandwick's links with the AOC, through IPR, also helped give it a good base of information about the Australian Olympic movement. After our meeting with David, we decided to give the job to Shandwick. We had the meeting Friday and Fuller delayed his trip home until Sunday. We called all the senior members of our team into the office on the Saturday so he could be fully briefed.

When I was next in London I gave presentations to the firm and spoke to all the Shandwick staff who would be working on the campaign. Shandwick was to link up with the communications division in our office and become its European arm. They were instructed to penetrate every Olympic sports federation in Europe; every part of the Olympic media in every town where an IOC member lived; all the sports ministers in the governments and all the sporting administrators at the provincial level. They weren't to go near IOC members — that was the province of official members of our lobby team — but they were to create a kind of macro-momentum about the Sydney bid in Europe. It became a very successful partnership.

Shandwick came up with a number of creative ideas for keeping in contact with the members. These included sending a series of postcards of Sydney every week in the last six weeks of the campaign and doing a survey of international athletes to see which city they preferred for the 2000 Games. And, of course, we had the entire Australian diplomatic network working for us. If Shandwick ever wanted to throw a cocktail party in Europe for, say, sports writers, the ambassadors always helped, embassy premises if necessary.

It was a hectic time for all of us. I was travelling so much in the end, I had to carry four passports. They kept getting filled up with visas. There was always a valid visa for one country in one passport, and another in another. An expired passport would have a current visa for, say, Mexico and other passports would have visas for next stop, Jamaica. At immigration counters I was forever looking through my passports saying, 'One of these passports is current, but the visa for your country is in this other one here.' People looked at me strangely.

It was exhausting but I had some fascinating experiences travelling around the world, lobbying for that extra vote.

I did a big sweep through northern Africa in April-May with Deeta. We went Paris, Algiers, Casablanca, Tunis and Cairo. Then she went home and I went down to the Sudan and up to Riyadh, Saudi Arabia. It was my first big foray into the region. My close relationships with the Egyptian NOC helped me make contacts.

It was a fascinating experience of many different cultures. I learned about the difference between the Berbers and Arabs, something I hadn't realised before. North Africans are wonderfully generous people and we were always invited into homes.

In Algeria we met Mohamed Zerguini again and his wife Zakia, who I liked very much. Zerguini was 71. He had been a very famous and brave soldier in the French army and had risen to colonel in the Algerian army. He had fought the French and been badly wounded. He had been a minister in the Algerian government and an ambassador.

His son, Yancine, who was a doctor, and his daughter-in-law, Doudja, looked after us there. They both spoke English whereas their parents only spoke Arabic and French. Deeta could speak to Zerguini and his wife directly in French, even if I couldn't. Yancine and Doudja took us out to a truly memorable lunch of beautiful fish and Algerian white wine and to visit Doudja's parents. Yancine specialised in sports medicine, so when I got back to Australia I got a lot of papers on sports medicine and sent them to him. That kept that relationship going. Doudja was very interested in a book that Deeta was reading, *Perfume* by Patrick Suskind, a novel about a scentless man obsessed with odors and scent making in France 300 years ago. So I sent that to her when I got back.

There was a 9.30 pm curfew in Algeria at the time. There had been problems with fundamentalists and if you didn't get home by 9.30 you had to stay where you were, so dinners were always hasty affairs. But we still enjoyed the local cuisine.

Zerguini was a devout Muslim and didn't drink alcohol but went to the trouble of getting whisky and French wine for our visit. One night they cooked a lamb for our dinner. We stood around the table and took pieces off and ate it in one course, then we went back to the table and sat down and had another course. It was just fantastic.

And the men kissing — I wasn't at all used to that. Zerguini gave me a big kiss on both cheeks. But he meant it. We also saw Roman ruins there — some of the best in the world.

In Casablanca we saw the IOC member in Morocco, old Mr Benjelloun, one of the 14 life members of the IOC. He was 81 and had been a member for over 30 years and wore a fez. His wife was very ill, and is now sadly deceased. We visited her in her bedroom and somehow — I don't know how — she got up to welcome us. We took coffee in a great big room with no windows and a couch all the way around the walls with little coffee tables everywhere in their old Moroccan house.

Then I flew across to Cairo and down to the Sudan to see General Gadir. I was amazed at the poverty. The remnants of the British occupation were still there, old buildings just about falling down but typical of British architecture of the time. The hotel where I stayed in Khartoum was virtually empty. There were no faxes — only a telex machine. It was 120 degrees. At one stage I went down to the swimming pool but it was so hot, I couldn't stay there. It was a very lonely experience.

General Gadir had been a member of the military and a government minister in the 1970s. A keen footballer in his youth — he had played for the Sudanese national military team. He became an IOC member in 1983 but this only lasted until 1987. In the late 1980s he was imprisoned for four years by the military regime and could no longer be a member. Released in 1990, he was re-instated.

According to my book of IOC members, General Gadir had a wife and two sons. So I bought them gifts at the airport in Cairo on the way. I had heard the boys were very young, so I bought two Walt Disney toys. I bought a scarf for Mrs Gadir and I had a colorful watch like a Swatch with me. Scarf and watch set aside for Mrs Gadir, the toys for the two boys.

I went to the general's house with Michael Ortega from the Australian embassy in Cairo. It was to be one of those men–only dinners common in that region. The men would bring in the food and take away the plates. You would never see the female members of the household. But Michael and I arrived at his house before the other guests, so I asked the general if I could meet his family. When they came out, there were two boys — and a 14 year old daughter. I thought, 'Oh, no. I'm one present short.'

My mind was racing. I decided to give Mrs Gadir the scarf and the daughter the watch. They were all lovely kids and they couldn't believe that somebody had actually asked them to come out to the front of the house and say hello. Michael explained to me later that General Gadir had two wives and it was the wife in his other house who only had two boys. It was one of those unexpected situations that I was able to fudge my way through.

The next day, General Gadir said, 'You have no idea what that meant to the little girl. She has not slept the entire night. She stayed awake playing with the watch. That was the only watch like that she had ever seen.' This little person from the Sudan couldn't believe she had been given a watch. A simple thing for some people can mean a lot.

In the Sudan I also met Hassan Agabani. Agabani was very wealthy, with homes in London, Cairo and the Sudan. He was married to a Danish woman.

My Egyptian contacts recommended I see him. The treasurer of the Egyptian Olympic Committee, Dr Sulieman, was on the African Athletic Association. Dr Sulieman told me that the most important person for me to meet in north Africa was Agabani. Agabani was not an IOC member, but he had a long standing interest in sport and the Olympic movement. He was an African delegate to the International Amateur Athletics Federation — a senior member of the IAAF council — and was very influential in athletics in Africa. The African delegation to the IAAF was one of the power bases that its chief, Primo Nebiolo, depended upon. Agabani was also very close to another influential IOC member from Africa, Charles Mukora of Kenya, also on the IAAF council.

During my visit to the Sudan Agabani invited me to lunch. I drove out from Khartoum to his house with Michael Ortega. Suddenly, we turned off the bitumen road. There was no roadway, just desert. I was thinking, 'I hope we don't break down here.' Eventually we saw what looked like a deserted Arab village of mud-brick on the horizon, but it turned out to be occupied.

We drove through the village and arrived at a big fancy gate of what looked like a ranch, the gate to Agabani's house. We went inside and walked out onto the verandah and, to my surprise, we were overlooking the Nile. The house was air-conditioned. At the lunch there were only men. General Gadir was there and several others wearing their traditional flowing robes — which I guess are quite cool — and very striking white headdresses.

Agabani was very helpful and warm. I could see that he had quietly decided that he would look after me. He was a very cultured man and he just said, 'I'll do what I can for you.' It wasn't until I met up with him later at the World Track and Field championships at Stuttgart and watched him operate in the IAAF environment that I appreciated how influential he was.

The next visit was not so fruitful. I went on to Riyadh for what was supposed to be a meeting with Prince Faisal of Saudi Arabia. We had a very high-profile ambassador there, Malcolm Leder. Saudi Arabia was an important country for Australia's sheep and other exports, and it was an important diplomatic post. We couldn't confirm our appointment with Prince Faisal but the embassy told me to come anyway. When I arrived in Riyadh I was told that the appointment would be tomorrow. I waited for a few days, constantly being told the appointment would be tomorrow, tomorrow. . . But the appointment just didn't come off and I decided to leave. I thought as soon as I'm gone, they'll say, 'Now I'll see him.' Which they did. I had travelled across the world to meet Prince Faisal in his home country, but I just couldn't get to see him. It was the only time that happened to me with an IOC member. I felt sure it was his minders who were putting off the meeting, not the prince himself. But I felt for our ambassador.

In May we were to host President Samaranch. An official visit, it was the first to Sydney by the president during our campaign. The IOC president doesn't cast a vote unless the voting is tied. But President Samaranch was clearly a powerful man. His views would count for a lot.

There was a lot of public interest in his visit. A staggering 150 members of the media were accredited to cover his visit — more than for the visit of US President Bush in 1992.

The president had just been in China for the East Asian Games in Shanghai and extensively feted there, reports said. He had three days in Sydney. Of course I knew him by then, but Kevan Gosper and Phil Coles knew him better and they argued strongly for a very low key visit.

They recommended that he be taken around by minibus and that there should be no luxury limousines, no police escorts and no official dinners — only cocktail parties so that he could be back to his hotel by 7.30 pm, giving him time to catch up on his office work and work on his book. That's what he wanted, so that's what he got. And he loved it. As he explained to me during his trip, 'I'm not 50. I'm 72 and I just can't stay up too late.'

There was a state reception at the Art Gallery of NSW to show him the 10 works of art which were to be loaned to the IOC Museum in Lausanne for its official opening the next month. Even then we got him back to his hotel early. Kevan and Judy Gosper came out especially for it, which was terrific of them. Kevan was always there, looking after the president all the time.

I didn't make any long speeches. I always kept my remarks down to about 90 seconds. We didn't keep him roped off from the public, we let him move around and meet people. At Sydney Olympic Park, which he officially opened and laid a commemorative stone, or at the art gallery, we just let him wander around through the crowd. People came over to talk to him and he enjoyed himself.

During the briefings at the bid office I could see he was tired. I read him pretty well and I realised he didn't want too much detail. But he was very impressed with a lot of what he saw. Quite a few times he would say, 'I'd like you to send that to Lausanne.' He loved our schools program and wanted to have details of that sent back too. He was also most impressed with our corporate supporters' kit.

We had a chart done on where all the Olympic events would be and at what time of day. He said he'd never seen that before. He was amazed at the statistics our librarian, Melissa Petherbridge, could produce out of our computer. He wanted copies of it all.

He also met children from the schools program at our office. They presented him with a scrap book full of reasons why Sydney should win the Games and gave him a boomerang to make sure he returned in 2000. He met three students from South Sydney High School who greeted him in Spanish and Leigh Habler, a student from the school who had swum in the Barcelona Games. There was also a dance performance by four Aboriginal students from La Perouse. He told the school children, 'I am very happy to be in Sydney and I hope to come again, many, many times — maybe also in the year 2000.'

He always had a gift for everybody — construction workers, school children. Everybody. There was always something in his pocket — little momentos like key rings and coins. We gave him a helicopter tour of the facilities we planned to use for the Games. We went from Darling Harbor, out to Sydney Olympic Park at Homebush, and the rowing course at Penrith. When we got out to Penrith, I said, 'Mr President, that's it. That's the plan.'

'Excellent.' And he just took his earphones off, looked at the window and didn't want to know any more until we got back to Sydney.

The next morning he toured Darling Harbor and the Sydney Football Stadium. He said he was much more impressed with these facilities than he was with Sydney Olympic Park. Sydney Olympic Park was still under construction so it was hard to compare, but he did understand we were proud of it.

In the middle of his visit, I was also dealing with another difficult issue within our organisation. News came that David Smithers, chairman of our Finance Commission, who was an accountant with Coopers and Lybrand, was to be charged by the Australian Securities Commission in connection with the preparation of the prospectus in 1988 for the float of the Budget Corporation. Smithers was a very close friend of mine. I had known him for 25 years and liked him very much. Somebody had got into the ear of the premier and Bruce Baird about it and suggested that Smithers should no longer be on the board of the Games bid. I talked to Smithers about it. He explained to me the background to the allegations against him. He said he would be fighting the charges and he said he wanted to stay on the board. I told him, 'David, as far as I'm concerned, everybody's innocent until they're proven guilty and I'll defend you.'

I decided to research the facts of the matter to satisfy myself about the seriousness of the charges. With David's permission, I spoke to his lawyer, Paddy Jones from Allen Allen and Hemsley, about the facts of the case. One of my partners from Corrs, Andrew Stevenson, was also to be charged over the same pro-spectus. So I also spoke to the managing partner of Corrs to see what advice had been given to the firm on the matter. I went back to Bruce Baird and gave him all the facts I had been able to put together on the matter and I argued that there was no reason for us not to support Smithers. As far as I was concerned, he should stay on the board. I called Smithers a few times to explain to him what I'd done.

I met up with him when President Samaranch was making his tour of Sydney Olympic Park. David's wife, Isabelle, had just had her photograph taken with the president and David said to me, 'I can't believe that in the middle of Samaranch's visit, you're looking after me as well.'

'Sure. Why wouldn't I?'

He was terribly grateful. But it would have been terrible if he had been forced off the board. The push for him to resign continued for a while, but in the end Premier Fahey, Bruce Baird and everybody else decided to do the right thing and let him stay. It was a very important matter for me. The fact that the president of the IOC was visiting at the same time didn't mean I couldn't make the time to check out the facts of the matter and make sure 'justice' was done. President Samaranch, of course, never knew what had been going on behind the scenes and the visit went off without a hitch.

The prime minister put on a special lunch for the president at Admiralty House. (The dining room at the prime minister's

Kirribilli House was considered too small). The prime minister and the president seemed to get along particularly well. Both were big-picture people who were very knowledgable and interested in world affairs and they understood each other immediately.

President Samaranch came with his daughter, Maria Teresa. We had met her in Barcelona where she was the official liaison officer for our team. Every team in the Olympics had to have one and — in a brilliant move — John Coates had got Maria Teresa, who lives in Barcelona, to be our liaison person. She became very much a part of the Australian team in Barcelona. A great woman, full of Spanish vitality, she proved to be a wonderful person to accompany her father on his Sydney visit. Deeta took her out to see the clothes at fashion designer Trent Nathan, who was preparing the clothes for the Sydney bid team to wear to Monte Carlo and she did some shopping. The Samaranchs gave Deeta a Louis Vuitton handbag as they left and it was the start of a very good friendship.

By this time, Margaret, my assistant, and President Samaranch's secretary, Annie, had also become firm friends. So I made Margaret the visit officer with the responsibility of arranging all the details and accompanying them throughout the visit. Margaret became friendly with President Samaranch too. She agreed to take some paperwork back to Lausanne for him when we went to the opening of the Museum in June. After she delivered it, the president gave her a beautiful pair of glasses in the Olympic colors which he had bought especially for her. Later, at the World Athletics Championships in Stuttgart, she met Annie again and told her she had put new lenses in them. Annie invited her up to the president's suite to show him. I was about and said, 'I'm coming too.' So there I was, tagging along with my secretary to get another chance to chat with the president.

During his visit to Sydney, President Samaranch made some encouraging remarks. He told the reception at the art gallery that if he were asked his impression of the outcome of the race for the Games, he would 'have to say, as President of the IOC, that all the six bidders are on the same starting line. But after the start, maybe some will be faster than the others. And I think the Sydney bid could be really very fast.' In answering questions on another occasion, he said Sydney's chances of winning were 'very high'.

'How high?' he was asked.

'You are one of the favorites.'

But he also had a warning. The biggest mistake that Sydney could make at the moment, he said, was to think it was the winner. 'You have to fight to the last minute,' he counselled. Exactly what we intended to do.

When it was all over, we drove to the airport in the minibus and he said, 'Best bid city visit I have ever made. No dinners. Perfect.'

The only bad memory I have of the Samaranch visit is a personal one. When the arrangements were first made for the lunch with the Prime Minister, I was not invited. Bruce Baird wasn't either. I thought it was extraordinary and was concerned at what sort of message it would convey to the President if the chief executive officer of the bid was not invited to the Prime Minister's lunch. I made this point to the organisers. I was told it was a very small table and it would be difficult to seat extra numbers. Then I got world I could go. The lunch was to be one with wives and partners but seating was tight and only I could go. Deeta was not invited and she was upset by that. It was certainly not the Prime Minister's fault — he didn't submit a guest list. I didn't know what was going on behind the scenes. When I got there, after being told there wasn't enough room, there was an empty seat beside me at the table. When I told Deeta this she was very upset. I had to calm things down and tell her somebody must have made a mistake or there had been a last minute change. I didn't talk to anyone else about it until months later. I said to Bruce Baird, 'Intended or otherwise, my wife was deeply hurt and insulted by that incident.'

These hurtful personal situations come up in business from time to time, often when you don't expect them and usually when you can least afford them, given the amount of work that needs to be done. All I can say from my experience, especially in the position of CEO, is that you've really got to bite your tongue and get on with it. I had so much to do, I just couldn't afford to get angry. So I had to play a game with my own wife about there having been some mistake about the numbers, rather than joining her in being upset about it all.

But few people knew about that incident, and President Samaranch's visit was a success.

As we came closer to Monte Carlo, we crunched numbers constantly, trying to work out the voting pattern of each member. By then John Coates and I estimated we had over 50 first and second preference votes which gave us a clear win.

We developed a computer program that accepted each of the lobbyists' projections about how people would vote for each city through a number of rounds. We put it all into the computer to see what would happen. We went through all the scenarios — what would happen if Brasilia went out first? What would happen if Istanbul went out first?

Because Coates and I thought that we would get over half the votes to start with, the computer couldn't tell us the preferences because we had already won. Gabor Komyathy, Graham Lovett, Mark Jackson and Louise Walsh were more pessimistic — and the program actually worked for them. But on all scenarios, we won by the fourth round.

We wanted to see whether our tactics should change if preferences shifted. I don't think any other bid had that kind of technology. It was just another example of the level of professionalism we tried to bring to the complex art of winning the votes of some 91 individuals around the world.

16
Jostling for Position

In the true spirit of sportsmanship, for the glory of sport and the honour of our teams

oath sworn by Olympic flag bearers

The new Olympic Museum in Lausanne was a beautiful white building set into the hillside overlooking Lake Geneva. In central Lausanne, about a mile from Chateau de Vidy, the IOC headquarters, its first appearances are deceptive. You look upwards, past manicured lawns stepping up the hill, to what looks like a single storey building with columns out the front. But when you walk up the steps to the entrance, you see there were five stories excavated into the hillside, some below ground level. There is a lot of glass and a sweeping circular staircase in the entrance hall.

Built at a cost of $60 million it was designed by a member of the Olympic family, Mexican architect, Pedro Ramirez Vazquez, the IOC member who also designed the extension to the Chateau. The grounds were filled with sports sculpture given to the IOC over the years. Out the front there is a huge white kinetic sculpture whose pieces move to form the human body. The museum houses all sorts of historical records of the Games in a 15 000 volume library, a film and video archive and a collection of some 200 000 photographs. A whole section is devoted to the summer Games, another to the winter Games and a third to antiquities. You could see any Olympic 100 metres race on film and there were films of the events showing all the time. The Olympic flame is now housed there in perpetuity.

The museum was President Samaranch's pride and joy and its opening was set to co-incide with the 99th session of the IOC at the end of June. It was to be the last official gathering of all 91 members before Monte Carlo, an event no bidding city could afford to miss. We were all jostling for position as we turned into the home straight.

Australia had loaned several paintings for the opening of the gallery. There was Tom Roberts' 'Golden Fleece', and works by Arthur Streeton, Brett Whiteley, Sidney Nolan and several Aboriginal artists. The Chinese had loaned several historical pieces for the opening. They were a major sponsor of the museum, along with many of the big Olympic sponsor companies such as Coca-Cola. We wondered if being a sponsor would help us in our bid, but decided we just couldn't afford it.

The Germans loaned a most impressive bronze horse head that had come off the Brandenberg Gate in the war. But the German contribution also included a strange exhibition which felt almost repressive in a sense. I felt most uncomfortable in it.

On the ground floor, partly underneath the spiral staircase and partly to the side, was what looked like a big semi-circle of black marble. Bruce Baird walked straight through it. It was actually still water, about 12 centimetres deep, over a black base. He walked around the opening with his shoes full of water. Some decided that the pond was a wishing well and threw coins in it.

All the bid cities were represented but Lausanne was one of those meetings when we always seemed to be ahead of our opponents.

We knew the meeting would be a difficult one, logistically. Lausanne was a small city and, with so many people suddenly descending on the town, we knew rooms would be hard to come by. The IOC insisted that it made the bookings and that the bid cities would only be given six rooms each. But we knew that we would have far more than six people. The Premier, the Lord Mayor, the Whitlams and Charlie Perkins were coming in addition to our lobby team. We also needed enough staff to run a Sydney bid exhibition for several days. The IOC couldn't even tell us ahead of time where our rooms would be. We decided that we would have to take things into our own hands, so we rang our friends at Qantas.

Qantas booked twenty rooms for us in the Beau Rivage Hotel where some IOC members were staying. When everyone arrived and the other bid cities saw our accommodation they were furious. They complained to the IOC but the staff said we had better accommodation because we were better organised.

We got there two days before the opening to set up our exhibition. Margaret was tipped-off that the IOC executive was going to have its own private inspection of the exhibition rooms. When they came through, our exhibition was ready. The entire Sydney team was there handing out material while the others were still unpacking boxes and building their exhibitions. The comment was made again about us, 'They're always organised.' I was proud — being ready ahead of time was one of those things that showed our professionalism. As Napoleon said, 'To be defeated is acceptable, but to be surprised is unforgivable.'

Shandwick stressed the need to continue to make an impact through the final months. It was important to have something new to release. After more than two years of campaigning, we knew we would have to work hard to keep up awareness of our bid.

We chose the Lausanne meeting to unveil the new Sydney bid team uniform, designed and donated by Trent Nathan, about $100,000 worth of clothing. Obviously, there was a limit on how many uniforms we had, so we decided that everyone going to both Lausanne and Monte Carlo would get an outfit. The men were given a navy jacket and two pairs of trousers — one in navy and one in dark grey. The women were given two suits — one in navy and another in an olive green color called taupe. Because of the distinctive design, you could see that whichever color mix people wore, they were all part of the Sydney team. There was a blouse, a jacket, slacks and either a long or a short skirt for the women, as well as matching handbags, belts and leather shoes. Trent gave us two ties for Lausanne. There was a deeply colored one and a very striking navy blue one with big white spots. The outfits looked great. Many people commented on them. The blue-and-white spotted ties made a real impression at our press conference and throughout the visit.

The Manchester team had worn its bid tie for two years and it was beginning to look boring. But the Sydney team was noticed as having a fresh, new look. It was a good strategy which was well timed and worked.

We generated more tension among the bidding cities on the final night when there was going to be a cruise on the lake. We were initially told only two representatives from bid cities could go onboard. For us it would have meant the Premier and Lord Mayor. But I said to Kevan Gosper it was a bit tough: our people had come a long way. I asked if six could come; six people per bid city had been allowed to other functions. So Gosper saw President Samaranch and got permission for all bids to have six.

But about an hour before cast-off, the president said he wanted to see us. About ten of us from Sydney went and Samaranch said, 'Now, you're all coming on the cruise?'

'Well, look, Mr President, the rules are actually six each.'

'Oh, no. I want you *all* to come. Everyone. All the Sydney people.'

There were 30 of us in total when we boarded. The other cities only had two. None of them had even heard that they had permission to have six. We told them that the president specifically asked that all the Sydney team come. But they were not amused.

Bob Scott from Manchester was really upset. At one stage he was standing by himself and not looking well. His marriage was breaking up under the strain of so much travel over the previous few years and I think it was all taking its toll. So I asked him to come and sit with us.

By then the China issue was serious and the subject of much discussion. There was also a private meeting in which Joao Havelange tried to tell the Latin American IOC members how to vote: Brasilia first. No-one thought Brasilia had a chance. It was a strategy to try to split the first-round votes. If it worked, it could have seen Sydney eliminated in the early rounds, leaving the Games to Beijing. And if Brasilia had managed a healthy first-round showing, it could have augered well for another Brazilian bid for 2004 and China would have been obliged to throw its weight behind it. Several South American friends told me what had happened. They were very angry that anyone would try to tell them how to vote. Roque Munoz Pena from the Dominican Republic reportedly got very angry during the meeting and said no-one was going to tell him how to vote.

There were tensions in our camp too. Charlie Perkins had also spoken out on human rights at a press conference which created some controversy but that was not the real problem. Perkins had arrived on the Sunday and attended the press conference on Monday morning. We had wanted him in Lausanne for a presentation about our cultural program. I had written him a memo about what was to happen during the week and what events I wanted him to attend. It was the same memo I wrote for every other person on the trip, and they weren't offended. But Perkins was out of sorts about it. He went on a cruise on the lake on Monday afternoon and was uncontactable, so he missed an event I wanted him to go to. Next morning he packed his bags and stormed off.

We had a quick meeting of our strategy team as soon as we found out. Bruce Baird said he thought Perkins might still be at the airport and if I contacted him and apologised, we might be able to persuade him to come back. Everyone else said I shouldn't have to apologise because I had done nothing wrong. But I was prepared to apologise to anybody if it would help. But we couldn't find him. We wondered whether he would criticise us when he got home. He didn't.

We may have done better than the other bid cities at Lausanne, but the trip also had some logistical lessons for me. Again we were travelling with a reasonably large party and again I was being bothered with all sorts of minor issues. I had appointed Paul Clark from our Sydney office to manage the trip but it became apparent that he was just not senior enough. With so many VIPs, it was hard for him to handle all their requests and problems. Whenever anything went wrong, everyone seemed to come to me. It was terribly diverting. I would be trying to look relaxed, talking to an IOC member, and people would come up to me and say, 'X wants you. Y wants you.'

When I got home I decided that the problem had to be dealt with, so I appointed Bob Elphinston as manager for Monte Carlo. I told Bob, 'I don't want people to drive me nuts. I need to go there and do a job. You look after things.' He was to be in charge of the whole team — if anyone had any problems about bookings or travel or where they had to be or what they had to do or anything else, they were to go to him. He was to run the operations and I was to be head of the lobby team. And, of course, I knew he would do a great job. It would leave me free to move around among the members and have last-minute conversations before the vote.

Now I know why generals always appear to be walking around not doing much. They can't plan a battle if they are distracted by all sorts of minor tasks and staff complaints. They have to have their mind free to concentrate on the big picture.

By this time, the Whitlams had become an important part of our extended lobby team. They had done a great job entertaining all the black African members who visited Sydney. When they went to Lausanne they met them all again. Gough always got a great reaction from these people.

We decided to use them on a major lobbying trip through central and southern Africa in the final weeks of the campaign. The trip was led by John Coates, because of his strong connections in the region, and also included Perry Crosswhite, the executive-director of the AOC.

Ross Turnbull tried to help out by organising a jet for them to charter from South Africa. Turnbull and his group had good contacts in South Africa and they were talking to Anglo-American there about trying to use one of their planes. It didn't come off and we had to charter another plane for the trip but I remember John Coates acknowledging the Turnbull group's contribution.

Gough and Margaret were 78 at the time, and Margaret walked with the aid of a stick, but they kept up a gruelling pace around Africa. They went to Mauritius, Mali, Ivory Coast, Toga, Cameroon and Uganda. BHP had a big gold mine in Mali, the biggest business in the country, and the company looked after them there. They were to go to the Congo but they couldn't get in for some reason. They went to Zimbabwe, Swaziland and South Africa where they met Nelson Mandela.

Gough privately briefed himself on the history and the politics of all the countries. He was an authority by the time they got there. Gough was often able to refer to meetings he had with the friends and colleagues of the African members. Many French-speaking black leaders go through Paris and he had met a lot during his time as Australian Ambassador to UNESCO. And of course Gough often mentioned the fact that Margaret was a great swimmer as a young girl and probably would have swum in the Olympics if they hadn't cancelled them because of the war.

Christine Woodall, a visit officer who speaks fluent French and Spanish, went with them and Sam Ramsamy, head of the South African Olympic Committee, helped us out with contacts and appointments. The Whitlams were a wonderfully relaxed, interesting and well-travelled couple, and thrilled to be part of it all. They were always very accommodating and never seemed to mind being piled into the back of a bus or being bundled into a car with everyone else.

Gough lost his passport in Mali. Perry Crosswhite often handled all passports and processing by immigration authorities. After they had gone through customs at Mali airport, Perry gave the passports back to everyone. A few days later, as they were checking out of their hotel, everyone was making sure they had their passports. Gough said Perry still had his passport. Perry said he didn't. But Gough said, 'I have never carried my passport. It is always carried for me.' But Perry was insistent that he had given Gough's passport back. Gough's temperature started to rise. In the end, they opened Gough's suitcase in the lobby of the hotel. They went through his clothes. Socks and underwear were flying in the air. Then Margaret, almost regally, walked over, put her hand in the inside pocket of a suit that was in the case, and found the missing passport. Gough shouted a well-known Australian expletive. Margaret quickly followed, 'And that, ladies and gentlemen, is the last word from a former prime minister of Australia.'

John Coates tells another story about their trip to Swaziland. They met the king of Swaziland and his four wives, who took them out to dinner at a restaurant. Coates, Gough and Margaret were talking to the Prime Minister at one table while Perry Crosswhite was seated at another with members of the Swaziland Olympic Committee and some other guests. When dinner was finished, Coates and Gough escorted the Prime Minister out to his car. When they came back, Margaret exclaimed, 'John, a man there just exposed himself.' The man had actually stood up at the table and urinated next to it.

'Which one was it?' Gough asked.

'It was that little journalist over there,' Margaret replied.

'Wouldn't you know it. Another press leak.'

Sydney's big selling point was our technical superiority. We didn't offer the supposed attraction of a market of a billion people or being a potential economic superpower undergoing major change at the turn of the millennium. We had no deals to offer the power brokers. But we believed we were the city which was simply the best place to hold the Games for athletes, officials and spectators. Our Games were The Athletes' Games. If people were serious about the quality of facilities, the transport, health and communications infrastructure, if they wanted to pick the city where the athletes would be happiest to compete, it had to be Sydney.

That meant the report of the IOC's Evaluation Commission was going to be very important to our case.

Its report on the technical competence of the bidding cities in 1990 was a turning point in Atlanta's campaign. Although the *rankings* were never publicly announced, it became well known in the Olympic movement that the committee had raised questions about whether Athens could handle the Games, citing worries about its finances, transport, pollution and security. Before that, conventional wisdom had it that Athens *had* to have the Centenary Games. After it was released, senior members of the IOC, like Canada's Dick Pound, started to look seriously at other candidates. Both Melbourne and Atlanta had high-quality technical bids. But it was always going to be difficult to give the Games back to a city which had already had them before when there were other strong competitors. The Atlanta team were great lobbyists, so the pendulum began to swing to the US, even though Los Angeles had staged the Games in 1984.

By mid-1993 we had a few hints that Sydney was going to do very well out of the Evaluation Commission's report. Ian Dose and Hamish Fraser put together a publicity campaign aimed at maximising worldwide impact from the report and what we hoped were Sydney's excellent results. But in early July, about a week before the report was due to be released, a journalist working for a German news agency was leaked the report and wrote it up. The story went worldwide. We just couldn't believe our luck. It was staggering. The journalist did his own rankings, not the report's. He said Sydney was first by a good margin on its technical merits. Beijing ranked fourth. Although the official report was soon released, the German's rankings seemed to stick as the story was reported around the world.

We cancelled our campaign. We couldn't have had the same impact in our wildest dreams. The story broke while I was in South America again. As I travelled, I could see the reports in Uruguay, Brazil, Venezula, Chile and everywhere else. Newspaper headlines read:

SYDNEY NUMERO UNO
SYDNEY: EL CANDIDATO PREFERITO
SYDNEY FAVORITO!

The Commission said the Sydney bid offered 'conditions over and above what is required by the IOC . . . a solid bid and a safe environment.' It said the compact nature of the Sydney bid was a 'great asset' and agreed that our bid was designed to give the needs of the athletes top priority. 'One Olympic village, enabling all participating athletes to enjoy the Olympic experience, is a positive factor.' We were particularly pleased to see the theme of the importance of the athletes taken up in chairman Gunnar Ericsson's covering letter. He urged members 'to think of the most important criteria for the athletes and the youth of the world'.

Our financial plan was described as 'conservative, professionally prepared and credible'. But I thought the report's remarks on possible problems with Australian quarantine and the equestrian events was a bit unfair. It said Australia's quarantine requirements 'may cause inconvenience for a few countries' although it didn't see this as causing any major problems. It never came up again as an issue.

I thought the commission was a bit kind on the Beijing bid which it described as being 'realistic' and 'solid.' It said China could stage the Games and that Beijing had a good bid committee. But they said it was weak in a number of areas — including sporting facilities and telecommunications. Beijing said it had built facilities for 17 of the 25 Olympic sports, but the commission said all of these needed modifications. Seven needed major changes. There was concern about Beijing's ability to provide a clean environment, free of pollution. But the one area which was singled out for concern affecting all aspects of its bid was the language problem. The commission said special attention would have to be given to having English and French speakers available in all fields, particularly where there was to be contact with the general public.

The Commission noted that Manchester had yet to build many of its facilities and raised questions about its proposals for accommodation of the athletes. But it was particularly forthright on the subject of Brasilia. It recommended the Brazilian capital should withdraw, saying that it was not equipped to handle the Olympics. But Brasilia refused. The leader of the bid was the daughter-in-law of the country's new president and she declared they would be staying in the race.

Even though the Evaluation Commission's report did not rank cities in order of merit, it was now clear to everyone in the IOC that our bid was technically very superior to Beijing's. And that made voting against Sydney more difficult.

Selling the technical merits of our bid was partly covered by courting all 25 summer Olympic sporting federations. Bob Elphinston and Graham Lovett were in charge of this. We always made sure that whenever we met officials from any of the sporting federations, we handed out fact sheets giving full details of the venues and staging of their particular sport. Over the last five months of the bid, we produced a series of five sports magazines, each providing all the technical details on how we planned to stage five different Olympic sports. At all the major events we attended, we were always giving out fact sheets and talking about the technical side of our bid, stressing the importance of sport and the athlete.

We backed this up with a sophisticated computer graphics program which showed illustrations of all the venues from all angles, regardless of whether they had been built or not. It was state-of-the-art interactive television. Atlanta had something like it designed for them by Georgia Tech, and everyone thought it was the best toy they had ever seen. We wanted to be at least as good as they were, so we spoke to IBM and Arthur Anderson which had links through its US offices into the latest of this kind in-the-round graphics program. At first we just had it on our office computers but later we put the program on laptops and travelled with them. They were programmed to answer any question about our bid in English, French and Spanish. They could show the designs of all our facilities and tell what day which sports were supposed to be on. No-one else had anything like it. Atlanta had done it four years before, so why wouldn't everyone follow its winning example?

I flew to Mongolia to meet Shagdarjav Magvan and sign a co-operation agreement between the Australian Olympic Committee and the Mongolian Olympic Committee. I took Sean Burke as my translator. Sean spoke Russian and had looked after Shagdarjav during his visit to Sydney.

Mongolians have two standard drinks — non-pasteurised mares' milk which they drink all the time from big saucer-style cups they hold in two hands, and vodka. On our first day in the capital Ulan Bator there was a ceremonial welcome for us and there were big pitchers of mare's milk. Now I don't like milk at the best of times, but I had great trouble with the mares' milk. I drank it the first time, but when the jug came around again I just couldn't drink any more. I said to Sean, 'I'm going to say I'm allergic to this.' I discovered that he couldn't drink vodka. He'd overdone it once as a youth and couldn't tolerate it any more. So we did a deal. He drank all the milk and I drank all the vodka. Wherever we went I drank double lots of vodka and he drank double lots of mares' milk, for which I will remain forever grateful.

We had the formal signing ceremony in a big tent in a dachau on a hillside outside Ulan Bator. It was a big old concrete building which had been used by the Russians. It's not the sort of thing that we would think glamorous but in Mongolia it was regarded as pretty smart. We played a game of snooker there and drank two bottles of vodka. It was a funny game because the snooker ball they used was like a tennis ball and it only just fitted into the pockets. If you were slightly off line, the ball wouldn't go in. It took hours to play one game. Our skill levels were no doubt impaired by the amount of vodka that was being consumed.

The next day we went on a picnic about 80 kilometres from Ulan Bator. There were rolling green hills with not much to see except shepherds looking after the cattle. It was pouring with rain and the dirt roads turned to mud. We were travelling in a convoy of 4WDs but we still got bogged. We had to get out of it by rocking the car back and forwards. We finally got to the picnic site, all of us pretty cold. It was in a big tent. They were cooking our lamb. They killed one and chopped it up in front of us. They put in some of the lamb in an old steel urn, then some water and herbs, then they took some red hot rocks out of the fire and put them in. More lamb and herbs and water and hot rocks until the urn was filled to the top. They put the lid on and put it on the fire. We were all sat there drinking vodka, except for Sean, of course, who was getting stuck into the mares' milk.

Someone decided it was time to check how the lamb was going, so they eased the lid over to one side. I was sitting right next to it. The lid blew off and water and fat and everything went all over me. I was covered in lamb and fat and herbs from head to toe. When I got home I had to dry-clean my trousers five times to get out the smell. Once they realised I wasn't burned they all laughed and there was more fun and drinking. When it was finally cooked, the lamb was very tasty. The water became soup which we drank from big bowls. Then they passed around the red hot rocks, flicking them from hand to hand, which really kept us concentrating.

I stayed in a hotel with dowdy old carpets and worn out furniture. It was cold, there was only an old heater in the room. I visited the museum of natural history in Ulan Bator. It was a very cold building but it had what we were told was one of the world's best collections of fossil pre-historic animals. It was around the time the movie *Jurassic Park* was showing, so I was conscious of dinosaurs. The skeletons were huge and it was all very impressive.

I kept up my contact with Magvan after that. He saw me as a friend; the person who made the effort to come to see him in his country. Hardly anyone else ever did.

I also made close friends on my trips to South America. I made two visits there in the last few months of the bid. I saw Flor Isava again in her home town of Caracas in Venezuela both times. Flor was marvellous: forthright and independent. Many IOC members had impressive sporting records, but Flor had been a national golf champion, national tennis champion and national equestrian champion in showjumping and dressage. She was a member of the Venezuelan Olympic equestrian team for the 1956 Olympics in Stockholm. (The equestrian events were held in Sweden because of Australia's quarantine laws that year.) She had the most impressive trophy room I had ever seen.

I also got very close to Agustin Arroyo, the IOC member from Ecuador, and his children and his wife's children from her first marriage. When they knew I was coming the second time they rang me and said, 'You're not staying in a hotel. You must stay in our house.' Arroyo was initially evasive about which city he was going to vote for. His children were all saying to him, 'You've got to vote for Sydney.' One of his daughters actually said she didn't want him to come to her house if he wasn't going to vote for Sydney! By the end, I felt he wasn't going to vote for us. If he did vote for Beijing, he was entitled to. And in my discussions with him, he did have some very sound reasons for wanting to have the Games there. Of course, I felt differently but he was entitled to his opinion and we still became good friends. It was one of the things I noticed towards the end of the lobbying process — I was getting closer to some of the members and their families than many people I knew in Australia.

As we were pushing ahead, in the final days of our marketing campaign, there was an unnecessary diversion which involved some media heat and light — but not a lot of substance.

In early August, just before we were due to go to the IAAF track and field championships in Stuttgart, a media controversy flared up concerning Bruce Baird and Nick Voinov, the son-in-law of a Romanian IOC member, who got a temporary job at the NSW State Rail Authority.

It was really a minor issue, only slightly connected with the Games, which got blown up out of proportion. But it upset Bruce

Baird and was not something we needed in the final weeks of our quest to win votes.

The Romanian IOC member, Alexandru Siperco, had a daughter who had applied to emigrate to Australia with her husband, Nick. Phil Coles knew Siperco and told him we would keep an eye on them. It was one of those things anyone would do for a friend or colleague. Phil drove out to the airport and welcomed them, and they were placed in government migrant accommodation in Auburn. After a few weeks, I got Sue Bushby to see how they were going. They both were struggling with English, so we asked the Romanian community in Sydney to keep an eye on them. Sue would visit them or give them a call every so often.

She discovered they were lonely. We thought a television set might be helpful. We asked Philips, who were a sponsor of the bid, if they could make an old set available. They said they couldn't, so we asked if there was any objection to the bid office loaning the Voinovs one of the sets Philips had loaned us. They said it was all right, but as the sets were on loan, the Voinovs would have to return it at the end of the bid.

When Sue took the television out there, she could see that they were really battling. They had no jobs and warmed themselves by turning up the oven and leaving the door open. At one of our early strategy meetings it was mentioned that the Voinovs were doing it tough and hadn't got work. Someone around the table said, 'What does the guy do?'

Sue Bushby said he was an engineer. Bruce Baird said, 'I'll see if I can do anything.' In November 1992 Nick got a job as a temporary engineer with State Rail.

Now, if anyone else around the table had any connections with an operation that used engineers they would have helped. But John Coates, Peter Montgomery and I were lawyers, Geoff Wild was in advertising and Graham Lovett was in the sports business. There was nobody who had a natural ability to pick up the phone to someone in the engineering business except Bruce Baird. Baird always saw himself as just part of the committee. He never carried on about being the minister. He just rolled up his sleeves and made his contribution.

A month or two later, Sue Bushby went out to Auburn but found the Voinovs had moved into a flat in Maroubra. They wanted to be near the sea. They had arranged it all themselves and, again, we had nothing to do with it.

We had nothing to do with them migrating here. They paid their own fare and were in their own accommodation. And they had to give the TV back. The fact that the whole issue got blown up by the local press was most unfair to Bruce.

All Bruce did was make a phone call. We do it in the private sector all the time — I've employed many kids in my law firm because their dad was giving us business.

The Olympic family were totally supportive of Bruce, even if the Australian media weren't. They just said, 'We wouldn't expect anything else. You are part of the Olympic family. We all help each other.'

Bruce was feeling down at the World Track and Field Championships in Stuttgart over the Voinov matter, worried that he may have hurt the bid. But everyone was saying, 'Bruce, don't worry. It has been very appreciated by the Olympic committee that you tried to help a son-in-law.' Of the 1200 journalists from around the world at Stuttgart, not one of them thought the Voinov issue important enough to mention.

The World Track and Field Championships was the last major international sporting event before Monte Carlo. About 50 or 60 IOC members were going, so we had to be there.

The event had the potential to provide an eleventh-hour advantage for the Berlin bid. Having so many members in the country just before the vote gave the German bid an extra opportunity to impress members. Sydney had its chance for extra visits when it hosted the GAISF conference in 1991, but Berlin's big opportunity was a lot closer to the vote than ours'.

We knew that in Stuttgart the city and all the facilities would be excellent. There had been some suggestion that Stuttgart had been the preferred candidate for the 2000 Olympics but the Germans switched it to Berlin after The Wall came down.

But Stuttgart would provide fertile ground for lobbying for us too. We were going to run a hospitality room and distribute a special newsletter and brochures on Sydney's facilities for track and field. Then we learned that bid cities were to be charged for all exhibitions and hospitality areas — and charged a lot. When we had the GAISF conference we gave all the bidding cities space for exhibitions and hospitality in Darling Harbor for nothing. We thought it was a bit unfair to charge us for space in Stuttgart.

The events were held in a beautiful stadium in lovely grounds with wide pedestrian walkways leading up to it. The organisers had sold all the space along these walkways for stalls to sporting equipment manufacturers and other merchandisers. They offered us the right to do the same. But we didn't want to freight over merchandise and run a shop for ten days. And even if we did, the cost of the space would have been prohibitive anyway. We just said, 'Forget it. We're not interested.'

But we weren't deterred. Ian Dose, Margaret and Alan Hoskins went around all the hotels where the media and the representatives from the sporting federations were staying and the press centre, and distributed our brochures and newsletters which helped make up for our lack of an exhibition stand. None of the other cities took a stall either and the organisers were upset because it caused a shortfall in their budget.

We discovered the Berlin bid had a hospitality room in the IOC hotel while none of the rest of us were allowed to have one. We were surprised. Germans are normally pretty fair about these things. All the other cities were angry and the word was reaching the members. It ended up hurting Berlin as much as it helped them.

Other hiccups didn't help the German bid. The hotel where the IOC members were staying was quite new but it was not good. Room service was an hour late all the time and the members were complaining. We thought, this isn't doing Berlin any good at all — and Germany was paying for all those members to be there!

At Stuttgart I met up with my friend Hassan Agabani from the Sudan and watched him operate among the IOC members and the IAAF officials. I appreciated his significance in the movement more and more. He would often call me over and pass on a bit of information. He was a great colleague to have and a good source of intelligence. I went out to dinner with him one night and he kept saying to me, 'Rod. Things are fine. Things are fine.'

I was happy with how our lobby team went in Stuttgart — I thought we were consolidating our position nicely.

The Brazilian team finally announced its withdrawal from the race at Stuttgart, apparently to concentrate its efforts on the 2004 Games. After the Evaluation Commission's critical report, some IOC members questioned whether they should even bother to visit the city. It was becoming increasingly difficult for them to maintain any momentum. Brasilia's withdrawal meant that the possibility of the 16 Latin American members feeling morally obliged to support Brasilia in the first round — thereby reducing first-round votes for Sydney — was now over.

A lot of signs were emerging, suggesting that this time voting would be different; that people would vote more on the merits of cities rather than as a members of any voting blocs or in some complicated system of preferential patronage. The concern about the potential dangers of sympathy voting in the early rounds had already been translated into an IOC decision not to announce the votes for each city between rounds. Members were also showing a desire to see the game being played much more on its merits.

In the past there had been a lot of talk about the Latin countries always voting as a bloc. This time around the view that there was one solid Latin American voting bloc which could be directed by one or two IOC power brokers was no longer applicable. Flor Isava and Willi Kaltschmitt from Guatemala were all saying, 'There's going to be no more capricious voting. We all saw what nearly happened in Birmingham. The best bid is going to get the votes.' They said that after the vote for the winter Olympics in Albertville in February 1992 and they were still saying it at the end.

Brasilia's withdrawal removed another competitor for first round preferences and made it easier for a strong technical bid such as Sydney's to succeed. And that was all we wanted.

17

Monte Carlo Matchpoint

September 23, 1993. That date is engraved on our minds. There's no room here for next time.

Staffer, Sydney 2000

In January 1993 a staffer in the bid office told the *Sydney Morning Herald*, 'September 23, 1993. That date is engraved on our minds. There's no room here for next time.' From the beginning everyone who worked on the bid knew we were working towards one moment in Monte Carlo at 8.20 pm on 23 September in the Stade Louis 11 when President Juan Antonio Samaranch would announce where the Olympic Games would be held in 2000.

It was to be the end of a game in which there were no second prizes, no silver medals.

In theory, the winner should have already been decided in the minds of the IOC members by the time we got to Monte Carlo for the IOC session almost a week before. The winning team should have already made firm friends of more than half the members and convinced them of the soundness and superiority of its technical bid. In the conventional wisdom of the Olympic movement, a candidate city couldn't expect to win the Games in the final week but it sure could lose them.

Monte Carlo is the capital of the principality of Monaco, an independent state on the Mediterranean Sea, at the foot of the southern alps of France not far from the Italian border. The country has some 30 000 well-off inhabitants living in an area of about two square kilometres — one of the largest concentrations of wealth in the world. The city was built on a hillside with narrow streets, which makes it hard for cars to get around. An elegant, rich person's resort, it has good restaurants — and of course the casino — but it is very expensive. Most of the time it is a pretty quiet town. I'm sure it really buzzed when the Grand Prix motor racing was on, or the tennis, but I have never been there during any of the festivals. There was glamor associated with the name, but it wasn't the sort of place I'd go for a holiday.

Prince Albert, the only son of Prince Rainier and Grace Kelly, and heir to the Monaco throne, was the youngest member of the IOC. A charming man, always extremely friendly to me and the others on the bid, he had been to Australia a number of times and came to the GAISF conference in Sydney in October 1991.

For me, that final week at Monte Carlo was always going to be very much a working week — culminating in what was to be the most critical presentation of my professional life. The trick was to make sure our team looked and felt perfectly relaxed. I wanted ours to be the sales team which was totally confident of the quality of its product; professional and well informed; relaxed and assured — just there to have one last round of meetings with the customers, to give the product one final high-quality presentation before, hopefully, closing the deal.

I knew exactly what we should do that week. Take over the town — create an Australian atmosphere in the city so that everyone knew we were there. We were going to have Sydney 2000 banners, street performers, a didgeridoo player, a Sydney 2000 koala and Sydney 2000 kangaroo walking around. Our supporters would wear their colorful orange Sydney 2000 tee-shirts and the official team would wear their smart new Trent Nathan outfits. We would have events arranged for the media and the corporate supporters while our lobby team moved discreetly but effectively among the members. Every minute of every day in Monte Carlo, everyone on our team would know exactly what to do.

Australia was to be represented by a high-profile high-class varied team: Evonne Goolagong Cawley, Kieren Perkins, Dame Joan Sutherland, Paul and Annita Keating, John and Carolyn Hewson, Gough and Margaret Whitlam, Ros Kelly, John Fahey, Nick Greiner, Bruce Baird, Bob Carr, Frank Sartor, Sallyanne Atkinson, Charles Perkins and Donald McDonald.

Everyone would be friendly, confident and enthusiastic and everything would run smoothly. That was the plan.

Behind the scenes was more than a year of intensive planning and the combined experience of 12 years of Australian work in bidding for the Olympics. Nothing was to be left to chance. All the lessons we had learned from previous trips in taking away large groups, all the experience that we had gained from our previous presentations, everything that the Australian Olympic movement had learned from making three consecutive bids, would all come into play in Monte Carlo.

Our planning for that crucial week got underway when we made our preparations for the GAISF conference of October 1992. GAISF's headquarters are in Monte Carlo and every second year it held its annual meeting in the city. We saw the meeting as an opportunity for us to check out the city and do our homework for September 1993.

I decided that somebody in the office needed to be totally responsible for the logistical organisation for Monte Carlo 1993, someone who would make sure all the hotel bookings and transport were right and everything worked when we got there. I gave the job to Paul Clark. Paul was a senior NSW public servant who had done of a lot of organising for the opening of the Eastern Creek Grand Prix motor racing circuit. I thought he had the experience to plan our campaign logistics. Most of 1992 he was preparing bid books, but that work was winding up.

I also decided my assistant, Margaret, who was well organised and very close to the IOC staff and the secretaries of key members by then, should go too.

Paul and Margaret went to the GAISF conference in Monte Carlo to prepare for the next year — check out hotels, restaurants, availability of limousines and translators, and anything else we might need. They spoke to Danielle Roland, the former GAISF employee appointed to run the Monte Carlo session in 1993. She was at the GAISF conference and available to talk to anyone about the 1993 session — but I don't think any other bid city bothered. Margaret and Paul quizzed her on what everything would be like for that final session the following year. If Wal Murray and Graham Richardson thought rooms, coffee and other seemingly petty details were important we were not about to neglect them. All the bid cities were given a tour of the Sporting D'Ete, which was to be the venue for the presentation in 1993. We photographed and videotaped the whole place so we could show it to Greg Daniel, the chairman of our Communications Commission and everyone back at the office. Nothing was to be left to chance.

My legal background had given me a solid grounding in the need for attention to detail. It might sound fussy, worrying about limosine bookings 12 months ahead of time, but we knew we would have a big party of VIPs. Monte Carlo was a small city with limited resources: the citizens may be wealthy, but there's only 30 000 of them. If we got in early, we could have our pick of facilities. Any bid city that left things to the last moment could find themselves in trouble. If we were going to convince people we could run an Olympic Games, our team could not afford to be looking harassed by organisational problems on the last week.

At the GAISF conference, we also renewed our acquaintance with a man who had become a friend of the Sydney bid — Dr Luc Niggli. Executive director of GAISF, Dr Niggli lived in Monte Carlo. He knew John Coates well as they worked together on the organisation of the GAISF conference in Sydney in 1991. He was a very valuable fellow and we liked him a lot. He was due to retire as head of GAISF after the conference, so Coates asked him to become a consultant to the Sydney bid when he stepped down. He was to become part of the team and our man on the ground for our preparations for Monte Carlo 1993. He was very influential and we knew he could help us put everything in place.

A very proper man, Niggli said he couldn't accept any payment until after he retired from GAISF. When I saw him at Monte Carlo in October 1992 he looked sick and, sadly, he died a few months later. We made a payment to his estate for the couple of months he survived after he retired from GAISF when he was theoretically part of our team. A dear man.

As soon as we got back from the GAISF conference, I spoke to Greg Daniel, and asked him to start preparation for our presentation at Monte Carlo. At that stage it was going to be a full hour. We were looking at an exercise which could cost about $500,000, so we sure didn't want to be rushing it at the end.

Greg convened a sub-committee to prepare it, including Don

Morris from Mojo, Alex Hamill from George Patterson, Wilf Barker, who had been involved in the Brisbane presentation, Warwick Hastie and Mike Wrublewski, chairman of the Sydney Kings basketball team. I talked to them. So did John Coates. Kevan Gosper gave them his views when he was next in Sydney. Phil Coles, who had seen several presentations as IOC member, spent time with them, telling them what the audience was like and the good and bad things that had been done in the past.

We had to pick our speakers. We knew we could only have about six — and four picked themselves. You had to have the Premier, John Coates as head of the Australian Olympic Committee, Kevan Gosper as the most senior Australian figure in the IOC and me as the chief executive of the bid. We had to have an athlete and as far as everyone was concerned there was only one choice. Kieren Perkins had set records in the pool at Barcelona and was a very articulate, presentable individual. If we could get him, he was the one.

Daniel's committee came up with the idea of using a child in our presentation. We remembered the impact that a child's voice had in our video presentation to the Pan-American Sports Organisation meeting at Mar del Plata in Argentina earlier in 1993. That success convinced people that a child was right for Monte Carlo. And once it was decided, we had to have a child from one of the twinning schools. Enter Tanya Blencowe, move over Shirley Temple.

We heard Paul Keating could probably be there. We were very keen to have him. Keating is a very saleable guy. Britain's Prime Minister, John Major, would be there to support Manchester. Bob Hawke had gone to Tokyo in 1990, part of the presentation for the Melbourne bid and it was noted. We knew it would send out a very strong message if our Prime Minister was there. I had always personally liked both of the Keatings. They were an extremely impressive couple in themselves, and they sent out many appropriate signals about Australia — multiculturalism, youthfulness, style, the importance of children and the family. Their story was a great one: the boy from Bankstown who left school at 15 and became Prime Minister; the idyllic tale of meeting the air hostess on a plane and wooing her around the world.

I said at one of our board meetings that I was also keen to

have Annita in the presentation. I knew she spoke several languages and she had made a striking impression on members in
Barcelona. Simon Balderstone from the Prime Minister's office
said it would be unprecented for Paul and Annita to speak at the
same functions as they had a general rule about not doing so. He
said Annita didn't make many public appearances. It was a good
idea but it could be difficult to organise. At the next Board
meeting Simon said he was a bit more hopeful of getting her to
do it and, of course, in the end she did and she was magnificent.

As we began to formulate our plans, we decided that the presentation needed a producer. We had met a guy called David Mason
when he was doing a documentary for Channel 7 on the bid.
Everyone liked it. We interviewed a number of people, but
Mason got the job.

He then had to work up a treatment — who was going to say
what and what sort of visuals would be running while people were
speaking. The board took a very deep interest in it all. Mason
came to monthly meetings, showed us videos and took us through
the whole presentation as it developed.

There were differences of opinion about our style. I wanted a
presentation which fitted the Share the Spirit theme — young,
bright, informal, enthusiastic and colorful. I believed we would
go wrong if we did not go back to our original creative themes.
We had spent so much time getting it right early in the bid, it
was important to return to our origins and present a consistent
image. Phil Coles argued that we needed a more cultured
approach with classical music like Vivaldi because it had
impressed the members before. But I was very firm: we shouldn't
be changing our image at the last minute.

Gough Whitlam's former speech writer, Graham Freudenberg,
was retained to write the speeches which were then fine-tuned
by John Coates and myself. Then we got Neil Flett from Rogen,
the communications consultancy we used to train our staff in
speaking and presentation techniques, to advise us on our Monte
Carlo presentation. We started rehearsing individually from
about July. I put a lectern in my office. Every time I had a spare
15 minutes, I would close my office door and practise it. I must
have read my speech over 60 times. I can still say it.

We started rehearsing in earnest together in mid-August. Paul Keating came to the Sheraton Wentworth Hotel twice for rehearsals. We thought it was fantastic of him to make the time to do it.

At our first rehearsal we met Tanya Blencowe for the first time. A few people started to get worried about using a child. What would happen if she got nervous? Wouldn't adults be safer? But Tanya was just fine. Bruce Baird took a close interest in the rehearsals and made valuable comments. I also asked Donald McDonald to look in on them because I had a very high opinion of his judgement on artistic matters.

In the beginning I only made modest suggestions and people were still debating whether we should use 'Waltzing Matilda' or Vivaldi or 'I Still Call Australia Home' for the background music. But it was at the second rehearsal at the Sheraton that I really began to worry. I was unhappy with the videos for the presentation and I made my feelings perfectly clear. I thought a lot of the visuals were flat and boring. I couldn't understand why we had been spending so much money and getting such uninspiring stuff. It was not good enough and I let everyone know. Afterwards, Donald McDonald said to me privately, 'Thank God you said that. I was thinking the same thing.' My outburst seemed to galvanise everybody. Some of the videos were reworked. The background music was changed to use the Share the Spirit theme song, which I wanted.

The strategy committee decided it would be a good idea to make ourselves known to Australians living in Monte Carlo, some 800 of them, most of them couples.

I was talking to Lloyd Martin at the Opera House one day and he said, 'You should meet my sister-in-law from Monte Carlo. She's in Sydney.' Roxanne Clayton recommended that I make contact with Carole Davis, an Australian girl who lives with the European manager of the Loews hotel group. The Loews Hotel in Monte Carlo has always been one of the big convention hotels of the city, used by the IOC for the GAISF conference.

When I first went to Monte Carlo, Carole arranged a dinner for me to meet some of the Australians there. It included Mr and Mrs John Swaine, who had once owned the RM Williams company, Bob Cowper and his wife Dale, and a Mrs Wright whose husband Kerry represented Reg Grundy in Europe.

I told them what was going to happen in September 1993 and asked if they could help us. They said, 'Just tell us what you need. We know all the restaurants, the tennis club and the golf club. We'll do anything we can for you.' So when Margaret went back to Monte Carlo twice in 1993 she met Carole, who helped us with our arrangements. As it happened the IOC allocated the Loews Hotel for most of our staff. Most of the corporate supporters were also booked in there so we also used it for our corporate hospitality suite.

In the meantime I met another Australian resident of Monte Carlo, Richard Wiesner, while he was on a visit to Australia. He and his wife, Dianne, have a lovely villa and offered it if we needed it. They also helped out where they could, particularly in the critical moments in early September when there was a host of last minute arrangements to be made.

Having Australian contacts on the ground in Monte Carlo was a godsend in those final months. If we needed to measure up a room for something, they would be down there with a tape measure. They sent a lot of local detail which would have been difficult for us to get without the cost of sending someone over there again. And, as locals, they were so much better informed about how the place really worked than any visitor.

After Lausanne, of course, I had put Bob Elphinston in charge of organising it all. I had realised that Paul Clark was not senior enough to handle all the logistics for such a huge operation and it was not fair to ask him to do so. It needed a firm, experienced general manager and that's what Bob was. So he was supervising it all in our office with the assistance of Paul, Margaret, Silvana Griffin and Alan Hoskins.

It was a great comfort to me to know that Bob was handling that side of it. I thought I had learned my lesson in Barcelona about the importance of having a good operations manager, but it was only after Lausanne that I realised the importance of that person having seniority. It took a bit of time, but by Monte Carlo, which was the most important trip of all, we finally *did* get it right.

After the Mediterranean Games in Montpelier, France in June, Ian Dose and Silvana Griffin went to Monte Carlo for more planning. Margaret flew down to Monte Carlo again after the IAAF meeting in Stuttgart in August.

There was much debate on the board about who should go to Monte Carlo. There were some anxious times — at one stage not all the board members were on the list. Bruce Baird took a strong line: people should only go if they had a job to do. We were not paying them back for three years work by giving them a trip.

So some senior members of our staff got left behind and some junior members came. The decision was based on services, skills and needs, not seniority. Sue McElhone was our receptionist. She went to run the corporate support suite. She used to be the receptionist in the Premier's office. She had welcomed every corporate supporter into our office for three years, some of them many times. They all knew her and liked her, so she was the best person for the job.

Right up until the end there were issues of cost and how many people would be in our party. We had concerns about how the public saw it. There were obvious political sensitivities about going away with a large group. There was the question of whether we would take spouses with us. Until that time, board members on bid business travelled first class. Donald McDonald said he would prefer to travel business class and take his wife. Everyone agreed it would be a good solution and that's what happened. The bid company only paid for business class air tickets.

But only board members' wives went. As throughout our representation was in line with the IOC's. IOC members would be taking their spouses and it was the spouses of our board members who had entertained them on their trips to Sydney. We ended up with a party of 70 people going to Monte Carlo. People were constantly putting up 'good reasons' why we should take more, but we had to be pretty tough about it.

We had to cater for our corporate supporters. Atlanta had a very large support team for the decision in Tokyo and a number of our corporate supporters said they would come to Monte Carlo. We wanted to use them to create a Sydney 2000 community around us. So we organised a program of activities for them. We got Qantas involved in looking after them. We fitted them out with our orange Sydney 2000 tee-shirts and gave them corporate supporters kits and Sydney 2000 flags to hang out of their hotel windows.

We were allowed to take 80 media representatives but about 120 flew out of Australia for Monte Carlo, some direct and some travelling as part of the prime minister's international tour. We briefed journalists and corporate supporters in our office before we went so everyone would know what to expect.

We prepared a detailed briefing book for everyone going on the trip with a map setting out details of hotels and events and facilities and a complete itinerary for the week. Margaret and Lynne Jones masterminded all the travel bookings, a tough job, trying to hold seats for 70 people in planes months ahead and accommodating people's last minute changes. We got civic permits for our street performers. We booked up the hire cars and arranged all the drivers in advance.

In my own planning, from the beginning of 1993, I made a point of keeping the last three weeks before Monte Carlo relatively free. I deliberately did not schedule any international lobbying trips after 31 August. There were three reasons for this. I wanted to be able to take an emergency trip if one became necessary. I wanted to be around the office for the last days of planning and rehearsing for Monte Carlo. And, the most important reason, just to let myself slow down and get my breath back after so much travelling. I recalled the fatigue of Barcelona and focussed on the importance of being fresh for Monte Carlo. My jogging regime had certainly helped me get fit and cope with the thousands of miles of air travel I had done that year, but it was also important I be mentally refreshed as well. I briefed the key people going to Monte Carlo, including journalists, corporate supporters and other VIPs, but this was not difficult because the information was all at my fingertips by then.

I wrote a paper for our team saying it was critical that we all looked relaxed and happy. We had done the work, built the relationships. We didn't want or need to chase people around lobbies. We shouldn't be tense with one another. We were taking enough people to make sure it all worked. That was my fundamental direction to everyone who was going to Monte Carlo and it was the message I took on board myself. I knew what stress was about by then.

There are people who say they work better under stress. As a lawyer I was used to working long hours to tight deadlines and juggling a number of different things at a time. It was part of my life. But there is a fine line between pushing yourself and your team hard, and fraying at the edges in way that causes problems in your relations with your clients and your staff. Step over that line — particularly when you are the CEO — and you can jeopardise the very thing you have been working so hard for.

I pressed Mahmoud Elfarnawani on whether I needed to make a last minute trip back to North Africa. But he assured me that our votes were solid. That was the last trip I might have done, but — thankfully — he insisted it wasn't necessary.

My strategy of having a stress-free run up to Monte Carlo was working well. Everything was planned out and going smoothly. Everyone was working hard. We were on track. I suppose I should have expected something would go wrong.

Two weeks before we were set to go, a Sunday morning, I read the *Sun-Herald*'s page-one story and groaned:

Sydney Games
officials say:
<u>IT'S</u>
OURS!

No 'officials' were named — of course — but there were pictures of Phil Coles and myself. We were horrified. Any ordinary reasonable reader would have assumed that Phil and I were going around town boasting that we had the Games in our pocket. Nothing could be further from the truth. It was embarrassing. The Sydney bid team was often accused of being overconfident and arrogant by our rivals and we were particularly sensitive to the need to be humble and cautious about the outcome. We knew the IOC would read the story — it monitored everything. If the IOC believed Sydney was complacent and arrogant just before the vote, it could damage the bid.

I went down to the paper's Broadway office and I told the editor, Andrew Clark, 'You've really hurt us.' Andrew said the paper would not publish a correction because it believed the story to be true. But he said he would give us space to put another view in next week's paper. We did, but the headlines were unfortunate three weeks before the vote.

The final days in the office in Sydney getting ready to go Monte Carlo were horrendous. To get 70 people and all our gear away was never going to be easy. But we had 90 odd personal gifts for the IOC members and another 90 for their spouses, we had all the stuff that was to go in the hospitality suite, everything for the exhibitions and gear for the street performers. In total, there were 39 tonnes of cargo, all packed in our office. The boardroom was covered in satchels, a mountain of them. We were in the office half the night and all weekend, packing. I remember Silvana Griffin's daughter sitting in the middle of the boardroom table packing satchels one weekend. Silvana brought her in because it was the only way they could spend some time together. It was a time of huge effort, great expectation and nervous enthusiasm.

A member of staff told the *Sydney Morning Herald* what was it was like to work on the bid. 'There's a huge level of commitment to the bid in this office. I don't think anyone comes to work here unless they have a passion. They don't come here because it's a job.' You can only imagine what Australia could achieve if a lot of our workers — and their bosses — had the same commitment to organisational goals.

By September, the bonds between everyone in our office were very strong. As we came closer to Monte Carlo, people didn't want to be with anyone else — we had become such a cohesive team. I was very proud of that.

So we all packed up and went to 'heaven' as we called it then.

Paul and Margaret and other staff went ahead to set things up. Margaret rang me with daily reports. By the time I arrived, on the Friday before the announcement, they were all set up.

When I hit Monte Carlo I felt like a million dollars. Because I had taken the time to slow down, I was happy and relaxed, just how I wanted to be.

Our team had set up a hospitality suite in the Hotel De Paris, one of the main hotels where the IOC members were staying, which looks onto the Place Du Casino. The IOC had booked each bid city an identical suite but on different floors.

Peter and David Grant, who ran an exhibitions business in Sydney, had built picture boards which showed the entire skyline of Sydney Harbor. The mural was designed by Jamie Gordon. It went from floor to ceiling, with Centrepoint, the Opera House, the Harbor Bridge, pictures of beautiful blue skies and water and seagulls and clouds around the walls. At a bar at the end of the room, there was a boomerang and at the other bar there was a surfboard which made it look as if you were at Bondi Beach. No other bid city had done anything like that.

When you came into our suite, you walked in over the Harbor Bridge, through the pylons and down into the room. The mural was arranged so that there was a sweep of Sydney Harbor next to the window, and the window actually did look out over water. It was the Mediterranean of course but it blended in perfectly, next to the blue of the Pacific on our picture boards. Opposite the window was a giant picture of the Opera House with a huge white sail which we got the IOC members to sign. Peter and David didn't charge us anything for their professional time for setting it all up: not a penny.

Our corporate hospitality suite was at the Hotel Loews. Overlooking the Mediterranean, the Loews was built out over the roadway which is used for Grand Prix races. It was one of those universal American hotels with no particularly unusual character — but very efficiently run. Our staff and a lot of our corporate supporters stayed there. A short walk around from the Loews, as you turned into the Port de Monaco on the sea wall, was the Calypso Restaurant, a popular meeting point for Monte Carlo locals. It was a brasserie-style restaurant with good seafood. We had arranged for the Sydney bid team to take it over. There were Happy Hours with cut-price drinks between 6 and 7 every evening and the place became a meeting point for everyone connected with the bid. It was decked out in Sydney 2000 finery and became the informal home for all our supporters. If anyone needed an extra Sydney 2000 tee-shirt or a lapel pin they could get one there. I was too busy to drop in but I heard that Prince Albert visited a few times.

We had all sorts of little gifts for the IOC members. For members who like golf, we got Greg Norman to sign caps and gloves and photographs. Sir Donald Bradman signed cricket bats and posters. Dame Joan Sutherland signed books for the opera lovers. Evonne Goolagong signed photos for the tennis lovers. Nick Farr-Jones signed souvenirs for the rugby fans. We gave Henry Adefope a gardening book. For others we had Olympic coins. We had wattle brooches for a lot of the wives. The twinning schools had all done little projects for their members.

Drizabone supplied us with 90 of their distinctive raincoats for next to nothing. We delivered baskets of Australian produce to every member in their hotel room with an invitation to visit our hospitality suite.

We made sure there was plenty to do for the corporate supporters and others who had made the effort to come. We had celebrity lunches with Gough and Margaret Whitlam, Dame Joan Sutherland, Kieren Perkins, Evonne Goolagong and television stars, Ray Martin and Liz Hayes, who were covering the event for Channel 9. Margaret Whitlam did a guided tour of the picturesque nearby French hill town of St Paul de Vence.

John Fahey had a reception one night on the Pistou Terrace on the roof of the Hotel Loews which had a great view of the sea. There was a golfing day at the exclusive Monte Carlo Golf Club. At the Monte Carlo Tennis Club, Evonne Goolagong played in tennis round robin and had a few other friendly games. Kieren Perkins gave swimming lessons to Monaco youngsters. We had three performing groups, Stretch, Etcetera and the Great Bowing Company, wandering around the streets of Monte Carlo, as well as our big kangaroo and koala. It showed some of the contrasts of Australia. The five members of Etcetera walked around in business suits and solemn hats and ties. A group of Aboriginal musicians with a didgeridoo, played outside the Hotel de Paris, the haunting sounds attracting members to our hospitality suite.

Our corporate supporters hung their colorful Sydney Olympic flags from their hotel rooms. They looked great — but the Monte Carlo organising committee took a dim view of it. Fluttering flags, they said, contravened the city's outdoor advertising regulations and we had to ask everyone to take them down. We would have liked to have them out for the whole week, but they had achieved their aim. People knew that the Sydney 2000 team was in town.

We looked after the media. We set up a media centre in the Hotel Metropole where Deeta and I and most of our VIPs were staying. We held twice daily press conferences. The first was at 7 am to co-incide with night time television news and deadlines for the Australian newspapers. The second was at 5 pm, in time for Australian breakfast television and the evening deadlines of the European media. We wanted good coverage both at home and abroad. It was important for us to keep the Australian public informed and excited about our bid, but it was also important to keep ourselves highlighted in the international media which would be read by the IOC members. It was all part of the process of maintaining interest and a sense of freshness as we came to the end of a sales campaign far longer than any election campaign. We had news stories for every press conference. It was all planned in our media office in Sydney before we went by Ian Dose, Andrew Woodward and Hamish Fraser, and it ran like clockwork when we got there. On the first day I arrived in Monte Carlo, we gave a press conference announcing the homestay program for relatives of athletes which was to be co-ordinated by Rotary. The program would offer free bed-and-breakfast accommodation in Sydney during the games for up to two relatives of each of the 10 000 athletes expected to attend.

At another press conference we showed a film on the environmental aspects of the Sydney bid featuring endorsements from Tom Cruise and Nicole Kidman. We invited Paul Gilding, the Australian who was the executive director of Greenpeace International, and Karla Bell to the press conference. Gilding described the Sydney bid as 'the one which has taken the environment most seriously'.

Our press conferences raised considerable international interest. No other bid cities had planned them. At one stage Manchester must have felt the pressure was on and they decided to hold a press conference. Bob Scott opened it by saying he was only doing it because journalists wanted it. He said he had nothing new to say, but would answer questions. Fine, but it seemed to me that if you want good media coverage you have to put work into planning a press conference, the same way you would in planning any other important meeting. If you hold a press conference with nothing to say you are wasting everyone's time, just as if you called an important business meeting with no agenda. And if you don't set the agenda at such events, chances are someone else will and it may not be to your advantage.

The final week was for crucial last-minute lobbying. We set down clear rules on who was and who wasn't to go near the IOC members in Monte Carlo. We didn't want well-meaning supporters bothering members we knew were already on our side, or irritating others whose votes may have been finely balanced. Only official members of the lobby team were allowed near members. We worked out ahead of time which member of our team would be concentrating on which IOC members.

This meant I had to explain to even very senior people like sports minister Ros Kelly, who was there representing the Federal Government until Paul Keating arrived later in the week, that all the last minute lobbying was to be left to the official lobbying team. She understood and we organised a special program for her, including supporters' lunches and press conferences.

We made the same point to everyone in our pre-Monte Carlo briefings. One of these briefing sessions was attended by Judy Patching, an AOC member who was a veteran of the Australian Olympic movement. Judy had been involved in managing Australian Olympic teams from Rome in 1960 to Munich in 1972. He was secretary general of the Australian Olympic Federation (as it was then called) for 12 years to 1985 when he was succeeded by Phil Coles. A distinguished naval officer in World War 2, Judy was a very dedicated Australian with a great sense of fairness and purpose. Well known to the International Olympic Committee, he had gone to Barcelona with us to add strength to our lobby team. He and his wife had flown up from Melbourne for the briefing. I was explaining to the audience that we wanted our supporters to wear their tee-shirts and make sure that it looked like Sydney was in control of the town — but that we also wanted them to stay out of the way of the IOC members. I think some people in the audience thought we were being a bit tough. But Judy got up and supported me:

'I've been through all this. Those last days will be a frenzy. We shouldn't get in the way. These people know what they're doing.'

He was the emeritus campaigner giving public support to what we were trying to do. He knew how important it was for us to be following through our strategy in these final days. It could be crucial to the success of our bid. I appreciated Judy's comments very much.

We also arranged lunches and social functions with IOC members in advance. So when members arrived in town, the other teams would ask them if they were free for lunch and they would have to say they were booked. Sometimes people did not want to commit themselves ahead of time, but generally it worked. It was one of those small things which showed up the importance of planning and being well organised.

There were some touching moments for Deeta and I when we met up with people from the Olympic family who had become our good friends. We spent some time with Yancine, who came to Monte Carlo from Algiers with his father, Mohamed Zerguini. Three days before the vote, he presented Deeta with a bracelet — a Berber-style silver piece with sharp gems on it that you could imagine a Berber woman wearing. It was several hundred years old. He said to me, 'I have only ever given this gift once before — and that was to one of the wives of a member of the Atlanta team when I thought they were going to win. And I'm giving one to your Deeta as a good omen. I don't ever give them unless I think people are going to win.'

As the decision approached, the odds moved against us. London bookies made Beijing favorite. We wondered if someone was actually placing bets on as a public relations trick. Someone made inquiries and found out that a bet of $5,000 to $10,000 would have changed the odds in our favor! But we couldn't justify using public money for that sort of thing.

In the press, particularly the British press, there were suggestions that the Sydney bid was falling away and our own press picked it up. We said it was going to be close but we felt we were holding our ground. SBS Television quoted a Chinese official mentioning the possibility of boycotting the Atlanta Games if Beijing didn't win. Media controversy followed. It was hot news in Monte Carlo for about 36 hours. Some people thought it had hurt Beijing's bid, but the Beijing team told the IOC there was no question of a boycott. The controversy died down. I learned during the bid a lot of media controversies can be quite illusory. You worry about them, they generate a lot of heat and light, but people need more evidence that just a media report before they change their minds on an important issue such as their vote.

The international Olympic press — mainly British — were there in full strength. They regard themselves as the real experts on the bidding process. Most of them thought Beijing was going to win. They kept saying to us over and over again, 'Beijing's got it.' And I kept saying to them, 'You don't know what you are talking about. It'll be fine.' But they did irritate me a little because, in the end, I thought they didn't know as much as we did. Had they drank vodka and mare's milk with Shagdarjav Mavan in Ulan Bator?

Nicole Jeffrey from the *Australian* interviewed me a few days before the vote and asked me how things were going. I said, 'Things are fine, Nicole. The only thing that's going to worry us from now on is if one of the major powerbrokers makes a strong move against us and is effective.'

The big power brokers I had in mind, of course, were Joao Havelange from Brazil, the head of football; Mario Vazquez Rana, the head of all the NOCs; Primo Nebiolo, the head of world track and field; and President Samaranch himself. The *Sun-Herald* story published before we went to Monte Carlo had reported that Mario Vazquez Rana from Mexico told Paul Keating during a visit in September that he had originally favoured Beijing but was shifting his view towards Sydney. There were also rumors that the president favored Beijing — but I never found him to be anything other than even handed.

Then, all of a sudden, in the last 48 hours before the vote, we got tips that Havelange was making a move; that he was encouraging members to vote for Beijing. The reports we heard said he was targetting members from third-world countries in Latin America and Africa where he had a lot of influence. I went straight to Kevan Gosper and said, 'You've got to try and stop him. It's the one thing we can't lobby against. We're not in the room with him and we don't know what's going on.'

Gosper spoke to Havelange. Kevan said there was no problem

about who he supported — he was entitled to his own opinion — but he shouldn't criticise Sydney. Havelange had spent some weeks in Australia during the World Youth Soccer championships and he knew what it was like. Gosper is six foot four and can be quite formidable if he wants to. I wasn't present at their meeting, but I understood he was direct. And he did it on the floor of an IOC session, so other members saw him do it. It seemed to steady things down.

We wanted to make one last-minute splash to hold the Sydney bid in the minds of members. We booked a Sydney Olympics 2000 color advertising supplement over the front page of the *International Herald Tribune*, which was sold in Monte Carlo, for the edition of 22 September. Qantas donated the cost of it and we had the newspaper slipped under the door of every IOC member that morning. It was a day before the vote because we wanted to give the members time to read it and have the message sink in. We had organised it well ahead of the Monte Carlo week, but as soon as we booked it, we began to worry that somebody else might steal our idea and do it on the next morning, the day of the vote. So we booked space so that no-one else could do the same thing as we did the next day. It was not all deadly serious that week. Geoff Wild had never worn a pager before. He was having lunch with Richard Carrion, the IOC member in Puerto Rico, one day when his pager went off. I had arranged to send a message to him which said: 'Lock up the vote Sunshine!' which he thought was very funny. We were under a lot of pressure but there were still moments for a little bit of fun.

I don't know how many times that week I walked from the Metropole to the Hotel de Paris, where most of the members were staying, and up to our hospitality suite; or how many times I walked down the hill to a meal, or up the hill to get into a car. There were street performers wandering everywhere and my mobile phone was always ringing. It was hectic, but well planned. The only anxiety I had was about my own presentation before the members on that last day. There was only one occasion when somebody didn't think things were going right and wanted to have a meeting. Graham Lovett thought we had too many people in the lobbies of the two IOC hotels. It was too obvious and we didn't need it. He was right — but I wasn't going to have a meeting about it. I got him to tell Bob Elphinston and we eased back a bit. But, overall, it was probably the most relaxed I had been on any of our big overseas trips.

The evening before the vote, the morning in Sydney, I did a radio interview with Alan Jones of 2UE who was broadcasting from the Hotel Loews. It was amazing how the media had educated themselves so quickly about the technicalities of voting for the Games. They all sussed out that, for us to win, we needed to start with 30 to 35 votes in the first round, then pick up preferences in subsequent rounds. By this time we knew there would be 89 IOC members voting the next day. Ivan Slavkov from Bulgaria was under arrest in his country. That meant we needed 45 votes to win. 'Unless you're going to start with 30 votes, you've really got a problem. Brisbane thought they did and Melbourne thought they did and they didn't. Do you really have them?' Jones asked.

And I thought, there's no point kidding around now. I've either got to stick my neck out or not. 'Alan, I don't think there's any doubt we've got them. We'll start with 30 votes.' And we did!

By then, we had just about done everything we could, bar the final presentation. That evening we went to a cocktail party for members of the Sydney team on a yacht in the harbor hosted by Kerry Packer's stepmother, Lady Packer, who lived in Europe. Deeta and I took Sam and Judith Pisar along and then we all went off to a ballet put on for the IOC members in the Monte Carlo Opera House. Colleen and John Fahey, Pauline and John Coates and Deeta and I were invited from the Sydney bid team. The ballet was to be followed by an official dinner which all the members would attend. But by this time I knew we were coming to the end of the road. I thought, 'I don't want to get too carried away about this any more.'

I met up with a good friend, Ashwini Kumar, IOC member in India and his wife, Renuka, at the ballet. He had been to Sydney and I had been to New Delhi where he lived. He really liked Deeta. We asked them what they were doing afterwards and he said, 'Why don't we just have dinner on our own and forget all this official stuff?' It seemed like a great idea. 'That just suits me fine.' So Renuka, Ashwini, Deeta, Alain Dainet, who had run the Paris bid for the 1992 Olympics, and I had a quiet dinner at an outdoor cafe across the road from the ballet.

I wondered what people would think of the CEO of the Sydney bid missing his last chance to be with 60 or 70 IOC members and having a private meal with one who probably was going to vote for Sydney anyway. All the other bidders were all over the IOC members at the ballet and the reception afterwards. But I thought it was better to stay relaxed and enjoy the last night before my big presentation. I suppose if we'd lost I'd would have kicked myself for being naughty on the last night, but it seemed to me that an important part of the selling process was for the sales team to keep themselves in a relaxed frame of mind.

If you get to the point where you look like you are desperate for that big order and you are down on your knees begging for it, you detract from the quality of the product you're selling. If you know it is good, why would you be going to those extremes? It seems you have to be able to get to a point in a sale or a deal where you should be able to be relaxed and gracious and not be seen to be begging. As you give your final presentation, you have to be able to say to yourself, 'I know these people well, they know our product. I'm really here to say, hasn't it been great?'

Four years before, in Tokyo on the eve of the decision on the 1996 Games vote, Atlanta changed the pillow slips in all the bedrooms of the IOC members in the hotel. When they went back to their rooms, the members found a new pillowslip which said, 'Go to Sleep with Georgia on Your Mind.' We got the twinning schools to write a letter to their individual member and tied a ribbon around it and put it on their pillows. So the last thing the members got before they went to sleep was a little message from their own school children saying, 'Please give Sydney the Games.'

Thursday, 23 September 1993: Five cities would present for 30 minutes with 15 minutes of questions each. Presentation order was Berlin, Sydney, Manchester, a break for lunch, Beijing, Istanbul and the report by the Evaluation Commission. Then the vote at 6 pm in the Salle des Etoiles of the Sporting D'Ete, a circular congress building in a park beside the sea.

Each of the bidding cities had put up their exhibitions in other rooms in the Sporting D'Ete. We already had three rehearsals during the week at Monte Carlo — in addition to rehearsals back in Sydney — so we all knew what we had to do.

That's when I got a cold. I sucked about 40 throat lozenges that day. I thought, 'This is *not* the day to lose your voice.' I got some advice from Alan Grover from the Australian Olympic Committee, cox in the rowing eight that came second in the Mexico Olympics. Obviously a cox has to keep his voice. He told me lemon and honey was the only thing to take. So I took heaps.

That morning all the people involved in our presentation gathered in a room in the Metropole. I think our minders decided that was the way to stop anyone going missing.

We had a warm up session with Neil Flett, who wound us up like a football coach before a game. He told each of us to go to the lectern and shout. We had to look at each person and shout out their name and then shout out the numbers from one to ten. So it was, 'John, one, two, three, four, five, six, seven, eight, nine, ten. Rod, one, two, three, four. . .' When little Tanya had to shout to the premier she couldn't bring herself to call him by his first name. So it was: 'Mr Fahey, one, two, three, four . . .'

Neil Flett told us, 'There's absolutely no need to worry because you have your words. They'll be on the lectern. Don't try and wing it. Don't ever feel as though it's going to get away from you.' That was always the message: if in doubt, don't ad lib, go back to the speech.

There were 12 members of our team who would be on the platform for the presentation. Only eight would speak — Paul and Annita Keating, Kevan Gosper, John Fahey, Kieren Perkins, Tanya Blencowe, John Coates and myself. The others were Phil Coles, Frank Sartor, Bruce Baird and Sallyanne Atkinson. Sallyanne was our understudy. If anyone fainted or got sick, she was to give their speech. She had a complete set of them. She had sat in on the rehearsals and played Annita Keating. She christened herself 'Mum' and she would knit in rehearsals. She was a real pro. She had already done a presentation for the Brisbane bid and she wouldn't have blinked if she suddenly had to get up and fill in for someone. It was great just knowing she was there with us.

Kieren was given the task of looking after Tanya and making sure she was all right. He did a great job of talking to her and keeping her calm, but I think it was Kieren who was by far the most nervous of the two.

It was one of *the* moments of my life, heading off together as a team for the presentation. When we got to the hall, we were greeted by all our supporters, standing in a huge line outside under a covered walkway cheering us on. It was pouring rain.

We hadn't expected a welcoming party. Each city was allowed to have 100 supporters in the hall, behind all the IOC members, during their presentation. Our supporters were supposed to be seated before we got there. But the Berlin team was a bit behind time and our supporters had to wait for the German supporters to come out.

So when we walked in, we walked through a corridor of Australians wishing us well. I've never been in anything like that before. It must be what it feels like to run out onto the football stadium as a Wallaby; it's as close as I'm ever going to come to that anyway.

I remember Bonita Boezeman, the managing director of Time Life in Australia, saying, 'Break a leg.' I didn't know it was a curious theatrical expression of good luck, but obviously she meant well. I could see my assistant, Margaret, who was busy putting the special passes we needed on everyone's name tags. When she looked at me, I could tell she didn't know whether to say 'good luck' or not. I could see Donald and Janet McDonald and the Wilds waiting there.

People were patting us on the back and saying 'good luck.' And the press were all over us, saying, 'Do you think its going to be OK?'

I remember Kieren Perkins using that wonderful showbiz expression, 'Hey. It's going to be all right on the night.' But it was pretty tense, walking single file through all those people, into the room.

All the IOC members were sitting in the front rows of the hall, in order of protocol. Behind them were our supporters. Up front, on the stage, was President Samaranch and the other members of the IOC executive board, looking at the audience. The team making its presentation was positioned near the front but off to one side. We spoke facing to the members and our supporters, while the president and the TOP team actually watched the presentations on television monitors.

We were the only group to have synchronised visuals showing while people spoke. So when John Fahey spoke about trains and buses, they appeared on the screen behind him. Thanks to our rehearsals, everything went off smoothly.

I spoke last. Nothing but a spotlight. I didn't feel nervous. We had rehearsed so much. I wanted my speech to have a high-minded tone. Just as I had at the GAISF conference in Sydney in 1991, I wanted to make my final presentation one which touched on both the ideals and the obligations of the Olympic Charter.

I reminded the members that 70 per cent of our venues for the Games were ready, or almost ready. That ours would be The Athletes' Games, where, for the first time in a modern Olympics, all the competitors and officials would be able to walk together from the village to the opening and closing ceremonies. I spoke of the strong environmental principles encompassed in our bid, of Sydney being a city of safety and friendship and of Australia's unbroken commitment to the Olympic Games. We were not saying 'Sydney is the best', we were saying what we were planning would be wonderful for the whole Olympic movement. So I said, 'Our pledge to you today is that a successful Sydney bid will protect and promote' all the principles and traditions of Olympism. I concluded, 'Our fervent hope is that the choice you make today will give Sydney the honor of delivering to you an Olympic Games in the year 2000 which will strengthen even further the glory of the Olympic movement.'

John Coates and I had to answer the questions. I didn't know what they were going to ask so I was prepared for everything. I had initially proposed to have Bob Elphinston with me to handle some of the technical questions — but at the last minute they said he couldn't be there. So John Coates, who was already part of the presentation, was the one to help me. I had a crib book with me specially indexed so that I could find anything quickly. Sallyanne looked after it for me and handed it to me after my speech.

When it came to the questions, they were all kind. Prince Albert of Monaco asked a question on the cultural program. Paul Wallwork from Western Samoa asked about sporting assistance to Olympic committees. Denis Oswald from Switzerland asked about ticketing and the access of athletes to events.

John and I answered them without looking at the crib and we were happy with our answers.

Somehow the ambience and the power of our presentation all seemed to work.

At the end of it, the IOC members were all filing out of the room for a coffee break. As they came past, they said, 'Congratulations. Well done,' but I think they said that to everyone.

And then our 100 supporters came out. They were tremendously supportive and thought we were wonderful. Some of them were crying. I think they lived through every second of the presentation like we did.

After that, my feet never seemed to hit the ground. Tanya and I were whisked off for a live television cross to Australia. Channel 9 had a tent set up in the grounds and Tanya and I were sheltered underneath beach umbrellas to avoid the heavy rain as we rushed down to it, to do the interviews.

Then we had a general press conference. People quizzed us about how Tanya had gone and how everything else had gone.

Then there was a celebrity lunch for all the corporate supporters with Kieren Perkins, Evonne Goolagong and John Brown. I went to it but I don't remember eating.

There was nothing more I could do.

At 6 pm that evening we were due at the Stade Louis 11, at the southern end of Monte Carlo for the announcement ceremony. It was held in an indoor basketball arena underneath the football stadium. Deeta and I decided to wear our Akubra hats to show we were Australian through and through.

It was hell in the hall, trying to get everyone seated. Each bid city was treated equally for the seating, so we were all given a narrow bloc of six seats across, stretching down the back of the hall, like a long thin rectangle. I sat in the front with John Fahey and John Coates but most of our team was in the rows behind us.

The narrow shape of our seating meant that we had to keep moving people back as more important people came later. Bob Elphinston had to keep asking people's wives if they would go back a row. Deeta was moved back and was unhappy about it. There were near riots, but everyone was eventually seated. Berlin was on one side of us, Manchester on the other. There was a good spirit between the teams. At one stage, the Chinese girls choir started singing, so we responded by singing Waltzing Matilda. The other teams answered with their own songs but our lot eventually managed to drown everyone out.

The pressure was building up, but I felt composed. I suppose I'm just a terribly fatalistic person. I believe if you can't control something in life, then you shouldn't worry about it. I knew we had done the best we could.

John Fahey was a nervous flyer and often carried a St Christopher medal. Five minutes before President Samaranch got up on the stage Colleen Fahey lent over and gave John a St Christopher which he held in his left hand. John was a heavy smoker and he couldn't smoke in there, so he was fidgeting and moving around.

As the IOC members filed into the hall, the whisper went around our team, 'She's got the scarf on. She's got the scarf on.' Flor Isava, the IOC member from Venezuela, had become a great friend of the Sydney bid team. She had told us that if we got into the final round of voting she would wear the floral Sydney scarf when the members came back into the hall after they had finished voting. Because of the new rules about keeping the totals secret, she wouldn't know the result, but she would know if Sydney was one of the final two. If we weren't she was going to have the scarf tied to her handbag. I wasn't going to look at Flor when she came in. I didn't think I needed to know at that point. But the others couldn't resist and Coates was beside me saying, 'She's got the scarf on. She's got the scarf on.'

As President Samaranch started speaking, John Fahey gripped my hand.

But I felt perfectly calm. I just looked at President Samaranch and thought, 'You're going to read out "Sydney".' And when he did, I felt a tremendous surge of relief; a feeling of, 'Oh well. That's that.' I hadn't quite expected I would be dragged to my feet by an exuberant premier.

I went up onto the stage, amid all the chaos and the confusion, but I tried to keep out of it all. The press were all around and the politicians were being interviewed. My head was aching and I moved to the back of the stage. Then, through the crowd, a man came up. It was Samuel Pisar — the survivor of the Holocaust, the teenager who had come to Melbourne to be educated and went on to become a top international lawyer, President Samaranch's own personal counsel, adviser to the IOC for more than a decade, a man who knew the movement backwards, the man who had been so concerned how Deeta and I would handle defeat. He just looked at me. It felt like ten seconds. It was probably one. He shook my hands and just said, 'I don't know how you did that.'

Then he walked off the stage.

18

Towards the 27th Olympiad

Citius. Altius. Fortius.

Olympic motto, literally 'Faster, Higher, Stronger'

Home. When I realised how enthusiastically Australians had reacted to the news I really became, for the first time, emotional about it. Until then I had been so focussed on achieving our goal that I had no idea that it would have such an impact.

In Monte Carlo I was in a sort of semi-detached mood after the decision. But when we got back and saw the televised scenes of people erupting with joy at the decision — at Sydney Harbor, the Sports Centre at Homebush and even in Melbourne — tears came to my eyes. The enthusiasm was amazing. I had never expected the tickertape parade down George Street but it was wonderful to see the people of Sydney so enthusiastic about the news augured well for the 2000 Games. When I was invited to join the parade there was one thing I wanted to make sure of — that Bob Elphinston was there in the car with Deeta and I. He wasn't going in the car behind us — he was going in our car. Bob had been such a powerhouse of support for the bid and for me for more than two years. He never got much publicity but I could never have done what I did without him. He's a wonderful guy, he deserves a lot of credit and he will be a valuable member of the team which organises the Games.

Everyone wanted to hear about *how* we had done it. I was inundated with requests to speak, to tell the story, reveal the method of how Sydney won. I accepted a lot of them between September and Christmas 1993. I'd often show snippets from our presentation at Monte Carlo and was surprised at the emotional response they evoked.

I got hundreds of letters from people all over Australia, but there was a hand delivered one I particularly remember.

It was about a week after I got back, at a speech at the Powerhouse Museum in Ultimo. A stern looking woman in her fifties came up and handed me a letter and said, 'I'd like you to read that.' I figured she was from one of our 'twinning' schools.

'I hope this isn't a problem for me,' I said, a little warily.

'No. I'd like you to read it.'

There wasn't even a hint of a smile.

I read it driving back to the office. It was a very moving letter. She wrote about going to listen to the announcement on the morning of 24 September. She had driven to Central, near the railway station, and parked. She walked down towards Circular Quay where the celebrations were to be, but for a long time she didn't see anyone. She wondered if she was going to be the only one there. But then she started to see the crowds and realised that thousands had turned up. When Samaranch's words came over the loudspeakers some guy had just picked her up, whirled her around and put her back down again. She was a pretty conservative woman — the headmistress of a school. She said it was the greatest moment of her life *as an Australian*.

It was that way for many, a great moment in our history. Nearly everyone I speak to can still recall where they were and what they felt when they learned the news on that day.

So, with the wisdom of hindsight, why did we win? From the start, as I've made clear, I always believed Sydney had a very serious chance. We were always one of the front runners — the trick was to translate that into victory.

Some of it had to do with geography. The IOC likes to see the Games shared around the world. The summer Olympics were held in Asia in 1988, Europe in 1992 and will be in the Americas in 1996. There was a good argument for the 2000 Games to come to Oceania — or at least the Asia-Pacific region. Unlike Melbourne, Sydney had not hosted a Games before. In the bid for the 1996 Games, the IOC knew Melbourne was perfectly capable of staging another successful Olympic Games — the report of the Evaluation Commission told them that. But it is extremely difficult for a city to be able to host a Games twice, particularly when there are strong alternatives. And in the last 20 years the bidding for the right to hold an Olympics has become far more competitive.

A lot of it had to do with being well prepared, which is important no matter what business goal you are trying to achieve. Nothing beats extensive preparation. By the time Sydney got the final nod from the Australian Olympic Committee in March 1991, the NSW Government knew exactly what needed to be done to stage an Olympic Games and was well down the track in planning the venues. Once it was decided that Sydney was the Australian city to bid this time around, the state government and then the bid office moved ahead very quickly in planning and construction. Having a strong technical bid was one of our best assets. The task of the bid office was two-fold to make sure that was true — and get that message across to the members.

Our commitment to making Sydney The Athletes' Games was also important. Sydney not only provides a wonderful scenic setting for the Games, but its weather in spring, when they will be held, should be ideal for the athletes. Australia has always been committed to the ideals of the Olympic charter. Australians have always believed in the importance of fair play and making friendships through sport. We were not an economic superpower wanting to use the Games to strut our stuff on the international stage — we were always just a country whose citizens loved sport and had a high respect for the Olympics and Olympism, who just wanted to stage a great Games for everyone.

And looking back, you'd have to say Australia bidding for the third time in a row was a big advantage. It showed the Olympic family that we were a country which was serious and persistent about holding an Olympics. Our key lobby team members — Gosper, Coates and Coles — already had strong knowledge of the bidding process and firm friendships with IOC members. Before I was involved, the Australian Olympic movement had a detailed up-to-date knowledge of all the rules and conventions of lobbying, what was important in the bidding process, which way members were likely to vote. The recent experience of everything that had happened in the Melbourne bid, what Atlanta had done right, the connection of people like Sallyanne Atkinson way back from the Brisbane bid helped us avoid all sorts of traps for new players, of which bidding is full. Any city starting from scratch two years before a decision will have to work incredibly hard to learn the ropes.

We had the unequivocal support of our State and federal governments and the AOC. They were always behind us, which was very important to the IOC. There was also a strong degree of public support and the Australian business community got right behind us. While it created some headaches for me, the emergence of the Ross Turnbull's group showed how committed senior members of the Australian business community were to having Sydney host the Games.

A lot of credit has to be given to Nick Greiner, the premier who made the commitment to go ahead with the bid. Greiner had the foresight to appoint some of the best talent that Sydney and Australia could offer on the bid committee and our commissions. We had some of the highest calibre people in Australia, leaders in their fields, assisting the bid in all sorts of ways. John Fahey followed him with an equally strong commitment to the Games — to doing all we could to win, and also making sure that everything was done in the right way.

The Atlanta bid set new standards. But I'd like to think that ours were even higher — that ours was the most professional bid for an Olympics ever run.

The Atlanta bid and Sydney's success confirmed the importance of having the right team. This will be critical for any city wanting to host a Games. The bid team has to be young enough so that the IOC members believe the bidders will still be around for the Games themselves — but they can't be so young that they are inexperienced. They have to be good public presenters — basically the leaders in their field, the cream of that city's business, cultural and sporting communities.

As in business, there's the product and then there's the sales team. You have to get the product right — but the key thing was building firm relationships with the IOC members. They liked us and they wanted to do business. We worked hard to build those friendships. We didn't rush it but we took a professional approach to building up relationships, and finding what was important to the members as individuals. It's important in business or any sales pitch. We maintain those relationships as we work towards the Games themselves.

Since the decision, many people have asked me about the details of the vote at Monte Carlo — who voted for us, who didn't, what happened between rounds, how the votes shifted. We won by 45 votes to 43 in the fourth round of voting. Frankly, I had expected to get more votes than we did. I hadn't expected it would be as close. But in the end we won. No amount of debate and discussion about who voted for whom will change that fact. I have a pretty good idea about most of the people who supported us. As for the others, well, I'll never know.

For those with a taste for analysis may like to study, as we did, the previous two voting rounds for a summer Olympics:

1986 LAUSANNE	1	2	3		
Barcelona	29	37	47		
Paris	19	20	23		
Brisbane	11	9	10		
Belgrade	13	11	5		
Birmingham	8	8			
Amsterdam	5				

1990 TOKYO	1	2	3	4	5
Atlanta	19	20	26	34	51
Athens	23	23	26	30	35
Toronto	14	17	18	22	
Melbourne	12	21	16		
Manchester	11	5			
Belgrade	7				

And compare this with how they voted on this occasion:

1993 MONTE CARLO	1	2*	3	4
Sydney	30	30	37	45
Beijing	32	37	40	43
Manchester	11	13	11	
Berlin	9	9		
Istanbul	7			

* A total of 89 IOC members cast votes for the first two rounds. One member, David Sibandze from Swaziland, withdrew at the end of round 2, leaving 88 IOC members voting.

The only concrete observation you could make was the shift in votes from the first to the second rounds when Istanbul dropped out. Now, maybe one could assume that five of the people who had voted for Istanbul in round 1, transferred their votes to Beijing in the second round and the other two voted for Manchester. But we knew the member in Turkey, Sinan Erdem, pretty well and he had assured us that if Istanbul dropped out, he would vote for Sydney. It's a secret ballot and you never really know what happened.

Frankly, it surprised me that 43 members were prepared to vote for Beijing. Dick Pound from Canada told me he had voted for Beijing because he believed it would spread the message of Olympism to more than a billion extra people. He's entitled to his opinion but to have a regime build up the importance of winning a Games to such political heights, I think, is frankly dangerous for the Olympic movement. Some of the events that have happened in China since September 1993 have only served to prove my point. After we won many people came up to me and said Sydney's success had saved the Olympic movement. I think there was something in that.

There is a postcript to our narrow win and the final round's even number of voters. A Spanish journalist asked President Samaranch what he would have done in the event of a tie between Beijing and Sydney. He said he would have gone to the executive board for directions on how they would prefer he used his casting vote. When asked what the board would have recommended, he said, 'Sydney'.

But there's no point mulling over the vote. It's important to get on with the next thing: the challenge ahead. The task is now to organise the best Games in the history of the Olympic movement.

I am no longer part of the day to day operations of the office where I spent so much of my life from 1991 to 1993 but I remain a part of the Sydney Olympic Games Organising Committee, or SOCOG as it is more generally known. It is an acronym which Australians will hear much more of in the years to come.

I take away a lot of fond memories of the bid — of Paul Wallwork and his rugby and Ray Connif, of sailing with Jacques Rogge, of my friends Ashwini, Mzali and the wonderful Flor Isava. Samuel Pisar remains one of the most impressive people I have met and I will never forget his gentle concern about how we would handle defeat. I have nothing but the highest respect for the work and the commitment of John Fahey, Nick Greiner, Bruce Baird, Kevan Gosper, John Coates, Phil Coles — and of course Bob Elphinston. They were all dedicated to making the bid a success and fine Australians. And I'll always value my friendship with President Samaranch who has worked so hard and done so much for the Olympic movement.

One of the great things I got out of the bid was an appreciation of Spanish culture. The Australian culture is still very much Anglo-Saxon. We really have little idea of Spanish culture and the the Spanish/Latin approach to life. There is a different attitude — to culture, to enjoying life, to relationships between men and women, to family life. I began to appreciate it in my time in Barcelona and my trips to Latin America and in my meetings with the 'Latin' members — from President Samaranch to Flor and Agustin Arroyo and Mario Vazquez Rana. There's another rich culture in the world which Australians should take more time to understand and appreciate.

So now Sydney and Australia is busy preparing for the 2000 Games. There will be many young Australians already training and thinking about those Games. To those I have one message: if you have a chance to represent your country, take it, go for it. These days there is a whole new career path open to successful athletes. Devoting time to sport doesn't have to consign you to penury for the rest of your life. You'll only get one chance in your life to represent your country. The Games will be very special in Australia's history.

The 1956 Olympics in Melbourne showed the kind of legacies that a country gets from a Games for the next 50 years. Those Games created some fantastic memories for Australians and legends that live on like Dawn Fraser, Betty Cuthbert and Murray Rose. The 2000 Games will see the emergence of another generation of Australian sporting heroes who will be part of our lives and those of our children.

I don't have any doubt that Australia will stage a great Games. It will be a great two weeks to be in Sydney. For those of us involved in organising the Games, there are some important points to keep in mind. We need to make sure that it will be the Games for the whole of Australia. Melbourne's were in 1956. The Games should not be just about Sydney — it should be about Australia. We should keep this in mind in all our planning — from the ticketing to the torch relay. Chances are Australia won't see another Olympic Games for a 100 years after 2000. We've got to make sure it's the Games for all Australians.

But we need to go further than that. The 2000 Games should be the Games of Oceania. There is a great hidden culture in Oceania that the rest of the world should see. I can imagine an opening ceremony which brings together the cultures of all the people in the region — with grass skirts and flower headdresses, mud people from PNG and Maori hakas, gentle Fijian rhythms and Samoan grace. And Aboriginal and Torres Strait Island music most of all. Add some Australian rock music. It could be a pageant which moved through the years of history — from the early days to the modern day, with Aboriginal and islander music followed by the music of modern Australia.

It would be a knock out.

But we also need to be very sensible about delivering the budget. It's highly achievable. We did a good, realistic budget for the bid, on which we delivered. We should do that for the Games themselves. The 2000 Games doesn't need to be a Rolls Royce Games. Just because it's Olympic doesn't mean everything has to be gold-plated. The IOC doesn't expect extravagance — and indeed it would be worried if costs got out of hand. Barcelona showed that cost-saving is acceptable and works.

We need to show the world that we are proud of having the Games — particularly from 1996, after the Atlanta Games. We should put the Olympic flag at the top of Centrepoint as big as we can make it. Atlanta is very proud to be staging the 1996 Games and we should be too.

When I think of the wonderful staff I had on the bid — my superb assistant Margaret, Bob, Silvana, Ian, Hamish, Melissa, John, Sue Bushby, Sue McElhone and everyone else, working nights, weekends, Christmas Day — I am reminded of the words of US President Theodore Roosevelt:

It is not the critic who counts, not the man who points out how the strong man stumbled or where the doer of deeds could have done better.

The credit belongs to the man who is actually in the arena; whose face is marred by dust and sweat and blood; who strives valiantly; who errs and comes short again and again; who knows great enthusiasms, the great devotions, and spends himself in a worthy cause; who, at the best, knows in the end the triumph of high achievement; and who, at the worst, if he fails, at least fails while daring greatly, so that his place shall never be with those cold and timid souls who know neither victory nor defeat.

And that's the message Australia should carry as it prepares for the 2000 Games. Let the credit belong to those in the arena, trying for success, with the sweat and dust of effort on their face. Let's not let our efforts be torn down by the critics. We may stumble but we will have a great Games in 2000. It's a great opportunity for the country.

A study by accountants KPMG Peat Marwick estimated that Sydney winning the Games would boost the Australian economy by $10 billion until the year 2004, bring 1.2 million extra tourists to Australia and create 195,000 new jobs over a 10-year period. Many people argue that being awarded the Games has already started to have an impact on our economy. Some people set the date for when the Australian economy started to pull out of the recession from the date Sydney won the Olympic Games. Maybe we did have something to do with it. But the Olympic Games is much more than that.

The 2000 Olympics will be the greatest peacetime event in Australia's history. The Melbourne Games were fantastic but we will surpass ourselves in 2000. It will be something that all Australians will never forget. For many people, it will be the greatest time of their lives; and an event which lives on in their memory. After 2000 Australia may not get another Olympic Games for another 100 years. Those Australians lucky enough to be alive in 2000 will not only witness some marvellous sporting performances but they will be touched by that unbelievable spirit of friendship and comradery that is part of the Olympics.

One of the reasons Australia won the bid for the 2000 Games was that we convinced the Olympic Family that we — the staff in our office, the Olympic Movement in Australia, the Prime Minister, the Premier, the children in the twinning schools, the workers out at Homebush and every other Australian who shared the spirit cared about the Olympic ideals. Australia is a nation which genuinely does stand for the goals and principles which are the very foundations of the movement. It was up to those of us lucky enough to be directly involved in the bid to get this message across.

It will be one of the most important moments in Australian history when they light the flame at Sydney Olympic Park. At the start of a new millenia Sydney will be the focus of the Asia-Pacific region and the world will watch.

I can't wait to be there.

Appendix 1
Sydney Olympic 2000 Bid Limited Staff

Jo'anne Abignano
Oscar Andreazza
Virginia Bagley
Justine Baker
Chris Barnum
Nicky Bethwaite
Gavin Blatchford
Corinne Blatter
Christie Bourke
Helen Brownlee
Rosalyn Burns
Sue Bushby
Clare Carter
Sue Channels
David Churches
Paul Clark
Lauretta Claus
Alan Cunningham
Juliana Dignam
Peter Dolier
Ian Dose
Jane Drew
Bob Elphinston
Sally-Anne Farquhar
Amana Finlay
Hamish Fraser
Angela Garniss
Suzie Grierson
Silvana Griffin
Alan Hoskins
Sue Hunt
Mark Jackson
Robert Johnstone
Lynne Jones

Brad Kenworthy
Damien Keogh
Rosemary Kurtz
Karen Lange
Belinda Lovett
David Mason
Sue McElhone
Roderick McGeoch
Margaret McLennan
Lisa McMahon
George Mellick
Angela Meucci
Eddie Moore
David O'Connor
Melissa Petherbridge
Dennis Poropat
Bob Prater
Gemma Purcell
David Rathgen
David Roberts
Helen Rowley-Bates
John Shirley
Kevin Simmonds
Julie Symons
Susie Tuckerman
Justina Tulloch
Annalisa Turner
Ricky Walford
Louise Walsh
Peter Wejbora
Jannelle Witschi
Andrew Woodward
Peter Woolcott

Appendix 2

Sydney 2000 Bid: Committee and Commission Members

Sir Peter Abeles — Bid Committee

Wendy Adam — Transport Committee

John Alexander — Bid Committee

Dr Graham Ambrose — Health Care Committee

Dr Bernie Amos — Health Care Committee

Neville Apitz — Homebush Bay Committee

Steve Arnaudon — Sports Commission

Sally-Anne Atkinson — Bid Committee

Bruce Baird MP — Bid Committee, Executive Board, Strategy Committee

Wilf Barker — Communications Commission, Media Committee, Games Media Revenue Task Force

John Barraclough — Transport Committee

Sally Begbie — Cultural Commission

Jeremy Bingham — Bid Committee

Dr Ian Blackburne — Communications Commission

Dr Wayne Blackhouse — Equestrian Quarantine Working Group

Jim Bosnjak — Transport Committee

Adrian Boss — Design Review Panel

Beverley Bowyer — Environment Committee

Paul Boyce — Games Travel Subsidy Working Group

Bevan Bradbury — Corporate Support Committee

Gordon Brice — Security Planning Committee

John Brown — Bid Committee, Cultural Commission

Ken Brown — Sports Commission

Helen Brownlee — Community Support Committee

Bill Cairns — Building Commission, Finance Commission, Olympic Project Management Committee

Jenny Calkin — Accommodation Planning Group

Bob Campbell — Games Media Revenue Task Force, Media Committee, Communications Commission

Ross Campbell-Jones	Communications Commission
Edmund Capon	Cultural Commission
Andrew Cappie-Wood	Building Commission, Estimates Sub-Committee, Facility Operation Group, Homebush Bay Committee, Olympic Project Management Committee, Transport Committee
Bob Carr MP	Bid Committee
Ron Christie	Building Commission, Olympic Management Project Committee
Ann Churchill-Brown	Cultural Commission
David Clark	Bid Committee, Community Support Committee
Paul Clark	Security Planning Committee, Transport Committee
Michael Cleary	Bid Committee
John Coates	Bid Committee, Equestrian Working Group, Executive Board, Games Travel Subsidy Working Group, Strategy Committee
Peter Coe	Building Commission
Phil Coles	Bid Committee, Executive Board, Strategy Committee
Peter Collins MP	Cultural Commission
John Constantine	Sports Commission
Dr Brian Corrigan	Health Care Committee
Ron Cotton	Building Commission
Ken Cowley	Bid Committee
Richard Cox	Transport Committee
Frances Crampton	Community Support Committee
Phil Crane	Design Review Panel
Roger Crellin	Accommodation Planning Group
Perry Crosswhite	Sports Commission
Elizabeth Crundall	Community Support Committee
Greg Daniel	Bid Committee, Communications Commission, Corporate Support Committee, Executive Board, Monte Carlo Presentation Sub-Committee, Strategy Committee
John Davies	Health Care Committee
Dick Day	Transport Committee
David Denton	Building Commission, Media Committee, Security Planning Committee, Sports Commission

John Devitt	Bid Committee, Executive Board, Sports Commission
Sasha Dimitric	Transport Committee
Michael Donovan	Transport Committee
Dr Frank Doughty	Equestrian Quarantine Working Group
James Dunstan	Building Commission, Estimates Sub-Committee
Ron Eagle	Olympic Project Management Committee, Security Planning Committee, Sports Commission
Mary Easson	Communications Commission, Community Support Committee
Michael Easson	Bid Committee
Justice Marcus Einfeld	Bid Committee
John Fahey MP	Bid Committee, Executive Board
Graham Farrer	Accommodation Planning Group
Peter Ferris	Building Commission, Estimates Sub-Committee
Barry Flynn	Facility Operations Group
Brian Foster	Security Planning Committee
Lindsay Fox	Building Commission
Dawn Fraser	Bid Committee, Corporate Support Committee
Leon Fredkin	Design Review Panel
John Garvey	Security Planning Committee
Neville Goldspring	Facility Operation Group
Kevan Gosper	Bid Committee, Executive Board
John Grant	Communications Commission
Kerrie Green	Games Travel Subsidy Working Group
Julian Gregory	Accommodation Planning
Nick Greiner	Bid Committee, Executive Board
Wolfgang Grimm	Bid Committee
Bill Grounds	Homebush Bay Committee
Alex Hamill	Communications Commission
Ted Harris	Bid Committee, Executive Board, Building Commission
Warwick Hastie	Communications Commission, Community Support Committee
Steve Haynes	Health Care Committee
Geoff Henke	Bid Committee, Executive Board
Dr John Hewson MP	Bid Committee
Bill Hindson	Facility Operation Group
Eric Hitchen	Building Commission
Don Holstock	Transport Committee

Dick Humphry — Olympic Project Management Committee
Blair Hunt — Olympic Project Management Committee
Adam Jeffrey — Transport Committee
Alexandra Joel — Cultural Commission
Peter Jollie — Finance Commission, Communications Commission
Major Rob Joske — Security Planning Committee
Renata Kaldor — Bid Committee, Cultural Commission
Dr Ray Kaslauskas — Health Care Committee
Paul Keating MP — Bid Committee
Ros Kelly — Bid Committee
Mike Kennedy — Communications Commission, Community Support Committee
Reg Kermode — Transport Committee
Ian Kiernan — Community Support Committee
Brian Kirkham — Communications Commission
Greg Knapp — Accommodation Planning Group
Jan Land — Media Committee
John Landels — Corporate Support Committee
Superintendent Merv Lane — Transport Committee
Tony Lauer — Security Planning Committee
David Leckie — Media Committee, Communications Commission
Helen Lewis — Cultural Commission
Graham Lovett — Bid Committee, Building Commission, Executive Board, Health Care Committee, Security Planning Committee, Sports Commission, Strategy Committee
Tom MacDonald — Building Commission
John Malone — Building Commission, Design Review Panel, Estimates Sub-Committee, Homebush Bay Committee, Transport Committee
Norm Maroney — Security Planning Committee
Marlene Mathews — Bid Committee, Sports Commission
Len Mauger — Games Media Revenue Task Force, Media Committee
David McClune — Communications Commission
Neil McDermott — Games Travel Subsidy Working Group
Donald McDonald — Bid Committee, Cultural Commission, Executive Board, Monte Carlo Presentation Sub-Committee

John McInerney	Building Commission
Kim McKay	Community Support Committee
Craig McLatchery	Games Travel Subsidy Working Group
Judith Meppem	Health Care Committee
Phil Meyer	Estimates Sub-Committee
John Miller	Security Planning Committee
Peter Montgomery	Bid Committee, Sports Commission
Max Moore-Wilton	Games Travel Subsidy Working Group, Homebush Bay Committee, Transport Committee
Don Morris	Communications Commission, Monte Carlo Presentation Sub-Committee
Peter Morris	Estimates Sub-Committee
Keith Murton	Security Planning Committee
Sir Eric Neal	Bid Committee
Ian Neale	Finance Corporation
Noel Neale	Facility Operation Group
John Newcombe	Bid Committee
Professor John Niland	Building Commission
Diane Norvick	Accommodation Planning Group
Kerry Packer	Bid Committee
John Pash	Olympic Project Management Committee
Charles Perkins	Bid Committee
Laurie Power	Media Committee, Communications Commission
Prof. Neville Quarry	Building Commission
Bob Richardson	Estimates Sub-Committee
Bruce Robertson	Media Committee
Peter Roennfeldt	Communications Commission
Kevin Rogers	Security Planning Committee
Wayne Roycroft	Equestrian Quarantine Working Group
Steve Salter	Accommodation Planning Group
Colin Sanders	Building Commission, Facility Operation Group, Homebush Bay Committee
Frank Sartor	Bid Committee, Executive Board, Strategy Committee
John Saunders	Olympic Project Management Committee
Justine Saunders	Cultural Commission
Joe Schipp	Bid Committee
Trevor Schmidt	Bid Committee, Building Commission
Tony Selmes	Transport Committee
Geoff Sexton	Building Commission, Estimates Sub-Committee
David Smith	Communications Commission, Media Committee

David Smithers	Bid Committee, Corporate Support Committee, Executive Board, Finance Commission, Olympic Project Management Committee.
Dr Daniel Stiel	Health Care Committee
Colin Still	Design Review Panel
John Stott	Games Travel Subsidy Working Group
Dame Joan Sutherland	Cultural Commission
Rob Thorton	Equestrian Working Group, Games Travel Subsidy Working Group, Transport Committee
Allen Treanorv	Games Travel Subsidy Working Group
Andrew Turnbull	Finance Commission
Pam Tye	Sports Commission
John Valder	Bid Committee, Corporate Support Committee, Executive Board, Finance Commission
Peter Verwer	Accommodation Planning Group
Kim Walker	Cultural Commission
Pam Walker	Equestrian Quarantine Working Group
Ron Walker	Bid Committee
Richard Walsh	Cultural Commission
Brian Watters	Transport Committee
Dr Bill Webb	Health Care Committee
Graham Webster	Health Care Committee
Richard Wherrett	Cultural Commission
Nicholas Whitlam	Bid Committee
Geoff Wild	Bid Committee, Executive Board, Sports Commission
Dr Peter Wilenski	Bid Committee
Evan Williams	Cultural Commission
Richard Woolcott	Bid Committee
Mike Wrublewski	Communications Commission, Community Support Committee

Appendix 3
Corporate Supporters

GOLD SUPPORTERS
ANA Hotel
Australian Hotels Association
Australian Posters: 3M
Blake Dawson Waldron
Carlton and United Breweries
Catering Institute of Australia
Century Radisson Hotel, Sydney
Channel 9
Channel 7
Coca-Cola Bottlers, Sydney
Coopers & Lybrand
Golden Gate, Sydney
Goodman Fielder
Holiday Inn Crown Plaza, Terrigal on Sea
Holiday Inn Menzies, Sydney
Hotel Inter-Continental, Sydney
Hotel Nikko Darling Harbor
Hotel Nikko Sydney
Hyatt Kingsgate Sydney
IBM Australia
Kodak Australasia
Lilianfels Blue Mountains
Maritime Services Board
McDonald's Family Restaurants
Network 10
NSW Lotteries
Novotel Sydney on Darling Harbor
Old Sydney Park Royal
Philips Industries Holdings
Qantas
Registered Clubs Association of NSW
Sebel Town House
Sheraton Wentworth Hotel

South Sydney Council
Southern Pacific Hotels Corporation
St George Bank
State Bank of NSW
Sydney Airport Hilton
Sydney City Council
Sydney Hilton
Sydney Renaissance Hotel
TAB
Telecom Australia
The Park Lane, Sydney
The Regent, Sydney

PROUD SUPPORTERS
Advance Bank
Allen Allen & Hemsley
Amcor
Andersen Consulting
Ansett Airlines
Arnott's Biscuits
Arthur Andersen & Co
ANZ
Australia Post
Australian Airlines
AMP
Australian Picture Library
Australian Stock Exchange (Sydney)
Bayer Australia
Boral
BHP
Burns Philp & Co
Bus and Coach Association
Cabcharge Australia
Caltex Oil (Australia)
CSR
Castrol Australia
Clemenger Sydney
Coles Myer
Colonial Mutual
Commonwealth Banking Corporation
Concrete Constructions Group
Corrs Chambers Westgarth
CRA
Cunard Line

Davids Holdings
Ebsworth & Ebsworth
Ethnic Affairs Commission of NSW
Execon Pty Ltd
Fisher & Paykel
Fletcher Challenge
Fuji Xerox (Australia)
Gerard Industries
Honda Australia
Howard Smith Industries
Hymix (Australia)
ISIS/FHA Design
James Hardie Industries
KPMG Peat Marwick
Leighton Holdings
Lend Lease Corporation
Mallesons Stephen Jaques
Manufacturers Mutual Insurance
McLachlan Consultants
Mercantile Mutual Holdings
Mercedes-Benz (Australia) Pty Ltd
Michell Sillar
Multiplex Constructions Pty Ltd
NSW Department of Transport
NSW Taxi Council
National Australia Bank
National Mutual Life Assurance
Nestle Australia
New Blood and Old Money
News Limited
Next Millennium Film Makers
P & O Australia
Pearl & Dean
Penta Group
Pioneer International
Price Brent
Price Waterhouse
Prudential Assurance Company
Radio 2UE
Rider Hunt
Roads & Traffic Authority
Rochford Williams International
Rural Press
Shell (Australia)

Smorgan Consolidated Industries
Sparke Helmore & Withycombe
Streets Ice Cream
Sun-Herald *This Week* Magazine
Sydney Electricity
The Motor Inn & Motel Association
The Pot Still Press
Trent Nathan Pty Ltd
Triple M Broadcasting Station
Visa International
Time Inc Magazines
Tubemakers of Australia
Western Mining Corporation
Westpac Banking Corporation
White Industries Australia

FRIENDS OF THE BID
2GB
A. Royale
AAP Information Services
ABN Amro Australia
ACT Government
Adia Personnel
AGFA
Albury City Council
Alcan Australia
Alexander & Alexander
Allen Jack & Cottier
Ambrosoli & Thompson Pty Ltd
Ancher, Mortlock, Woolley Pty Ltd
ANI Corporation
Apocalypse
Armstrong Jones
Arnold House Pty Ltd
Artec Sound Vision
Arthur Stutchbury Pty Ltd
Atlab Australia
ATS
Austere Designs
Australia Day Council
Australia Television International
Australia Co-op Foods
Australian Earth Movers and Roadcontractors Association
Australian Society of CPA's

Avant Couriers
B & G Clark Indoor Plant Hire
Balsam Sports Systems
Barclays Bank Australia
Barclays De Zoete Wedd Australia
Barry Webb & Associates
Bayton Cleaning Company
Blackmores
Boral Building Services
Bowater Reding Industries
Brambles Industriesd
Britescreen International Pty Ltd
Brochure Flow International Pty Ltd
Brother Industries Pty Ltd
Building Owners & Managers Association
Canon Australia
Capcount Australia
Captain Cook Cruises
Cessnock City Council
Chameleon Touring Systems
Charles Parsons Group
Christies Pty Ltd
CIG
Cini-Little Food Service & Hospitality
City Link Messengers
City Rail
Clyde Industries
Com Tech Communications Pty Ltd
Comalco
Complete Sign Services
ComputerLand Parramattta
Connell Wagner
CPI Paperworks
Cunneen & Company Pty Ltd
DH Crosby Investments
Dandy Design
Darling Harbor Authority
Daryl Jackson Robin Dyke Pty Ltd
Datafile Wright Line
David Grant Special Events
David Jones
Denton, Corker, Marshall
Department of School Education
Doublet Pty Ltd

Drayton's Winery
Dubbo City Council
Dunhill Madden Butler
Duracell Australia
Email
Eurobodalla Shire Council
Federal Airports Commission
Feltex Carpets
Floormanager Pty Ltd
Florsheim Australia
Fordigraph TAC Pty Ltd
Fountainhead Pure Water
Freehill Hollingdale & Page
Fujitsu Australia
Geoff Pike & Assoociates
Glen Innes Municipal Council
Greater Lithgow City Council
Gresham Partners
Harden Shire Council
Harvey Norman Discounts
HCF of Australia
Henroth Investments Pty Ltd
HongKong Bank
Hume Shire Council
Huntley Hotel
Hurstville City Council
Hutchison Telecommunications
Intercity Hire
IPOH Garden (Australia) Ltd - QVB
Javelin Communications
John and Lois Ties
John B. Fairfax
Jones Lang Wootton
Juste Nous Catering
Ken Done & Associates
Kennards Hire
Language Professionals
Laservision (Australia) Pty Ltd
Lawrence Nield & Partners
Lewis Security
Lindemans Wines
Liverpool City Council
Lockhart ShireCouncil
Logical Solutions

Lotus Software
Louis Vuitton Australia
Macquarie Bank
Mastercut Gourmet Meals
Mayne Nickless
Media Monitors
Medical Benefits Fund of Australia
Meridian Asia/Pacific
Meriton Properties
Michael Dysart & Partners
Milk Marketing (NSW) Pty Ltd
Minale Tatttersfield Bryce & Partners
Modular Design Group Pty Ltd
Motorola
Mr Balloons
National Foods
Newstate Cleaning
OPSM Protector
Ove Arup & Partners
PA People
Pacific Mutual Australia
Pacific Waste Management
Pages Hire
Pakad Australia
Pancontinental Mining
Papoucci Imports
Park Hyatt, Sydney
Parkes Shire Council
Patrick Ryans Express
Patti's Hire
PC Ware Australia
Peddle Thorp & Walker
Penfolds Wine Group
Peter Weiss Pty Ltd
Philip Cox, Richardson, Taylor
Pluto Commercial Furniture
Pongrass Operations Pty Ltd
Prestige Portaloos
Prue Macsween & Associates
PSG
PWD
Qantas Express Parcel Service
QBE Insurance Group
Quality Presentations

Raine & Horne Parramatta
Real Estate Institute
Rebel Sports Warehouse
Rehame Australia
Retter Marketing
Rider Hunt
Rockdale Municipal Council
Rocks Catering Pty Ltd
Rogen International
Ross Turnbull & John Sample
Rothbury Vineyards Pty Ltd
Rothmans Holdings
Royal Agricultural Society
Royal Australian Institute of Architects
Royal Australian Planning Institute
Ryde City Council
Ryder Associates
Ryulstone City Council
Sainty & Associates Vegetation Management
Sales Development
SAP Australia
SBC Dominguez Barry
Scale Models Pty Ltd
Schroders Australia
Scitec Communication Systems
Shire of Wellington
Simsmetal
Sir Ronald Brierley
Snowy River Shire Council
Solarite Airconditioning
South Sydney Council
SPC Software Publishing
Spotless Catering
State Transit Authority
State Sports Centre
Stedmans Hospitality Personnel
Sturdy Holdings Group
Sutherland Shire Council
Sydney Events
TAFE
Taylor Thomson & Whitting
Temora Shire Council
The PA People
The Tetra Pak Companies in Australia

The Vaucluse Liberals
Thomas Cook
Tony Xpress
Tourism Brochure Exchange
Trafalgar Properties
Transfield Holdings
Tulloch Wines
Vale Metal Systems
Villeroy & Boch
Vipac Engineers & Scientists Ltd
WD & HO Wills (Australia) Ltd
Whitelaw & Chrystal Pty Ltd
WH Soul Pattinson and Co
Wingecarribee Shire Council
Wattyl
Westfield Holdings
Woodside Petroleum
Wormald Security
Wyong Shire Council

Index